The Making *of* Shakespeare's First Folio

The Making *of* Shakespeare's First Folio

EMMA SMITH

Bodleian Library
UNIVERSITY OF OXFORD

First published in 2015 by the Bodleian Library
Broad Street
Oxford OX1 3BG
www.bodleianshop.co.uk

ISBN 978 1 85124 442 3

Cover design by Dot Little at the Bodleian Library
Designed and typeset in 11½ on 16 Van Dijck
by illuminati, Grosmont
Printed and Bound in Great Britain by TJ International Ltd, Padstow, Cornwall
on TJ Woodfree Cream 80 gsm

British Library Catalogue in Publishing Data
A CIP record of this publication is available from the British Library

Contents

ILLUSTRATIONS

Colour plates

ACKNOWLEDGEMENTS

THE SPUR FOR THIS BOOK was the 'Sprint for Shakespeare' campaign to stabilise and digitise the Bodleian Library's copy of the First Folio (firstfolio.bodleian.ox.ac.uk): I am deeply grateful to colleagues across the rare books, digital library services, conservation, imaging and fund-raising departments of the Bodleian for their skills and energy in making that project happen. My thanks also to Amanda Saville, librarian of The Queen's College, Oxford, and to Samuel Fanous and Janet Phillips at Bodleian Library Publishing. This book is for my mum, Viv Smith, with love.

Introduction

IN LATE NOVEMBER 1623, Edward Blount finally took delivery to his bookshop at the sign of the Black Bear near St Paul's a book that had been long in the making. *Mr. William Shakespeares Comedies, Histories, & Tragedies* was the first collected edition of Shakespeare's plays, appearing some seven years after their author's death in 1616. Its 950 folio pages included thirty-six plays, half of which had not previously been printed, divided under the three generic headings of the title.

There was no fanfare at the book's arrival. There was nothing of the marketing overdrive that marks an important new publication in our own period: no advertising campaign; no reviews, interviews, endorsements or literary prizes; no queues in St Paul's Churchyard, no sales figures, price war, copycat publications or bestseller lists – in short, no sensation. Nevertheless, it is hard to overstate the importance of this literary, cultural and commercial moment.

The publishing cartel headed by Blount in partnership with the printing house of William Jaggard and his son Isaac did not know it, but they are responsible for giving us 'Shakespeare'. Without this book eighteen of Shakespeare's plays would have joined the many hundreds of early modern plays (the vast majority of all those performed) that have not survived; without this book there would be no *Macbeth* or *Julius Caesar* or *The Tempest*; without this book we would not therefore have lines like 'Some are born great, some achieve greatness, and some have greatness thrust upon 'em' (*Twelfth Night* 2.5.140–41) or Cleopatra's 'salad days' (*Antony and Cleopatra* 1.5.72) or even the most famous stage direction ever: 'Exit, pursued by a bear' (*The Winter's Tale* 3.3.57). As the playwright and poet Ben Jonson predicted in his dedicatory poem prefacing the collection, 'he was not of an age but for all time'. Shakespeare's reputation has rocketed culturally and geographically in the 400 years since this publication, but all that – everything from school syllabi to politicians' rhetoric, from Nahum Tate's happy-ending *King Lear* (1681) to *Haider*, a Bollywood *Hamlet* set in modern Kashmir (2014), from Internet memes to Shakespeare-themed rubber ducks, from YouTube parodies to elaborate arguments that these plays were not in fact by Shakespeare – all can be traced back to this moment in St Paul's Churchyard in 1623, when the book went on sale. The book we named in retrospect the First Folio is the beginning, that's to say, of a long and hugely influential afterlife, an incredible story of how a seventeenth-century London actor–playwright's work came to dominate Western literary culture.

If the First Folio's publication marks the beginning of the extensive and expansive reception of Shakespeare, it also marks the end of a protracted process, and of a period of considerable effort by its many makers. It is the product of a number of very specific social, cultural and commercial contexts, and of numerous individuals with different skills and different agendas. The book had been first advertised in the Frankfurt Book Fair catalogue of forthcoming English-language volumes in 1622, but it took another year for it to appear. In this study I work to illuminate that lengthy process of production and to fill out the details of how and why the book was produced, where the publishers got their copy to print from, and how it was marketed to early modern readers.

The Shakespeare First Folio is now an extremely valuable book: complete copies sell for more than £3 million at specialist auctions. Although by the standards of early modern books it is not rare – almost 240 copies or substantial part-copies survive, compared with, for example, just one complete copy of the first printing of *Hamlet* in 1603 – it is iconic. Its weight and heft give it a monumental quality, and it has accrued, for those institutions and individuals that own a copy, the aura of a precious relic, to be kept in a safe, handled reverentially with care and with gloves, and shown only to privileged visitors or kept in a display case for devout cultural pilgrims. It's in the nature of a relic that the circumstances of its production tend to be obscured. In this book, I argue instead that the First Folio is the product of recoverable human, technological and commercial enterprise, and that Shakespeare himself is only one agent in its preparation and realisation. This doesn't diminish the extraordinary literary achievement contained there, but it does apportion credit more widely.

I try to convey some of the contingencies, interruptions and obstacles in the preparation of Shakespeare's collected works, from the cost of imported paper to the employment of print-shop apprentices, and from difficulties in obtaining the rights to the plays to the increasing frailty of the master printer and stationer William Jaggard. Many different contexts shape the First Folio: the commercial realities of the early modern book trade, the rhetoric of noble patronage, theatrical practices, print-house techniques, civic and national politics alongside the politics of a family business. I aim to bring back into the story of the First Folio a diverse cast of characters worthy of one of Shakespeare's own plays, including men from the very different worlds of London commerce, industry, King James's court and the Globe Theatre. Above all, I try to link these questions with the book's content: the First Folio is not just any material product of the theatrical and printing industries, but a collection of unrivalled literary and dramatic interest. Sometimes book historians and collectors have been accused of indifference to literature, preferring the quantifiable and material object over its ineffable, transcendent subject matter. I come myself to this topic via a deep interest in Shakespeare's works, and thus try not to lose sight of what really matters: the plays.

The four chapters that make up this book cover the what, why, who and how of the First Folio. They ask what the book can tell us about early modern theatrical practice, about Shakespeare's own writing, and about publishing technologies. How popular was Shakespeare, and how far was the decision to publish his collected works an economic one? Where did the printing house get copy for the plays, and how was their typesetting and printing supervised? What can details such as stage directions, act and scene divisions, and the names of characters tell us about Shakespeare's writing practices and the way his theatre was organised? I try to recover the world into which Shakespeare's collected plays first emerged, and reveal a sampling of the immediate responses of its earliest readers.

A NOTE ON THE TEXT

The book you are reading is illustrated with forty images, but it is now easy to look at Shakespeare's First Folio in great detail online: the Bodleian's copy, received by the library in early 1624, has been digitised at firstfolio.bodleian.ox.ac.uk. The online Folio gives the opportunity to see the text as it hit the bookstalls of St Paul's in November 1623. In this book I quote, with some reluctance but for the sake of clarity, from the modernised text of the *Oxford Shakespeare* (2nd edition 2005). Where this differs importantly from the First Folio, I cite that work from the Bodleian's online edition. Quotations from other early modern texts have also been modernised for ease of reading.

ONE

The Plays &
their Presentation

NDER THE HEADING *Mr. William Shakespeares Comedies Histories, & Tragedies*, the First Folio includes thirty-six plays, divided by genre (PLATE 1). The comedies are, in order, *The Tempest, The Two Gentleman of Verona, The Merry Wives of Windsor, Measure for Measure, The Comedy of Errors, Much Ado About Nothing, Love's Labour's Lost, A Midsummer Night's Dream, The Merchant of Venice, As You Like It, The Taming of the Shrew, All's Well That Ends Well, Twelfth Night, or What You Will* and *The Winter's Tale.* The histories list *King John, Richard II, Henry IV Parts 1* and *2, Henry V, Henry VI Parts 1, 2* and *3, Richard III* and *Henry VIII.* In between the histories and tragedies sections almost all copies of the book also include *Troilus and Cressida,* which, for reasons discussed in Chapter 4, was not included on the catalogue page. The tragedies appear in the following order: *Coriolanus, Titus Andronicus, Romeo and Juliet, Timon of Athens, Julius Caesar, Macbeth, Hamlet, King Lear, Othello, Anthony and Cleopatra* and *Cymbeline.* None of Shakespeare's non-dramatic poems is included. Also missing are two plays where Shakespeare's part-authorship is not in doubt: *Pericles* and *The Two Noble Kinsmen.* Each play page has double columns of text boxed in with solid lines, and a running title across the top edged with a decorative border: the plays each take around twenty-three printed pages. The first letter of each play is a decorated capital. For the most part, stage directions are set in italic type towards

5

the right-hand side of the text, entries are italicised and centred, and act divisions, where they exist, are in Latin and marked out with horizontal rules. Each new play starts on a new page, and each of the three sections is paginated from page 1. At the end of each play, space permitting, is a decorative ornament, and some plays conclude with a list of characters.

The volume is introduced by a section of introductory material, including dedicatory epistles and poems: material that critics call 'paratext'. This paratextual material is crucial in shaping the impression of the book and, because it is where early readers would probably begin, it serves to guide their responses to the dramatic works that follow it in the First Folio. It can also yield some insights into the way the book was produced and its anticipated audiences. Therefore, it is worth spending some time on it before moving to the plays themselves.

The portrait

The first words of the First Folio are not by Shakespeare at all, but by his fellow dramatist Ben Jonson. Jonson writes a short poem 'To the Reader' as an extended caption to the facing page, an engraving of Shakespeare by Martin Droeshout, the engraver son of Huguenot immigrants, who is discussed, along with the other men whose work appears in the introductory material, in Chapter 3. Jonson's conceit here is of the inadequacy of the picture: 'O, could he but have drawn his wit / As well in brass as he hath hit / His face, the print would then surpass / All that was ever writ in brass!', and he concludes by urging the reader: 'look / Not on his picture, but his book'. The image of the picture that cannot capture the real nature of the subject is a familiar one, although in this case it seems to have been particularly appropriate. The now-iconic image of Shakespeare – the only portrait which is an undisputed likeness of the playwright – seems to have been difficult to achieve.

Droeshout's engraving shows a dome-headed, balding man with a light moustache and trace of stubble on his chin, wearing a starched ruff and a dark, restrainedly decorated doublet. It exists in three separate states, indicating that the copper plate was modified on two occasions. The first, apparently early in the printing process, since only a handful of copies of the First Folio survive with this first-state portrait, was to rectify the visual disconnect between Shakespeare's head and his ruff by adding hatched shadows to the ruff below his ear. The second modifications are less obvious and comprise some tweaking of the hair and the highlights in the eyes. Getting the portrait right was clearly important and worth spending time on (PLATE 2).

The choice and styling of this image for the title page is significant: Shakespeare is not pictured with the decorative border of laurel leaves typically associated with writers' portraits in this period – a style that characterises most of Droeshout's other surviving engravings. Rather, the layout of the book implies that he is not only its progenitor but also its main subject. The title page's focus on the name 'Shakespeares' in capital letters, and the large-scale portrait which takes up two-thirds of the space, may be the early foundation of our ongoing interest in Shakespeare's biography. The abiding sense, traceable back to the presentation of this first collected works edition, that the man and his plays must be deeply interconnected has continued to fuel perennial (and unanswerable) questions about Shakespeare's politics, or his religion, or his sexuality. The book presents us with a person, a personality, through his work. In passing, we might compare this with the elaborately architectural frontispiece chosen for Ben Jonson's Folio *Workes*, which included the author's poetry and court masques alongside his plays when it was published in 1616 – and which was really the only extant model in the English book trade for publishing vernacular plays in the folio format (for more on the folio format, see Chapter 2). The illustration here presents an allegorical figuration of poetic genres in a classical style to link the works with the learned past and situate Jonson's writing in a high-status tradition. It is significant that the production team for the First Folio opted for something quite different in commissioning a portrait of their poet to brand this book, leaning on the image of Shakespeare himself, rather than an image of scholarship or learning or the past, to market the book and locate its contents.

Heminge and Condell's dedicatory letters

Because book-buyers of the early seventeenth century bought their books unbound and took them to binders (see Chapter 4), the preliminary leaves after the title page with its portrait which do not have page numbers, nor any necessary narrative sequence, exist in surviving copies in different orders. The prefatory material includes printed letters to patrons and to the reader, four dedicatory poems, a list of actors, and a catalogue of plays or contents list. Like the blurb on a modern book or the publicity campaign for a current author, these features work to praise the writer. The material reconstructs Shakespeare as a commercially appealing figure, a kind of celebrity, by association with other starry figures past and present.

The two printed letters, both signed by Shakespeare's fellow actors in the King's Men, John Heminge and Henry Condell, propose a narrative of how the book was put together. Each has tantalising details about Shakespeare's writing practices from men who knew him and who had worked closely with him for two decades. However, since they are also both designed to flatter the book's aristocratic and commercial patrons, they cannot be read as an entirely accurate description of the Folio's provenance. They are in part a sales pitch, with the aim of making the book's contents more desirable.

The first letter is the dedication 'To the Most Noble and Incomparable Pair of Brethren' William and Philip Herbert (PLATE 3). The Herbert brothers were active literary patrons and recipients of dozens of dedications in books of this period. They, especially William, who had become Lord Chamberlain in 1615, had had a long association with Shakespeare's company. Heminge and Condell allude to 'the many favours we have received' and the 'favour' shown to 'their author living' (discussed in Chapter 3). They refer to the plays disparagingly as 'these trifles', 'the remains of your servant Shakespeare', requesting the Herberts' 'indulgence' for plays previously enjoyed 'when they were acted'. The gracious favour of the noblemen, the letter continues, itself transforms the quality of the modest gift: 'the meanest of things are made more precious when they are dedicated to temples'. This modesty topos is a standard pose in the literature of patronage, where two rhetorical terms habitually coincide: *hyperbole*, or excessive praise, of the gracious generosity and discernment of the noble patron, and *litotes*, or understatement, of the merits of the literary work presented. These terms cooperate to produce the mutually beneficial transaction of early modern literary sponsorship through which the value of both patron and text is enhanced.

There is a similar negotiation of artistic and economic value in the second epistle, 'To the great Variety of Readers'. In their opening, Heminge and Condell address a range of readers 'From the most able to him that can but spell', seemingly suggesting that Shakespeare's works are for everyone (questions of actual readership, in so far as we can judge them, are taken up in the Coda). But this idealised expansiveness is immediately undercut with the wry comment 'we had rather you were weighed': 'the fate of all books depends on your capacities, and not of your heads alone, but of your purses'. Heminge and Condell's prose is as much an advertising puff for their book as it is a description of its texts and its dead author: two imperative verbs – 'read' and 'buy' – struggle for prominence in a document that is as conscious of the book as an economic entity as it is as a literary one (see Chapter 2). It is in this commercial light – the insistence that 'whatever you do, buy' – that we need to interpret their statements about the collection and the underlying manuscripts.

Heminge and Condell go on to make two substantive claims about the works they have included in the Folio. The first is that the collection is complete; the second, that the texts are authoritative. Both statements have cast a long shadow over Shakespeare criticism and have shaped editorial policies for centuries, but, seen in their context within this economically inflected prefatory material, they have something of the sales pitch about them. Perhaps Heminges and Condell wrote here as brokers rather than as witnesses.

Assuring readers that the collection represented their author's work 'absolute in their numbers', Heminge and Condell made the implicit claim to publish the first 'Complete Works'. Unlike Ben Jonson's precociously premature folio of 1616 (Jonson's writing career would go on for a further two decades), this posthumous collection could therefore be presented as a total retrospective. As long-term associates of Shakespeare and as veteran theatre professionals, Heminge and Condell could claim to be in an authoritative position to review his entire works. The Catalogue to the First Folio organises some thirty-five plays under three generic headings: Comedies (fourteen titles), Histories (ten) and Tragedies (eleven). In fact almost all copies of the book contained a thirty-sixth play, *Troilus and Cressida*, for which the rights were apparently obtained after the catalogue page had been printed (see Chapter 4). Many early readers of the book added the title to the play in manuscript to the catalogue page in its position between the last of the histories, *Henry VIII*, and the first tragedy, *Coriolanus*. Of these plays, eighteen had been previously published and eighteen were in print for the first time. Without the Folio, that is to say, we might well have lost unpublished plays including *Macbeth*, *The Tempest*, *Julius Caesar*, *Twelfth Night* and *Antony and Cleopatra*: most theatre historians estimate that of the output of the professional theatres up to their closure in 1642, about one-sixth is extant, one-sixth is known about by references to titles or performances, but the majority, the remaining two-thirds, is lost without trace.

But it may be that this large number in the Folio does not in fact capture all of Shakespeare's plays. At least two play titles are associated with Shakespeare for which we do not have a text: *Love's Labour's Won* is mentioned in a list of Shakespeare's works by Francis Meres in 1598 (it is sometimes identified, as by the Royal Shakespeare Company in 2014–15 season at their Stratford-upon-Avon theatre, as an alternative title for *Much Ado About Nothing*); and there are performance records for *The History of Cardenio*, apparently a late collaboration with John Fletcher and taking its plot from the popular mock-romance *Don Quixote*. Neither makes it into the Folio. In addition to these 'lost' plays, at least one play attributed to Shakespeare, *Pericles*, published in 1609, was not included in the Folio – and the publication in 1634 of *The Two Noble Kinsmen*, co-authored with John Fletcher, added a further play to the Shakespearean canon that was not published as part of the 1623 collection. The publication history of the Folio also suggests that its inclusion of *Timon of Athens* was something of a plan B, and that there were such difficulties in getting the rights to *Troilus and Cressida* that the plan was to publish without it (see Chapter 4). But for a series of contingencies, that is to say, *Timon* and/or *Troilus* might well not have made it into the book. So there are plays which are quite firmly attributed to Shakespeare that do not appear in the Folio.

Further, scholars have long argued, largely on stylistic grounds, sometimes aided by computer analysis, about whether other plays

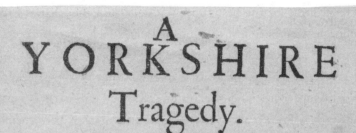

A
YORKSHIRE
Tragedy.

Not so New as Lamentable
and true.

Acted by his Maiesties Players at
the *Globe.*

VVritten by VV. Shakespeare.

At London
Printed by *R. B.* for *Thomas Pauier* and are to bee sold at his
shop on Cornhill, neere to the exchange.
1608.

FIGURE I   *A Yorkshire Tragedy*, attributed here to Shakespeare in 1608, but now generally thought to be by Thomas Middleton. *Bodleian Library, Arch. G d.41* (7).

should be attributed in part or whole to Shakespeare. These plays include *Edward III*, *Arden of Faversham*, *Woodstock*, *Locrine*, *Mucedorus*, the unpublished *Sir Thomas More*, and *Thomas Lord Cromwell*. It's a small testament to the almost scriptural quality that has accrued to Shakespeare that these marginal texts are known as his apocrypha, a word specifically and technically applied to those non-canonical books of the Bible excluded by the Protestant authorities during the Reformation. Many modern collected editions of Shakespeare include some of these additional and apocryphal plays: the revised Oxford edition (2005), for instance, includes *Edward III* and *Sir Thomas More*, as well as 'A Brief Account' of both *Love's Labour's Won* and *Cardenio*. In part these inclusions serve to differentiate the modern volume from its many predecessors and competitors, a phenomenon long familiar to Shakespeare publishing. When the Third Folio was published in 1663 it boasted on the title page that 'unto this impression is added seven plays never before printed in folio': only one of these, *Pericles*, has found a secure place in the Shakespeare canon despite the fact that two other plays, *The London Prodigal* and *A Yorkshire Tragedy* (now attributed to Thomas Middleton) had been identified as Shakespeare's in print during his lifetime (FIGURE I).

Can we feel confident that Heminge and Condell actively excluded rather than mistakenly omitted *Pericles* and *The Two Noble Kinsmen* and perhaps other plays too, and if so what was their operative principle of selection? Or, to put it another way, does the fact that it was not included by Shakespeare's fellow actors in their collected edition of his plays decisively scupper the claims of, say, *Edward III* or *Arden of Faversham*, or any of the other claimants to the Shakespearean canon? Perhaps so. But, equally, the inclusion of plays in the Folio may have actually been dependent on a pragmatic combination of practical and interpretative judgements. The rights to works already in print needed to be acquired from other publishers, and the cost of those might have been a factor. Take the case of *Pericles*, for instance. Being left out of the Folio has shaped *Pericles'* critical reception ever since, on the assumption that its omission says something about its aesthetic worth. If it wasn't worth putting in the Folio, the argument goes, it isn't really worth much of our subsequent attention. Heminge and Condell weren't interested in it, so why should we be? It might be in fact that this play, which was extremely popular in its own day, might have been prohibitively expensive to acquire (it went through five editions between 1609 and 1635, so it was obviously a marketable property for its publishers). Or we might hypothesise that, like many modern editors, Heminge and Condell took it to be only partly Shakespearean, and excluded it on that basis. The result is the same – no *Pericles* in the Folio – but our understanding of the value of the play and the implication of the processes of selection is completely different in each case. What is clear, though, is that collaborative works seem to be in danger of dropping out of the Folio. *Timon of Athens* (co-authored by Middleton) makes it only by a whisker; *The Two Noble Kinsmen* is not included. The Folio makes no mention of any other writer, and its presentational rhetoric works assiduously to construct a solo author, Shakespeare (see Chapter 3 for some of the playwrights it might have mentioned but didn't).

If collaborative works seem to be on the margins of the canon as established by the Folio, another aspect of Shakespeare's work is silently excluded. Had you asked the proverbial man in the Elizabethan street about Shakespeare you might well have received as an answer 'You mean the one who wrote *Venus and Adonis*?' *Venus and Adonis* was the first work by Shakespeare to be published, and the earliest appearance of his name in print (signing the dedication to the poem published in 1593). This erotic poem is based on an episode in Ovid's *Metamorphoses*, a text highly influential for Shakespeare's writing and which is also behind *Titus Andronicus*,

A Midsummer Night's Dream and many others. The writer Francis Meres noted in 1598 that 'the witty soul of Ovid lives in mellifluous and honey-tongued Shakespeare'.[1] The poem expands a short Ovidian episode into 1,200 rhymed lines describing Venus's fatal passion for a reluctant and beautiful young Adonis who prefers hunting over the goddess's invitations to 'smother thee with kisses'. It was Shakespeare's most sustainedly popular work in print, with sixteen known editions by 1675, joining and invigorating a fashionable sub-genre known as the epyllia, or 'minor epic', which also included Marlowe's *Hero and Leander* and poems by Nashe, Middleton, Marston, and just about every self-respecting well-educated young writer with an eye to the fashionable London literary market. Shakespeare probably wrote it when the theatres were closed due to plague, and dedicated it to the young Earl of Southampton, Henry Wriothesley.

By the time of the First Folio *Venus and Adonis* had been printed more than a dozen times – more than the two most reprinted plays combined – and that vagueness about the precise number is because some editions were, literally, read to extinction and no copies of them exist. But the poem was not included in the Folio. Perhaps Heminge and Condell, as men of the theatre, were not interested in their colleague's early forays into printed narrative poetry, the product of the theatre closures; perhaps this valuable literary property could not be acquired for a reasonable fee. For whatever reason, *Venus and Adonis* is not included in the First Folio; nor is its darker sibling *The Rape of Lucrece*, first printed in 1594 and, like *Venus and Adonis*, dedicated to the Earl of Southampton. Shakespeare's sonnets, which had been printed for the first time in 1609, were also omitted, as was the other occasional poetry, including the enigmatic sequence 'The Phoenix and the Turtle' (first published in 1601 as part of a work by Robert Chester titled *Love's Martyr*). As with the plays, there is a penumbra of potentially but not securely Shakespearean verse hovering on the margins of the canon: the poem 'A Funeral Elegy' by 'W. S.' was controversially attributed to Shakespeare after computer stylometric analysis and included in a number of editions in the 1990s, although even its initial advocates have now withdrawn from the attribution. 'Shall I die' has also been widely discussed as potentially Shakespearean; and in the twenty-first century a short, anonymous poem titled 'To the Queen' included in the RSC collected edition was publicised in the press under the tantalising headline 'Is there a lost Shakespeare in your attic?'[2] However extensive Shakespeare's uncollected verse hiding in the nation's attics might turn out to be, the fact remains that nothing of his non-dramatic poetry is included in the First Folio. Taken together with the omissions of plays detailed above, the literal accuracy of Heminge and Condell's claim to completeness can be seen to be somewhat shaky.

Their description of the manuscripts from which the Folio is printed is also questionable. We have no contemporary manuscripts of Shakespeare's plays, either in his own hand or in that of a theatrical scribe. Only the collaborative play *Sir Thomas More*, not published until modern times, may record Shakespeare's handwriting. Many scholars believe that this composite and probably unperformed play includes a contribution by Shakespeare, probably written around 1603–04 (PLATE 4). The early parts of the play dramatise an anti-foreigner riot in the London of Henry VIII (this had attracted the attentions of the dramatic censor, the Master of the Revels, because it was problematically topical in an Elizabethan London ill at ease with immigrants), and the scene attributed to Shakespeare has Sir Thomas More reproaching the rioters for their selfish lack of empathy with refugees. The play is now routinely included in modern collected editions of Shakespeare's plays.

Setting *Sir Thomas More* aside, the absence of Shakespearean manuscripts is not in itself unusual. Only eighteen manuscript play books from an estimated total of some three thousand plays of the period now exist.[3] What is unusual is Heminge and Condell's idealised description of those now-lost manuscripts: 'His mind and hand went together, and what he thought he uttered with that easiness that we have scarce received from him a blot in his papers.' Ben Jonson's retort 'would he had blotted a thousand' perhaps recognises that this description is adulatory rather than accurate – and further that it is the job of the writer also to be his own editor.[4] All professional writers redraft their work in the process of clarifying their thoughts and the shape of their texts: the idea that Shakespeare's works sprang fully formed from his invention seems implausible. However, following Heminge and Condell's emphatic assurances to the contrary, it has been hard for scholarship to accept the idea that Shakespeare, an active dramatist working with the same company for two decades, revised his own works. Their image is of the genius who does not need to work on his drafts or polish his writing. It focuses attention, like the iconic image of their author on the book's title page, on the singular and individual author–creator. This description has long been overinfluential on our view of Shakespeare's working practices, as we will see below in the discussion of *King Lear* and *Macbeth*.

Half of the plays included in the First Folio had already been printed before 1623, in small, single-play formats. The word 'quarto' describes a book made by folding sheets of paper twice to create four pages and eight leaves: it is a book format particularly associated with plays, pamphlets and other lower-end publishing. Heminge and Condell refer to these previous quarto publications when they tell their readers that 'before, you were abused with divers stolen and surreptitious copies', but that these plays are now 'offered to your view cured and perfect of their limbs'. It is true that Folio texts of previously printed plays are rarely identical with their earlier appearances, as is discussed below. For many later editors of Shakespeare, Heminge and Condell's statement was definitive evidence for the automatic superiority of the Folio text in such cases of difference. Scholars took at face value their statement about the relationship between these early texts. But, as some examples will show, it is extremely difficult to generalise about the differences between quarto and Folio texts.

Some of the differences, for example, are minor ones. When the captured Iago is directed at the end of *Othello* to look on the horrid consequences of his mischief – the bodies of Othello, his wife Desdemona and her servant Emilia – the quarto text, published in 1622, describes 'the tragic lodging of this bed' where the Folio has 'the tragic loading'. Either makes sense, and the cause of the difference is as likely to be a misreading of the manuscript either by a scribe or by the compositors in the print shop, as it is a purposeful change between two nouns. The Oxford edition of the play opts for the Folio reading here. There's a different explanation for one of the other differences between the two versions of *Othello*: censorship. In the 1622 text, Iago begins the play with the scoffing interjection 'Tush', and a few lines later uses the expletives 'God bless the mark' and 'Zounds!' (a contraction of the oath 'God's wounds'). These and other examples establish Iago's quarto speech patterns as quite different in tone from the poetic language of his military commander Othello. All these are absent from the text as printed in the Folio in 1623, because that text has had dozens of oaths and profanities purged in accordance with the Act to Restrain Abuses of Players of 1606 (we assume the manuscript behind the 1622 text pre-dates this Act). Other Folio plays have had the same clean-up treatment, and modern editors, including for the Oxford text, tend to reverse that to return to a saltier linguistic register.

Or if we turn to another play, *The Merchant of Venice*, there is a scene in which Portia and her waiting woman Nerissa discuss her hapless international suitors and take the opportunity to rehearse a comic catalogue of national stereotypes. In the text printed in 1600, Nerissa asks Portia about an Englishman called Falconbridge and then prompts 'What think you of the Scottish lord, his neighbour?' (1.2.74–5). Even though Portia's reply is not particularly negative – she is merrily dismissive of all nations' menfolk – the Folio text, reflecting a cautious change probably made under the reign of the new Scottish king James from 1603, replaces 'Scottish' with the more neutral 'other'. Jokes about the Scots were dangerous territory, as Ben Jonson found to his cost when he was imprisoned for one (see Chapter 3). Again, most modern editors would not follow the blander Folio reading here, but restore the more specific reading from the earlier text.

A final example for the moment – there's more on the different texts below, but at the moment we are just testing Heminge and Condell's assertion that the Folio presents perfected versions of the plays – is that of *Romeo and Juliet*. This tragedy is presented in the Folio without the famous choric Prologue beginning 'Two households, both alike in dignity / In fair Verona, where we lay our scene' (1.0.1–2). Missing this shaping sonnet, Folio readers are not informed at the start that this is a play in which 'a pair of star-crossed lovers take their life' (1.0.6), and do not begin their experience of the play with the strong sense of how it will end. Rather, the Folio play is less obviously predetermined (part of the purpose of the Prologue is to inform us that events cannot, however much we wish it, turn out differently in the end). Sometimes it's suggested that *Romeo and Juliet* misses out on being a comedy by a matter of seconds: the tragic ending is all about mistiming, as Romeo believes Juliet is dead and kills himself, only to have her awake on his dying breath and then take her own life. The Prologue makes this sequence unavoidable, written in the stars. No modern text of *Romeo and Juliet* would be willing to forgo this important opening statement. Heminge and Condell's account of the superiority of the Folio texts does not, in these instances and many others like them, accord with the judgement of later scholars.

In one way, however, scholarship has long been influenced by Heminge and Condell's description. Their apparent authorising of the Folio text over earlier printed versions was expanded by scholars in the early twentieth century who dismissed the quarto publications which varied most significantly from the Folio as unauthorised and incomplete: so-called 'bad quartos'.[5] These included versions of *Romeo and Juliet* as printed in 1597, of *Henry V* in 1600, of *The Merry Wives of Windsor* in 1602, and of *Hamlet* in 1603. Each of these texts in its early publication is substantially different from that printed in the Folio. Two of the plays, *Romeo and Juliet* and *Hamlet*, had already been individually published in revised form, and thus they exist in both 'good' and 'bad' quarto versions. Now, it may indeed be true that the early printing of Shakespeare's plays was in some sense unauthorised, in that we do not have evidence that Shakespeare himself was involved in their publication. Nor would we necessarily expect him to be, since play scripts were the property of the theatre company rather than the individual writer. Once they had been sold for publication the rights passed to the stationer. No dramatist could reasonably expect to publish his work under his own auspices or direction, and the very few who did, most prominently Ben Jonson, were exceptions. Shakespeare could not anyway have been directly involved in the preparation of the Folio unless work had begun long before its publication, since the playwright died in April 1616. Authorial involvement is thus not necessary for the First Folio's claim to authority.

Recent scholarship has been uncomfortable with the evaluative language of the 'good' and 'bad' quartos, and instead is interested in the way the play text as a dramatic script might legitimately exist in various different versions. And what may also be possible is that Heminge and Condell are using an established sales technique to denigrate rival or existing products. A keen playbook-buyer in 1623 might well already own some or all of the Shakespeare plays already published, making the premium price for the whole collected edition rather steep. A quick sum makes that clear. Paying 15 shillings – the generally accepted cost for the unbound Folio text, although binding would add anything from 1 shilling upwards to this (see Chapter 4) – for thirty-six plays means they cost the equivalent of fivepence each. This means the price compares favourably with the cost of buying individual play editions at sixpence each. But if you had already paid sixpence each for the eighteen plays previously available, you would have paid out 9 shillings on individual plays, plus the 15 shillings to get the other half only available in the Folio. The cost for the Folio would mean that you were paying again for those plays you already had, so that the equivalent price for the eighteen new plays in the Folio was tenpence each, plus binding. But by telling purchasers that this book supersedes any previous editions and that they need it for the 'cured and perfect' versions even of those plays they have already bought as well as for the previously unpublished work, Heminge and Condell add rhetorical force to their urgent request for customers (there's more discussion of the economics of the Folio production in Chapter 2).

A detail about the other work being undertaken alongside the printing of the Shakespeare Folio may be relevant here. In the years just prior to the Folio's publication, William Jaggard's print shop had been involved in a surprisingly controversial series of works on English heraldry and genealogy. These works had established a forceful commercial rhetoric of discrediting as lamentably error-strewn those previous publications which covered essentially identical ground. This experience may have made its way into the First Folio preliminaries (a copy of the First Folio, now in the Folger Shakespeare Library in Washington DC, was given by Jaggard on publication to one of the prominent heraldry adversaries, Augustine Vincent, forging a material connection between these different publications). It may not be unconnected that the next new edition of plays to be published in folio format, works attributed to the writing partnership of Francis Beaumont and John Fletcher, made much of the fact that the book was 'all new', and that since 'many Gentlemen were already furnished' with previously printed plays, 'I would have none say, they pay twice for the same book'.[6] Heminge and Condell try to pre-empt any similar complaint by stating that their plays are significantly superior to those already available in book form. As with their claim to completeness, this assertion may have as much to do with selling the book as with accurately describing its contents.

The dedicatory poems

The Folio also includes a series of poems in praise of Shakespeare and his works. Collectively they stress the book as a monument to the dead author, repeating Shakespeare's name and emphasising that the works are his lasting memorial. First is Ben Jonson's 'To the memory of my beloved author Master William Shakespeare and what he hath left us': two pages of rhyming couplets in which Jonson apostrophises his rival as 'Soul of the Age', 'wonder of our stage' and 'sweet swan of Avon'. Jonson places him in a literary pantheon alongside the medieval poet Chaucer, the Elizabethan poet Edmund Spenser, author of the epic *The Faerie Queene*, and Francis Beaumont, the Jacobean playwright and collaborator with John Fletcher: all three had been buried in Poets' Corner in Westminster Abbey, and Jonson urges them to move up 'to make thee a room' (in fact, Shakespeare had already been buried in Holy Trinity Church in his native Stratford-upon-Avon; it was Jonson himself who would ultimately be buried in Westminster Abbey, apparently standing up). Jonson's points of literary comparison are interesting ones: he links Shakespeare with the greats of the classical era, Euripides and Sophocles, Terence and Plautus, and also with writers of the Elizabethan past, naming John Lyly (who died in 1606), Thomas Kyd and Christopher Marlowe (who died in 1593 and 1594 respectively) rather than more recent writers. His famous assessment that Shakespeare had 'small Latin and less Greek' needs to be read in the light of Jonson's own considerable learning (the comparison with classical playwrights is also a display of Jonson's own literary sophistication, after all) as well as the increasing evidence of Shakespeare's own classical borrowings (See Chapter 3). Most notably of all, Jonson predicts Shakespeare's remarkable longevity: 'He was not of an age, but for all time.'

Jonson's theme that Shakespeare is 'alive still, while thy book doth live' is picked up by the other dedicatory poems. Leonard Digges suggests that the book will make Shakespeare 'fresh to all ages', and singles out one play in particular, suggesting that *Romeo and Juliet* will never be outdone. Hugh Holland asserts that 'the life yet of his lines shall never out'. These are memorial poems, juxtaposing literary survival against mortal decay. In this, perhaps unconsciously, they pick up the imagery of Shakespeare's own sonnets (not, of course, printed in the First Folio): the famous poem beginning 'Shall I compare thee to a summer's day', for instance, juxtaposes the transience of nature with the permanence of poetry, closing with:

> But thy eternal summer shall not fade
> Nor lose possession of that fair thou ow'st,
> Nor shall death brag thou wander'st in his shade,
> When in eternal lines to time thou grow'st.
>   So long as men can breathe or eyes can see,
>   So long lives this, and this gives life to thee.
> (Sonnet 18)

Using a similar contrast between the mortality of the author and the immortality of his works, Shakespeare's eulogists are also elegists, constructing the collection of plays, and the physical book itself, as Shakespeare's ultimate monument. At the very moment that 'Shakespeare' hits the London bookstalls, the book is projecting his literary afterlife into the future. The poets are right: the image of Shakespeare that has been transmitted to posterity is almost entirely dependent on the texts included in the Folio. But the Folio does not simply preserve plays: equally influential for the subsequent reception of Shakespeare's works is the persona of the author and his value that the book so sedulously constructs.

The lists of players and plays

Given that it was prepared, at least in part, by the King's Men actors John Heminge and Henry Condell, and given that it confines itself to Shakespeare's dramatic works, it is striking that the First Folio is rather reticent about its plays' performance history. Previous printed plays tended to advertise their theatre company prominently on the title page: the example of *King Lear* (1608) boasts that 'it was played before the King's Majesty at Whitehall, upon St Stephen's Night in Christmas Holidays' (admittedly, rather a bleak choice for the festive season: it's not quite *It's A Wonderful Life*). The title goes on to capitalise on the opportunity for promotion: 'by his Majesty's servants, playing usually at the Globe on the Bankside' (FIGURE 2). The King's Men continued to be the pre-eminent theatre company in London in 1623, with a repertoire including plays by the fashionable writing team of Francis Beaumont and John Fletcher, by Thomas Middleton, Cyril Tourneur and others as well as Shakespeare. An advert for their ongoing stage work might well have been expected in the Folio preliminaries.

But here in 1623 the Folio seems to have made a conscious decision to distance the plays from the theatre, perhaps as part of

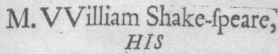

M. VVilliam Shake-fpeare,
HIS
True Chronicle Hiftory of the life
and death of King *Lear*, and his
three Daughters.

With the vnfortunate life of E D G A R,
fonne and heire to the Earle of *Glocefter*, and
his fullen and affumed humour of T O M
of Bedlam.

As it was plaid before the Kings Maiefty at White-Hall, vp-
pon S. Stephens night, in Chriftmas Hollidaies.

By his Maiefties Seruants, playing vfually at the
Globe on the *Banck-fide.*

Printed for *Nathaniel Butter.*
1608.

FIGURE 2 Shakespeare's *King Lear* as it appeared in quarto form, dated
1608: note the extended title. *Bodleian Library, Arch. G d.42* (5).

a strategy of pitching the volume upmarket. Although their status had somewhat improved since Sir Thomas Bodley's famous injunction to his librarian in Oxford in 1612 that he should omit plays as 'riffraff' and 'baggage books' (literally portable, small-format works), plays and theatre were still rather lowbrow entertainment forms.[7] Printing the plays in the prestigious format of a folio volume, associated with Bibles and learned books, may have been part of an aspirant marketing strategy of which suppressing the works' origins in the theatre was part. It may not be a coincidence that, although the Bodleian Library obeyed its founder's strictures when it came to quarto play texts – none of Shakespeare's works made their way into the collection at this point – it did obtain a copy of the First Folio at the beginning of 1624.

There are only three acknowledgements of the plays' previous life in the theatre. The first is a passing mention in the dedication to the Herbert brothers that they have previously enjoyed the plays 'when they were acted'. The second is Heminge and Condell's reassurance to the buying public that the plays have 'had their trial already' before theatre audiences. Finally is a list of 'the principal actors in all these plays' that appears as part of the prefatory material to the volume (PLATE 5). At the head of this list is Shakespeare himself. Opinions vary about how much he acted in his own and others' plays, although we do know from actor lists to Ben Jonson's plays that he performed in those as late as 1604. An old but unverified tradition suggests he played the Ghost of the murdered King of Denmark in *Hamlet* and the faithful old servant Adam in *As You Like It*, but this may derive from an assumption that his roles were minor or cameo ones. His position in the actors' list may suggest more extensive importance as a player. Richard Burbage, the tragedian for whom Shakespeare wrote major roles, including Hamlet, Macbeth, Antony and Othello, comes next. The order of the list seems to be, broadly, the chronology of actors joining the company: the first seven are the sharers who formed the Chamberlain's Men in 1594, and last on the list is John Rice, who became a sharer around 1620. These men, and their roles in Shakespeare's plays, are discussed in Chapter 3.

Last of the prefatory documents is a catalogue listing the plays included, but missing *Troilus and Cressida* (PLATE 1). The division of the plays into three generic categories – comedies, histories and tragedies – repeats the book's full title: it seems that the range of story types was an attractive feature to be stressed. It clarifies generic affiliations under these three headings: whereas later criticism has understood Shakespeare's works via new subdivisions such as 'problem plays' or 'golden comedies' or 'late romances' or 'Roman plays', the Folio's genres are evidently capacious enough to include the grimly venereal *Measure for Measure* as a comedy, or the fairy-tale romance of *Cymbeline* among the tragedies. Each play is given a page number, and each section appears to be separate because it has individual pagination.

The category 'histories' shows the clearest editorial intervention in preparing this aspect of the book's presentation. First, the Folio compilers have restricted the category to English history: the plays on Roman historical topics, such as *Julius Caesar*, are allocated to the tragedies. So too are the plays *Macbeth* and *King Lear*, where Shakespeare's major source was, as it was for plays on Henrys and Richards, the volume of history by Raphael Holinshed, his *Chronicles*. For readers in 1623 the category of 'history' is a distinctly national, rather than a strictly generic, one.

Second, the plays have been importantly reordered. Shakespeare wrote his plays on medieval English history achronologically – that is, he began with the later part of the story, the reigns of Henry VI and then Richard III. Subsequently he wrote the earlier material on Richard II and Henry IV and Henry V. Were the plays to be presented in the sequence Shakespeare wrote them, that is to say, they would be in this order: *2 Henry VI*, *3 Henry VI*, *1 Henry VI*, *Richard III*, *Richard II*, *King John*, *1 Henry IV*, *2 Henry IV*, *Henry V*, *Henry VIII*. In the Folio, by contrast, the plays are placed decisively according to historical chronology, from the historically earliest play, *King John* (King John died in 1216), to the last, the sixteenth-century material of *King Henry VIII*. The chronological logic of kings and their reigns trumps the chronological logic of the playwright and his plays. Further, each play was originally performed individually: the theatrical fashion for performing sequences of Shakespeare's histories is a twentieth-century one, influenced by the famous Wagnerian opera cycles performed at the Bayreuth Festival from the 1870s. But although many of Shakespeare's histories had enjoyed, and would continue to enjoy, considerable stage and print popularity as stand-alone plays, in the Folio their titles are amended to stress their serial quality.

For example, the play published here as *The First Part of King Henry the Fourth* had already been printed six times since 1598, largely because of the enormous (literally) popularity of its fat antihero Falstaff. In none of those editions did it bear the name 'First Part': it was simply *Henry IV*. The play printed as *The Second Part of King Henry IV* was thus more obviously a sequel – like a modern film sequel which adds 'II' to its title – when it was printed as an individual play in 1600. Here in the Folio catalogue, by contrast, it looks like the second part of an artistic diptych, always planned to have two parts. The arrangement of the plays in this category also stresses historical movement. The ending of each history play seems provisional in the Folio: the end of a chapter rather than anything more conclusive. Each play works to contain its traitors, crown its candidate and establish a tentative order – what Henry IV calls a 'frighted peace' (*1 Henry IV* 1.1.2), but turn the page and the whole shebang of kings and princes, lords and servants, loyalists and rebels, battles and conspiracies, jumps up for another bout. As the mordant Polish theatre director Jan Kott put it in his famous book *Shakespeare Our Contemporary* (English translation 1964), 'every successive chapter, every Shakespearian act is merely a repetition ... history is like a great staircase on which there treads a constant procession of kings.'[8]

We might think differently about the politics of *Richard II*, for instance, which ends with the deposition and murder of the king by his cousin Henry Bolingbroke, depending on whether we experience the play as a self-contained dramatic unit (it was described as a 'tragedy' when first printed), or whether we see it merely as one episode in a historical soap opera. The single play *Richard II* might seem to show that the uncrowning of a rightful king carries no real consequences, since the promise made by the play's bishop that God will protect his deputy on earth does not seem to be kept; but when we experience it as an episode, our attention is shifted immediately from the dead to the living, where Bolingbroke's reign, on the very next page, is dogged by the implacable political and psychological reverberations of his actions. Or take *Henry V*, where the final Epilogue reports that, after Henry's remarkable victory at Agincourt, his infant heir 'lost France and made his England bleed' (Epilogue, 12). These ironies are emphasised on turning the page in the Folio, to the sombre stage direction beginning *Henry VI Part 1*: 'Dead march. Enter the funeral of King Henry the Fifth'.

Sequence thus carries interpretative consequences in the Folio arrangement of the history plays, but it is not clear whether the other categories are ordered according to some meaningful pattern. They are not obviously chronological, since first of the plays is *The Tempest*, commonly identified as one of Shakespeare's last plays. Their arrangement doesn't appear to be thematic, although if a reader read the plays in order there might be some shaping of their response to later plays in the light of reading earlier ones.

Maybe *The Taming of the Shrew* looks a gentler play when read after its more affirmative cousin *Much Ado About Nothing*: another, but more ameliorative, version of the battle of the sexes. Perhaps it is easier to recognise what is unlikeable about Prince Hamlet when his play is sandwiched between the titular protagonists of *Macbeth* and *King Lear*. Modern collected editions sometimes follow the Folio's generic arrangement but are more usually now organised around Shakespearean chronology, in which *Taming* precedes *Much Ado*, and *Hamlet* comes well before the other two tragedies. Presenting his plays as part of his collected *Workes* in 1616, Ben Jonson also placed them in chronological order, including the date of performance for each play. Chronological order can serve to marginalise early plays in particular as juvenile or apprentice work, but here the Folio makes no such distinction. That's particularly clear in the history play section, where, as we have seen, the early works on the reign of Henry VI come after the later ones on Henry IV. But while the order of plays might have consequences for readers, it may well be that there is no purposeful sequence to the plays and they appear according to some more pragmatic reason, such as the order of manuscripts in the pile, or the date of delivery of copy (the order in which the plays were typeset and printed is discussed in Chapter 4). In any case, the catalogue with its page numbers theoretically allows readers to drop in and out of the volume wherever they please, rather than reading it from start to finish in the order presented.

The texts of the plays

Having thought extensively about the ways in which the para-textual material in the First Folio might have things to tell us about the practical, commercial and literary aspects of the book, let us now turn to think about the plays themselves. What clues do they hold about the provenance of their texts? How far do they seem to have been edited for the benefit of readers? What do they tell us about their theatrical lives pre-print?

The first thing to remind ourselves is that no play of Shakespeare's exists in an early manuscript, either in his own hand or that of a scribe. When editors imagine what the printers' copy for various plays might have been, their speculations are just that, speculative. We can attempt to deduce from the appearance of the printed texts some of the features that the now-lost manuscripts behind them might have possessed. Much of the work of textual scholars during the twentieth century has been the fantasy quest to imagine, and reconstruct, that lost authorial manuscript: in the provocative metaphor of the pre-eminent editor Fredson Bowers, to 'strip the veil of print from a text'.[9]

For some plays that unveiled version, the lost manuscript, seems to have been a neat, probably scribal transcription prepared by a professional writer for theatrical use or as a version for the printers. For others the printers can be shown to have worked from a previously printed copy, usually annotated, corrected, or cross-referenced with another source. Some plays suggest they are taken from Shakespeare's own working manuscript – sometimes graphically described as 'foul papers' – because of particular features associated with such documents. The relation to the 'foul papers' may be direct – we think that the copy for *Henry V* and for *All's Well That Ends Well*, *Coriolanus*, *Twelfth Night* and others was probably authorial manuscript. Or it may be that the Folio takes as its copy a previously printed edition that was itself typeset from such a manuscript.

Romeo and Juliet is set from a previous printing and can offer a couple of examples preserved from the lost manuscript. One feature associated with authorial copy is inconsistent speech prefixes (the abbreviated name of the character that indicates the speaker in the play text), particularly for minor characters. For example, Juliet's mother is labelled variously as '*Wife*', '*Old La.*', '*Mo.*', and '*La.*' in speech prefixes, and in stage directions as '*Capulet's Wife*', '*Mother*', '*Lady*' and '*Lady of the House*'. These names indicate her different roles relative at particular moments to other characters on stage rather than a coherent personality, and might thus capture the way the writer deploys or conceptualises his cast in the process of composition. A text that had been prepared for theatrical use would need to standardise these names to make it easier to generate a cue script – the roll of paper containing each actor's part, along with his cues.

A second feature of the play text suggests an origin, perhaps at one remove via an intervening printed text, in authorial drafting papers. After leaving Juliet after their first meeting on the night of the Capulets' ball, Romeo vows to get the Friar's advice, and speaks four lines about the coming dawn:

> The grey-eyed morn smiles on the frowning night
> Chequ'ring the eastern clouds with streaks of light,
> And darkness flecked like a drunkard reels
> From forth day's pathway, made by Titan's wheels.

Immediately after this the next scene begins with the Friar alone on stage, delivering an almost identical speech (PLATE 6). It's not likely that a performance text would retain this repetition, since it's not dramatically plausible that both characters should apostrophise the dawn in sequence. (The Oxford editors choose to cut Romeo's lines and leave the speech to the 'grey-eyed morn' to the Friar as he gathers botanicals into a basket for his medicines; 2.2.1–4.) The most likely explanation for the repetition seems to be that the manuscript underlying the print version of the play records Shakespeare's drafting process: he writes the poetic speech first, and only then decides who should speak it, probably giving it first to one character and then to the other, without properly deleting the unwanted version. So the printed text records something of the writing process; something that modern editors tend to tidy away in their search for a more authoritative text – and in the process it may also tell us something about how Shakespeare viewed the relationship between speech and character at this point in his career (the speech comes first, and then is given to the most appropriate character).

One last example in this category comes from the opening of *Much Ado About Nothing*. Here, the Folio text follows an earlier printing again, in its opening stage direction: 'Enter Leonato, governor of Messina, Innogen his wife, Hero his Daughter, Beatrice his niece, with a messenger'. Readers familiar with this comedy might justifiably be bewildered by one of these names: Innogen. It's striking that the play has no role for a mother to Hero. In the Folio, Innogen never speaks, and, after one further stage direction, fades entirely from the text. Indeed, the plot in which her father denounces Hero at the altar as 'fallen / Into a pit of ink, that the wide sea / Hath drops too few to wash her clean again' (4.1.140–42), might have turned out very differently had there been a mother to intervene. It seems that Shakespeare initially conceived of a family unit in which the mother was present (and indeed he is working from an Italian source story in which the mother plays an important role in rehabilitating her daughter's broken engagement). However, in the process of developing the plot, he apparently realised she was not needed, or, further, that her presence would impede an important element of the play: the maturation of Benedick when he alone chooses to believe Beatrice and Hero over his former military comrades Claudio and Don Pedro. (Although we now associate romantic comedies with a female audience, Shakespeare's comedies often have male coming-of-age as one of their dominant structural motifs.) So Innogen is what is sometimes called a 'ghost' character:

one whose presence can be faintly seen as a vestige of the writing process, and whose marked absence gives us an insight into the way the play changed during composition. The redundant mother is also, of course, exhibit A (or perhaps B, after Hamlet's mother Gertrude), in any discussion of the question asked by an influential academic article of the 1980s: 'Where are the mothers in Shakespeare?' (In this case the answer is: left on the cutting-room floor.[10]) Incidentally, these examples of Shakespeare at work further question that statement by Heminge and Condell that he never 'blotted a line'.

If these plays all seem to show traces of authorial drafting, other plays, on the contrary, show in their stage directions or other aspects a text that is closer to performance in different ways. The so-called permissive stage direction at the beginning of *Titus Andronicus* is a good example. This scene, the return to the city of the triumphant Roman general Titus, needs to fill the stage with the pomp and ritual of the victory procession, as the stage direction indicates: 'Sound drums and trumpets. And then enter two of Titus' sons. After them, two men bearing a coffin covered with black, then two other sons. After them, Titus Andronicus, and then Tamora the Queen of the Goths and her two sons Chiron and Demetrius, with Aaron the Moor, and others, as many as can be' (cf. Oxford 1.1.69). The stage direction names eleven characters (there are already four named characters on stage, plus unspecified numbers of tribunes, senators and followers) and wants even more, 'as many as can be'. It's a direction that has its origins in theatrical practice, not in the experience of reading a play, where the number of people on stage is constrained only by the limits of the readerly imagination, not by the actual numbers of acting personnel.

Plays offer clues to their own different genealogies, then, in the details particularly of stage directions and other technical elements of textual presentation. Importantly, there has been relatively little attempt to standardise the appearance of the plays when they are printed together in the Folio. The comparison with Ben Jonson's work on his collected *Workes*, published in 1616, is again instructive. Jonson himself saw his works through the press and acted as his own attentive editor, ensuring that each play was preceded by a list of its characters, its date of first performance and those who originally acted in it (this is how we know some details about Shakespeare's acting career, and about those of John Heminge and Henry Condell, as discussed in Chapter 3). Act and scene divisions are marked consistently in Latin, and each scene in a Jonson play has what editors call a 'massed entry': a list of all the characters required in the scene, whether they are on stage at the beginning or not. These are presented in a standardised small capitals format. The use of typeface, including italics and small capitals, is carefully deployed across the work, giving it visual unity and clarity of layout. Compared with this, the Shakespeare First Folio looks much more various and records a much more diverse set of underlying, now lost, printers' copy.

Let's take as a way into this issue of heterogeneity one particular feature of the text, the list of characters which was becoming a standard part of printed plays in this period, but which is present only intermittently in the Shakespeare Folio. Seven plays have a list of their characters, usually headed 'The names of all the Actors' and occasionally indicating the setting of the play: *The Tempest* – somewhat paradoxically – takes place on 'an uninhabited Island' and *Measure for Measure* in 'Vienna'. These lists are very unlikely to have been part of Shakespeare's original papers, and there is no particular use for them in the playhouse. Such lists become an increasingly common element in printed plays as part of that genre's move towards acknowledging the needs of readers: we would now expect this as routine. There is no other example, however, of such character lists coming after, rather than before, their play. This may be because the Folio publishers did not have extensive prior experience in play publication.

Sometimes the lists in the Shakespeare book contain interesting and even puzzling information. Only the character list tells us, for instance, that the mysterious Duke who disguises himself as a friar to oversee the plot of *Measure for Measure* is called Vincentio: his name is never mentioned in the play itself. In the list that concludes *Othello* (PLATE 7), we get a kind of clarity about the characters – Cassio is 'an honourable Lieutenant', Iago 'a villain' – that somewhat oversimplifies their functions in the play. The description of Bianca as 'a courtesan' is particularly problematic: *Othello* is a play in which all three female characters are accused of being whores, strumpets and otherwise sexually unreliable: it's part of the dynamic of the military world of male bonding into which the women unwittingly and fatally intrude. Iago tells us that Bianca, who is in love with Cassio, is a 'huswife that by selling her desires / Buys herself bread'. But Iago has a low opinion of everyone and can only equate sex not with romance or affection but with lust and animal appetite. Perhaps we should therefore read this character list as less the neutral and authoritative textual apparatus we might expect, and rather a continuation of the play's own derogatory rhetoric about its women. It is a part of the play world and written from within its values, rather than a neutral supplement to it.

Some of these lists have been used as evidence of the underlying manuscript behind the printed edition, a clean copy apparently drawn up by a scribe or another agent, for the print shop to work from. The playing company was, after all, unlikely to trust the printing shop with their own precious working copies. We know that the theatrical scribe Ralph Crane (discussed in Chapter 3) was in the habit of drawing up a list of characters to some of the plays he transcribed, because we have such a list for his extant manuscript copy of a play by Thomas Middleton titled *The Witch*. We also know that Crane worked on King's Men plays and we can surmise with reasonable confidence that he was probably behind the neatness of the first five plays in the Folio: his is the hand we can see in *The Tempest*, *The Two Gentlemen of Verona*, *The Merry Wives of Windsor* and *The Comedy of Errors*, the first four plays in the volume. He also almost certainly provided the tidied manuscript for *The Winter's Tale* and *Othello*. The majority of these plays have a character list along with other Crane trademarks, identified by T. Howard-Hill as a tendency towards massed entries, to embellished or more literary stage directions, to precise punctuation, and to consistent act and scene divisions.[11]

Later in the Folio, and unconnected with Crane's work, we get further character lists, but these begin to look as if they have been generated to fill out otherwise blank pages owing to miscalculations in the difficult art of 'casting off' – estimating from a manuscript the number of printed pages required (see Chapter 4). Thus *Timon of Athens* and *Henry IV Part 2* each end with a full page list of their characters in large type. The history play goes so far as to give a kind of map of the political factions fighting for supremacy by bracketing characters together as 'of the king's party', 'opposites against King Henry the Fourth' and, the ragtag companions of the disreputable Falstaff, 'Irregular humorists' (PLATE 8). The point here is that no one has done what a modern copy-editor would do, or what we are familiar with from a collected edition such as the Oxford or the Folger, which is to standardise this information for each play. Lists of what later editors would latinise as *dramatis personae* are present because of the independent initiative of the scribe, Ralph Crane, or apparently as a remedial feature in the printing shop, rather than as part of a unifying concept for the design of the whole book, or a sustained anticipation of readers' requirements.

This heterogeneity of presentation and the absence of overall editorial oversight can be found in just about every aspect of the Folio play texts, but the resulting inconsistencies can tell us a lot about the plays' previous lives in print, manuscript and performance. Take act and scene divisions, for instance. These are useful for readers since they can help to orient and pace the action and to indicate changes of emphasis, but they were less important in early outdoor performance, where, without elaborate scene changes, the plays probably ran quite fluidly from one scene to the next. Some plays are printed without any scene divisions at all. The Folio *Romeo and Juliet*, for instance, begins rather misleadingly with the heading 'Actus Primus. Scena Prima', but does not follow up with any other demarcated or numbered scenes or acts. The same is true of the second and third parts of the *Henry VI* plays, which were also written for performance in the outdoor theatres where such continuous staging was the dramatic norm. There was simply no need for this organisational hierarchy in the manuscripts from which the plays were typeset and printed.

But other plays, such as *Macbeth* or *The Winter's Tale*, which date from the later part of Shakespeare's career, are marked out with act and scene divisions, and in this they register the requirements of a different playing space. In 1599 Shakespeare's company moved to Bankside to their own theatre, the Globe, but they seem to have had a long-held ambition to supplement this with an indoor theatre, perhaps to extend the playing season in wintery weather and also to target a more exclusive audience. In 1608 they finally acquired the rights to perform plays in a smaller, indoor theatre in the district of Blackfriars. Plays were subsequently performed in both venues. The title page of the 1622 edition of *Othello*, for instance, advertises 'As it hath been diverse times acted at the Globe and at the Blackfriars, by his Majesty's Servants' (FIGURE 3). One feature of the Blackfriars was that because it was not lit, like the

THE
Tragœdy of Othello,
The Moore of Venice.

As it hath beene diuerse times acted at the
Globe, and at the Black-Friers, by
his Maiesties Seruants.

Written by VVilliam Shakespeare.

LONDON,
Printed by *N. O.* for *Thomas Walkley*, and are to be sold at his
shop, at the Eagle and Child, in Brittans Bursse.
1622.

FIGURE 3 The quarto of *Othello* (1622) shows that the play was performed at the Globe and at the indoor theatre of Blackfriars. *Bodleian Library, Arch. G d.*43 (7).

Globe, by natural light, it instead used candles for illumination. These candles needed to be trimmed or changed during the course of performance (PLATE 9). Plays intended for, or tweaked to be playable at, Blackfriars are thus organised around the act breaks necessary for this maintenance, which probably involved a few moments of music during a pause in the stage action. Act divisions thus became prominent as a practical necessity rather than as aesthetic structure, although writers were of course able to make dramaturgical capital out of these requirements. A number of Folio plays show these divisions and thus record one aspect of their performance tradition in the indoor theatre, although the now-standard citation of Shakespeare plays by act, scene and line number has to wait for much later editors for its development.

A Midsummer Night's Dream shows us how an early play initially written for the outdoor theatre was changed for performance in the indoor conditions. The play was first printed in 1600; like all the individually printed plays of Shakespeare except the late text of *Othello*, it does not have any act divisions. In the Folio an act break is introduced as Puck induces all the lovers to sleep so that he can rejig them into two couples so 'Jack shall have Jill, / Naught shall go ill', (3.3.45–6) and the Folio text instructs that 'They sleep all the Act' – that is, through the act break and on into the next scene. Some play texts are apparently printed in forms that recall their early life as Globe plays; others, like *A Midsummer Night's Dream*, from later adaptations for Blackfriars performance. This suggests that for the playhouse, scripts existed in a flexible form, to be updated as circumstances required. The working copy was the most recent rewriting of the play, and in many cases that is the version that has been printed in the Folio. That is in interesting contrast to most modern editorial procedure, which tends to privilege the first or earliest version as that closest to the author.

One final aspect of the texts that shows the range of their provenance is their varying representation of stage directions. These are inconsistently provided. Some plays have elaborately visual stage directions, apparently intended for readers to imagine the scene. In *The Tempest*, for example, the play's evocative stage effects are translated into detailed descriptions: 'Solemn and strange music, and Prospero on the top (invisible). Enter several strange shapes bringing in a banquet; and dance about it with gentle actions of salutations, and inviting the king &c to eat, they depart' (Folio 3.3.19). *A Midsummer Night's Dream*, by contrast, does not translate its magical stage business into narrative form, offering only unadorned exit and entrances.

The majority of plays have limited stage directions; this may be part of their flexibility for modern actors and directors. Comparing the elaborate apparatus of a play by George Bernard Shaw, or the extensive instructions about pacing and delivery found in a Samuel Beckett script, with the minimal stage directions of the First Folio is instructive and liberating. The ending of *The Taming of the Shrew*, for instance, has been a provocative source of disagreement and reinterpretation in criticism and the theatre. Katherine, the feisty daughter of Baptista, has been married off to an idiosyncratic fortune-hunter called Petruchio, who vows to tame 'this wildcat' (1.2.195) – depending on how you read the play, they are a well-matched screwball couple who respect each other's strength, or he is a sadistic misogynist set on breaking his wife's spirit. These wildly divergent readings come into particular focus at the end of the play, where Petruchio shows off his wife's new-found obedience by betting with his friends that she will come at his bidding. She does, and delivers a long and orthodox speech about the wife's duty to the husband, at the end of which she tells her fellow women to 'place your hands below your husband's foot, / In token of which duty, if he please, / My hand is ready, may it do him ease' (5.2.182–4). No stage directions clarify what, if any, physical gestures accompany these lines. We can immediately see that their meaning could be significantly modified if Katherine kneels or bends down and places her hand under her husband's foot, or if, say, she stands with arms folded daring him to ask her to do so. Petruchio's reply, 'Why there's a wench! Come on, and kiss me, Kate' (5.2.185), is similarly unchoreographed in the Folio text. Do the couple kiss, or not? (The romantic Oxford editors add a stage direction to say they do, but that's an interpretation not a fact.) And if they do kiss, is it forced or mutual – the silencing of Katherine or her rehabilitation, the final act of suppression or the longed-for consummation? The range of meanings this play has generated is thus directly related to its first appearance in print. The absence of explanatory stage directions is an enabling feature, allowing the play to be acted, directed and thus interpreted in any number of ways.

Behind the printed plays in the First Folio, then, are a range of prior documentations of their texts, many of them now lost. For the plays previously printed, existing print copies were a key source, but they were almost always marked up with some corrections and alterations, perhaps by one of the playhouse personnel. For the unpublished plays, some, particularly those printed early in the book, seem to draw on specially prepared scribal copies, and it may have been that the King's Men scribe Ralph Crane was intended to produce further neat transcripts, marked with his own idiosyncratic presentational style. Other plays were apparently set from authorial manuscripts or from prompt books belonging to the theatre, and these tend to show differences in the way they refer to characters in speech prefixes and the way they handle stage directions. The remainder of this chapter gives a little more detail, taking three plays as case studies in different kinds of Folio text: *The Tempest*, *King Lear* and *Macbeth*.

The Tempest

The Tempest was written around 1611 towards the end of Shakespeare's writing career, and was not published before the Folio in 1623. It tells the story of the magician Prospero, who lives on an island with his daughter Miranda and his servants Caliban and Ariel. The title tempest brings Prospero's old enemies into his power, and the play, set in real time (what Aristotle called 'unity of action'), shows how he brings them to the point of revenge, and ultimately steps back from it. Earlier critics were interested in the play's meditations on art, and on the character of Prospero as a figure of the artist in general, or an autobiographical portrait of Shakespeare in particular. When Shakespeare was finally commemorated in Poets' Corner in Westminster Abbey in 1740, it was with a life-size statue of him leaning his elbow on a stack of books and pointing to a scroll on which are written a variant of the lines from *The Tempest* in which Prospero bids farewell to his magic: 'The Cloud capt Tow'rs, / The Gorgeous Palaces, / The Solemn Temples, / The Great Globe itself, / Yea all which it Inherit, / Shall Dissolve; And like the baseless Fabrick of a Vision / Leave not a wreck behind' (PLATE 10). More recently, the critical interest of *The Tempest* has shifted, along with its performance traditions. As a play shaped by the early encounters between the English and the native peoples of America – and the play that gives us the phrase 'brave new world' (5.1.186) – it was powerfully associated in the later twentieth century with the history and legacy of colonialism. These readings have given a new complexity to the character of Caliban, bluntly described as 'a salvage and deformed slave' in the Folio character list.

The first play in the collection, *The Tempest* was apparently printed from a Ralph Crane transcript: we can see his characteristic use of parentheses, his elaborate stage directions, and his preference for providing character lists all in evidence in this text. In addition, as the Folio's greatest detective, Charlton Hinman, discovered, the first page of this play has been corrected at least four times, showing that particular care was taken in Jaggard's printing shop with the accuracy of the beginning of the book.[12]

Most striking, perhaps, are the stage directions in *The Tempest*. They are sometimes vague – 'Enter certain Nymphs' – but more often elaborate and detailed. As one critic points out, 'there are more adjectives, adverbs and elaborations than one would expect from an author or certainly from a prompt book': 'Thunder and lightning. Enter Ariel (like a Harpy) claps his wings upon the table, and with a quaint device the banquet vanishes' (3.3.52). This sounds 'more like an account of what happened onstage than an author's advisory notes for production'.[13] A 'quaint device' seems a reference to the mysteries of stage mechanics by someone watching the effect who doesn't know how it works, rather than by someone – Shakespeare or other someone else from the theatre personnel – who understands the pulleys, ropes and trapdoors intimately. Some of the incidental variations – such as whether speech prefixes are abbreviated to three or four letters – are actually tiny traces of different compositors working in Jaggard's shop (see Chapter 3 for more details). It seems as if one of the compositors was working with a box of mixed type, or hadn't got enough, since his work is marked by a high incidence of the wrong fount or typeface. It has also been suggested that the large number of colons and dashes in the play text are evidence of one of the compositors' particular punctuation preferences (Compositor B, see Chapter 3).

Because the play exists in only one early printed edition, a modern editor has relatively few choices to make about how to present the text for readers. The job of editing the Folio text here is one of standardisation of presentation, spelling, punctuation and capitalisation. There is one more difficult problem in the play, however: a problem of the interpretation of a particular word known to scholars as a textual crux. When Caliban, Prospero's slave, encounters Trinculo and Stephano, the drunken jester and butler from the shipwreck, he pleads pathetically for their affection. He promises:

> I prithee, let me bring thee where crabs grow,
> And I with my long nails will dig thee pig-nuts,
> Show thee a jay's nest, and instruct thee how
> To snare the nimble marmoset. I'll bring thee
> To clust'ring filberts, and sometimes I'll get thee
> Young seamews from the rock. Wilt thou go with me? (2.2.166–71)

Except the word 'seamews' is not found in the Folio, where Caliban offers 'scamels' instead. The word 'scamels' has proved very resistant to the kinds of editorial explanation that smooth out Shakespeare's meanings for us. It does not appear anywhere else, and nothing, except context, tells us what it might mean. A scamel (if that is the singular) seems to be edible, at least when young; it is perhaps not always or easily available ('sometimes'); it lives in or on rock. So it might be a plant (like filberts, or hazelnuts) or a creature (like the marmoset, a kind of monkey): a kind of shellfish, perhaps? Scouring all the books and dictionaries and examples of dialect, looking to the New World which informed the play's composition as well as to rural Warwickshire, the source of some of Shakespeare's unfamiliar vocabulary, for this mystery word, we have got no nearer than that this might be an error for the word 'seamew', an archaic version of 'seagull'. Some earlier editions emended the word on these lines (and, indeed, so does the Oxford edition). More recent editions tend to leave it as 'scamels', perhaps to capture the ultimate unknowability of Caliban, or the details of the natural world over which he alone in the play has mastery. Caliban snarls at Prospero and Miranda that 'You taught me language, and my profit on't / Is I know how to curse' (1.2.365–6), yet, despite this linguistic indoctrination, he remains something alien and other. 'Scamels' is/are also a moment of unreadability for the Folio text: perhaps a misreading by a compositor dealing with difficult writing, perhaps a word, now lost, intended by Shakespeare, it sums up some of the book's ultimate inscrutability.

King Lear

Unlike *The Tempest*, which had not been published before 1623, *King Lear* had appeared in quarto form in 1608 (FIGURE 2). The play is the story of Lear, king of ancient Britain, who divides his kingdom between his daughters, who turn against him. The pathos of his increasing madness, amplified by his crazed conversations on the heath with his fool, a (pretend) madman and a blind old courtier, is partly alleviated when he is reconciled with his young-est daughter Cordelia, but events turn against them and the play ends with their deaths.

The 1608 text (usually abbreviated in bibliographical discussion as Q) differs from the 1623 text (F) in a number of particulars: Q contains some 300 lines that are not in F, and F contains around 100 lines not in Q; the scene in which Kent and a gentleman discuss the turbulent events is present only in Q, as is the sequence in which a maddened Lear places his daughters in a mock trial; the final two lines of the play are spoken by Albany in Q and by Edgar in F; and there are hundreds of minor variants that individually and cumulatively affect overall and local interpretations. What are we to do with these differences?

Most modern editors of the play now believe that the two texts of *King Lear* record two distinct stages of the play's life and that F is a conscious and purposeful revision of Q. Many scholars would go further, and argue that *Lear* was written probably around 1605–06 and subsequently revised by Shakespeare himself three or four years later. If the revisions are indeed by Shakespeare, we can only speculate about why he might have undertaken rewriting that in some places is significant and in others merely fiddly. Was it that Shakespeare was dissatisfied with his work and wanted to tinker with aspects of its stagecraft and expression, or was the revision required by different theatrical conditions, such as indoor performance? Perhaps it was both. One difference can illustrate these possibilities. Both versions of *King Lear* include one of the most traumatic scenes Shakespeare ever wrote. Lear's daughter Regan and her husband the Duke of Cornwall torture the elderly Gloucester and pluck out his eyes on stage in the memorably callous phrase 'Out, vile jelly'. In Q, the text published in 1608, the scene ends with Regan exiting with the injured Cornwall, and a nine-line exchange between two servants talking together about what they might do for the wounded Gloucester: 'I'll fetch some flax and whites of eggs / To apply to his bleeding face'. The servants do not appear in the equivalent place in the Folio text of 1623, in which the scene ends with Cornwall's request to his wife: 'Give me your arm'. In part their absence from the later text asserts a harsher world-view in which there is not even the simple goodness of servants to counteract the cruelty of their masters – and there are other changes in F that might add to this bleak impression. This would argue that the scene was reworked to revise the tone of the play. It's in interesting – and heartbreaking – contrast to the romance plays of father–daughter reconciliation, such as *The Tempest* and *The Winter's Tale* that Shakespeare may have been working on at the same time. But the rewriting may have also, or instead, had a more immediately practical purpose. The servant dialogue may have been unnecessary in the theatre for which F was prepared, an indoor theatre which had act breaks for the trimming of candle wicks. The servants' role may be more about the practical business of theatre than about the empathetic business of the story. In both versions of the play, Gloucester has to reappear in the very next scene, in an encounter with his son Edgar, who is disguised as a Bedlam beggar. The servants may be there to temporise, to give the Gloucester actor a bit more time offstage to clean up after the bloody atrocity we have just witnessed. In the 1623 text of *King Lear*, restructured around the playing space of Blackfriars, the scene ends with the act break, which performs the same function of giving the actor time to prepare himself for the next scene. The revision thus has both practical and artistic motivations and consequences.

The rewriting hypothesis has meant, radically, that neither text can claim to be the sole authority, nor even the preferred one, and thus recent collected editions of Shakespeare have tended to publish each version separately, sometimes calling Q 'The History of King Lear', as its title page puts it, and F 'The Tragedy of King Lear' (see the *Oxford Shakespeare*). The comparison of the two texts throws up all sorts of intriguing variants which some critics have interpreted as a snapshot of Shakespeare at work. It is easy to see why this is an attractive hypothesis, since Shakespeare's working practices remain so obscure, but it may be wishful thinking. How important are the differences between the two versions? Is it significant that in Q, for instance, Gloucester discusses 'the division of the kingdoms' – the plural suggests they are already not a single entity – whereas for his F counterpart it is 'the division of the kingdom'?, or is that to overemphasise the kind of unimportant variation produced in the print shop? Lear's speech in F about his 'darker purpose' is six lines longer than in Q – does Shakespeare feel he, or his eponymous hero, needs to give a bit more motivation to introduce the fatal love test? A number of small differences are clustered around the plays' depiction of their endings. In Q the line 'Break, heart, I prithee break' is spoken by Lear, suggesting he wills his own death as he understands the terrible tragedy of Cordelia's. The same line in F is spoken by the faithful servant

Kent after the stage direction indicates that Lear has died, thus suggesting it applies to Kent himself. Whether this gives Lear more agency or more pathos at the ending is open to interpretation, as is the nature of his knowledge of what has happened. The Folio Lear dies saying 'Look on her, look, her lips / Look there, look there' – does this suggest he entertains a hope that Cordelia is still alive? And if so, is it better to die in a happy delusion or somehow more tragic to have failed even to acknowledge the truth of suffering? Is young Edgar, the play's only claimant to moral decency, the proper spokesman for the shocked concluding lines: 'The oldest have borne most. We that are young / Shall never see so much, nor live so long' (as in F) or should they be allocated to the senior, though compromised statesman Albany (Q)?

The scholarly discussion around *King Lear* as a possible example of authorial revision contradicts the impression Heminge and Condell try to present of their author as uniquely eloquent. Rather, we now imagine that Shakespeare did himself revise his works and, further, that this process probably explains textual variants in *Hamlet*, *Troilus and Cressida*, *Othello*, and perhaps others. Not all authors are their own best revisers: although evaluating the changes – do they make the plays better or worse? – is an unfashionable idea in academic circles, it is nevertheless an interesting one. It is commonplace to describe the changes to the Folio *Lear* as streamlining or more theatrical, for instance, but many modern directors have returned to Q for the mock-trial scene as a uniquely stage-worthy moment, or found in the unease of allocating to Albany the last words a more appropriate ending for this discomforting play. In printing the later revision of the text rather than the already printed version, the Folio compilers again suggest that what Shakespeare's theatre most valued was the up-to-date script, not the 'original'. Perhaps as the printers' correlative to Shakespeare's own reworkings, this play too has a high level of errors, press corrections and uncorrected errors (see Chapter 4): it's a play text that thus makes visible some of the efforts, creative and technical, that go into its production.

Macbeth

Macbeth appears in print for the first time in the Folio. Its depiction of Macbeth's partnership with his wife and their fraught decision to murder the Scottish king, Duncan, is darkened by the mysterious presence of three witches. Ghosts, apparitions and prophecies haunt this play, which is less interested in the causes of, but fascinated by the psychological consequences of, violence. Its location in the history of Scotland and its interest in witchcraft mark it as a play written with the company's new patron, James VI of Scotland and I of England, firmly in mind: the genealogies published in the fanfare of James's accession in 1603 claimed Banquo as one of his ancestors, and Shakespeare has tidied up some of the more troubling elements of the historical Banquo in his play. In addition, the play's interest in regicide and its depiction of the mind of the assassin register the oblique but definite reverberations of the Gunpowder Plot of 1605, the failed attempt by Catholic conspirators to blow up the Houses of Parliament and kill the king and his government.

Like *King Lear*, *Macbeth* is printed in the Folio from its most up-to-date theatrical version, and, as with *King Lear*, we think this version represents a revision of an earlier play. Unlike the previous example, though, there has been little suggestion that this revision might be authorial, but instead undertaken by another playwright, Thomas Middleton. And, more importantly, we can only deduce the earlier play from its traces in the revision: it does not, unlike the quarto of *King Lear*, exist as an independent text.

What might Middleton, a younger playwright writing for the King's Men in the latter years of Shakespeare's career and beyond (and discussed in more detail in Chapter 3), have added to the play?

The hunt begins with two songs that are cued in the Folio text, but their words are not given in full: 'Come away, come away' (3.5.34), and 'Black spirits and white' (4.1.44). It was common for song texts to be kept separate from play texts, but the words of these songs appear in Middleton's manuscript play *The Witch*, and are generally thought to have been shared between the two plays by Middleton (PLATE 11). In *Macbeth* they are part of scenes where the witches are joined by the figure of Hecate, and where their speech rhythms and use of rhyme change from their previous appearances. These are considered to be part of a revision by Middleton which had as one of its aims to develop the musical presence of the witches in the play. It's an interesting insight into what early audiences might have enjoyed and wanted more of – what Diane Purkiss has memorably dubbed 'the all-singing, all-dancing plays of the Jacobean witch-vogue'[14] – and a useful counter to our own stress on the psychology of the two human protagonists as the play's most abiding source of dramatic interest. It is proposed by the recent editors of a collected edition of the works of Middleton that his contribution marks about 11 per cent of the text of *Macbeth* as we have it – leaving Shakespeare with the major share of its writing.[15] But we should also note that the text of *Macbeth* seems distinctly short for one of Shakespeare's tragedies: only just over 2,500 lines, rather than the 3,900 lines of *Hamlet* or the 3,300 words of *King Lear* in the Folio. Perhaps this suggests a script cut for performance. Perhaps Middleton also excised some of the material he found in Shakespeare's play as well as adding to and revising other parts.

Part of the legibility of Middleton in Shakespeare's plays – he is also credited with co-writing *Timon of Athens* and with a similar adaptation of *Measure for Measure*, and other plays might well join that list as more investigation is undertaken – is based on stylometric analysis, often computer-aided. Authorship tests tend not to focus on exceptional linguistic elements but instead on the commonest words, phrases or syntactic patterns. One example registers the generational and educational difference between Shakespeare and Middleton. As Jonathan Hope has pointed out, two variable forms of common locutions coexist in early modern English: a choice between 'you' and 'thou' in the second person pronoun, and ' "-th" and "-s" as an ending or the third person singular present tense of verbs (e.g. "hath" versus "has")'. Both these variants have a more modern form – 'you' and '-s' – and an older variant – 'thou' and '-th'. On both of these examples, Middleton (a Londoner born in 1580) favours the newer variant and Shakespeare (born in a Midlands market town in 1564) the older. Further, their different use of the auxiliary 'do' form is distinct. Middleton's preference is for what modern English would call the 'regulated' form of the verb, as in 'I went home'. Shakespeare's strong preference is for the unregulated, now non-standard form: 'I did go home.'[16] Hope's work is an important reminder that the Shakespeare we credit with such linguistic inventiveness and fertility is also marked by a recognisably old-fashioned syntax, particularly by contrast with his younger collaborator Middleton. Middleton's work on *Macbeth*, then, was probably intended to pep the play up for a new revival and is further evidence that the actors who helped to coordinate the publication of the Folio were drawing on the most recent versions of the plays available to them.

The Folio plays and preliminaries together construct the Shakespearean canon. Their image of Shakespeare – visual and literary – has been a dominant theme in his subsequent reception. Their selection, however contingent, has shaped the ways we have often continued to think about Shakespeare's works, organised by genre and marginalising the non-dramatic poetry and the collaborative plays. We move next to focus on the years preceding 1623, to understand why the book was published and the context into which it appeared.

TWO

Shakespeare's Reputation

HE FIRST FOLIO is a book that has cast such a long shadow that the story before it became so famous is often overlooked. The eulogists presenting the volume to the reading public do such a good job in claiming the timelessness of the plays inside – most famously in Ben Jonson's phrase 'not for an age, but for all time' – that their specificity and the immediate context of their publication are often overlooked, considered irrelevant to their eternal literary value. Why was this book printed, and what was the economic, literary and political world into which it emerged? To answer these questions, we need first to examine Shakespeare's cultural presence in the preceding period and assess his print profitability for the Folio's publisher–investors.

Shakespeare in print before 1623

Shakespeare had been an author in print for thirty years when the First Folio was printed. His earliest printed books were the narrative poems *Venus and Adonis* (first published in 1593) and *The Rape of Lucrece* (1594); *Titus Andronicus* is the earliest known Shakespeare play edition, also in 1594. There was a Shakespeare publication in almost every year from 1593 to 1623, during which time forty-nine editions of nineteen separate plays were published. There has been useful – and quite heated – scholarly debate about the extent to which play books were a profitable opportunity for the printing trade, with the prominent book historian Peter Blayney arguing compellingly that, for the most part, published plays only more or less covered their costs and that only if there was a second edition would they turn any real profit. On the other hand, the analysis of publication trends conducted by Alan Farmer and Zachary Lesser leads them to conclude that 'plays were a highly successful portion of the early modern book trade'.[1] This unresolved argument gives an interesting shape to questions of Shakespeare in print: the evidence shows that some plays were apparently print successes but that others were not invested in by stationers even where they owned the rights (Edward Blount, for instance, registered the rights to *Antony and Cleopatra* but apparently didn't publish it until the collected edition of 1623). The picture is a varied one.

For ease of analysis, let's split Shakespeare's writing career into two approximate halves: the works he wrote for the Chamberlain's Men during the 1590s up until their incorporation as the King's Men in 1603, and the works from that period to his retirement about ten years later. In the first period the main focus is romantic comedies and works based on English medieval history. In the second, tragedies and the late tragicomic plays sometimes called romances dominate. Many of the plays from the first half of Shakespeare's writing career were printed within a few years of their performance. The records of the Stationers' Company, the body regulating publishing in the period, show that the rights to print Shakespeare's plays were frequently transferred from one stationer to another, suggesting that they were viewed as active and potentially profitable commercial assets. We can assume that plays were only reprinted when an edition had run out, so the number of editions is a fair guide to sales and therefore to popularity – with readers, at least. Based on this measure, Shakespeare's most popular work is *Venus and Adonis* (around eleven editions from 1593

A CATALOGVE

of the seuerall Comedies, Histories, and Tragedies contained in this Volume.

PLATE I   The First Folio's catalogue page, from which *Troilus and Cressida* is missing.

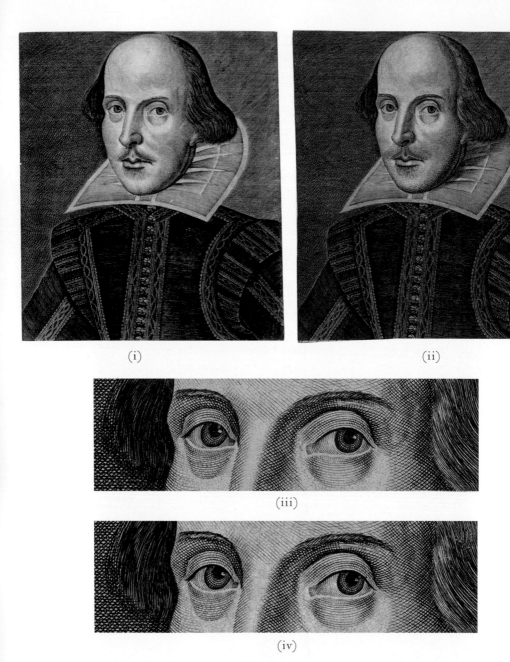

(i)　　　　　　　　　　　　　　(ii)

(iii)

(iv)

PLATE 2 (i) The first state of the Droeshout engraving. *G.11631* © *British Library Board.* (ii) The second state of the Droeshout engraving, with shading added on the collar. *By permission of the Folger Shakespeare Library.* (iii) The third state of the Droeshout engraving, with additional lights in the eyes, shown here above (iv) a detail from the second state. *By permission of the Folger Shakespeare Library.*

TO THE MOST NOBLE
AND
INCOMPARABLE PAIRE
OF BRETHREN.

WILLIAM
Earle of Pembroke, &c. Lord Chamberlaine to the
Kings most Excellent Maiesty.

AND

PHILIP
Earle of Montgomery, &c. Gentleman of his Maiesties
Bed-Chamber. Both Knights of the most Noble Order
of the Garter, and our singular good
LORDS.

Right Honourable,

Hilst we studie to be thankful in our particular, for the many fauors we haue receiued from your L.L we are falne vpon the ill fortune, to mingle two the most diuerse things that can bee, feare, and rashnesse; rashnesse in the enterprize, and feare of the successe. For, when we valew the places your H.H. sustaine, we cannot but know their dignity greater, then to descend to the reading of these trifles: and, while we name them trifles, we haue depriu'd our selues of the defence of our Dedication. But since your L.L. haue beene pleas'd to thinke these trifles some-thing, heeretofore; and haue prosequuted both them, and their Authour liuing, with so much fauour: we hope, that (they out-liuing him, and he not hauing the fate, common with some, to be exequutor to his owne writings) you will vse the like indulgence toward them, you haue done

A2

PLATE 3   The dedication to the Herbert brothers, William and Philip.

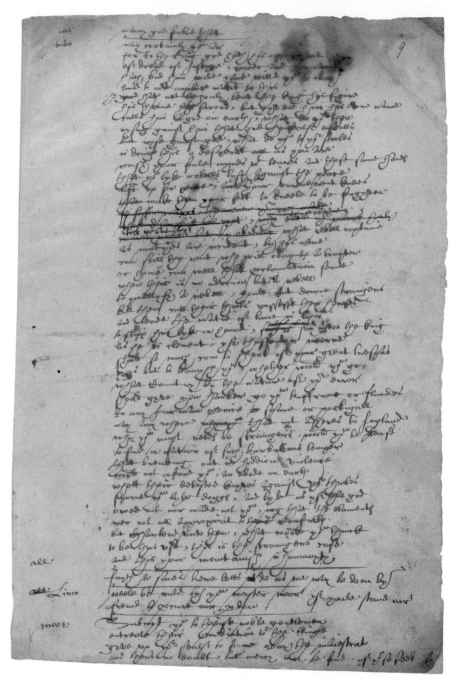

PLATE 4 Perhaps the only example of Shakespeare's dramatic writing in his own hand: part of the unpublished collaborative play *Sir Thomas More*. *Harley MS. 7368, f.9* © British Library Board.

The Workes of William Shakeſpeare,

containing all his Comedies, Hiſtories, and
Tragedies: Truely ſet forth, according to their firſt
ORJGJNALL.

The Names of the Principall Actors
in all theſe Playes.

WIlliam Shakeſpeare.	Samuel Gilburne.
Richard Burbadge.	Robert Armin.
John Hemmings.	William Oſtler.
Auguſtine Phillips.	Nathan Field.
William Kempt.	John Underwood.
Thomas Poope.	Nicholas Tooley.
George Bryan.	William Eccleſtone.
Henry Condell.	Joſeph Taylor.
William Slye.	Robert Benfield.
Richard Cowly.	Robert Goughe.
John Lowine.	Richard Robinſon.
Samuell Croſſe.	Iohn Shancke.
Alexander Cooke.	Iohn Rice.

PLATE 5 The Chamberlain's Men, later King's Men, as listed in the
First Folio.

And I will take thy word,yet if thou swear'ft,
Thou maieft proue falfe:at,Louers periuries
They fay *Ioue* laught,oh gentle *Romeo*,
If thou doft Loue.pronounce it faithfully :
Or if thou thinkeft I am too quickly wonne,
Ile frowne and be peruerfe,and fay thee nay,
So thou wilt wooe : But elfe not for the world.
In truth faire *Mountague* I am too fond :
And therefore thou maieft thinke my behauiour light,
But truft me Gentleman,ile proue more true,
Then thofe that haue coying to be ftrange,
I fhould haue beene more ftrange,I muft confeffe,
But that thou ouer heard'ft ere I was ware
My true Loues paffion,therefore pardon me,
And not impute this yeelding to light Loue,
Which the darke night hath fo difcouered.
    Rom. Lady,by yonder Moone I vow,
That tips with filuer all thefe Fruite tree tops.
    Iul. O fweare not by the Moone,th'inconftant Moone,
That monethly changes in her circled Orbe,
Leaft that thy Loue proue likewife variable.
    Rom. What fhall I fweare by ?
    Iul. Do not fweare at all :
Orif thou wilt fweare by thy gratious felfe,
Which is the God of my Idolatry,
And Ile beleeue thee.
    Rom. If my hearts deare loue.
    Iuls. Well do not fweare,although I ioy in thee:
I haue no ioy of this contract to night,
It is too rafh,too vnaduif'd,too fudden,
Too like the lightning which doth ceafe to be
Ere,one can fay,it lightens,Sweete good night:
This bud of Loue by Summers ripening breath,
May proue a beautious Flower when next we meete:
Goodnight,goodnight,as fweete repofe and reft,
Come to thy heart,as that within my breft.
    Rom. O wilt thou leaue me fo vnfatisfied ?
    Iuli. What fatisfaction can'ft thou haue to night ?
    Ro. Th'exchange of thy Loues faithfull vow for mine.
    Iul. I gaue thee mine before thou did'ft requeft it :
And yet I would it were to giue againe.
    Rom. Would'ft thou withdraw it,
For what purpofe Loue ?
    Iul. But to be franke and giue it thee againe,
And yet I wifh but for the thing I haue,
My bounty is as boundleffe as the Sea,
My Loue as deepe,the more I giue to thee
The more I haue,for both are Infinite :
I heare fome noyfe within deare Loue adue :
                       Cals within.
Anon good Nurfe,fweet *Mountague* be true :
Stay but alittle,I will come againe.
    Rom. O bleffed bleffed night,I am afear'd
Being in night,all this is but a dreame,
Too flattering fweet to be fubftantiall.
    Iul. Three words deare *Romeo*,
And goodnight indeed,
If that thy bent of Loue be Honourable,
Thy purpofe marriage,fend me word to morrow,
By one that Ile procure to come to thee,
Where and what time thou wilt performe the right,
And all my Fortunes at thy foote Ile lay,
And follow thee my Lord throughout the world.
                     Within: Madam.
I come,anon : but if thou meaneft not well,
I do befeech thee   *Within*: Madam.

(By and by I come)
To ceafe thy ftrife,and leaue me to my griefe,
To morrow will I fend.
    Rom. So thriue my foule.
    Iu. A thoufand times goodnight.   *Exit.*
    Rome. A thoufand times the worfe to want thy light,
Loue goes toward Loue as fchool-boyes frô thier books
But Loue frô Loue,towards fchoole with heauie lookes.

Enter Iuliet agaaine.

    Iul. Hift *Romeo* hift:O for a Falkners voice,
To lure this Taffell gentle backe againe,
Bondage is hoarfe,and may not fpeake aloud,
Elfe would I teare the Caue where Eccho lies,
And make her ayrie tongue more hoarfe,then
With repetition of my *Romeo*.
    Rom. It is my foule that calls vpon my name,
How filuer fweet,found Louers tongues by night,
Like fofteft Muficke to attending eares.
    Iul. Romeo.
    '*Rom.* My Neece.
    Iul. What a clock to morrow
Shall I fend to thee?
    Rom. By the houre of nine.
    Iul. I will not faile,'tis twenty yeares till then,
I haue forgot why I did call thee backe.
    Rom. Let me ftand here till thou remember it.
    Iul. I fhall forget,to haue thee ftill ftand there,
Remembring how I Loue thy company.
    Rom. And Ile ftill ftay,to haue thee ftill forget,
Forgetting any other home but this.
    Iul. Tis almoft morning,I would haue thee gone,
And yet no further then a wantons Bird,
That let's it hop a little from his hand,
Like a poore prifoner in his twifted Gyues,
And with a filken thred plucks it backe againe,
So louing Iealous of his liberty.
    Rom. I would I were thy Bird.
    Iul. Sweet fo would I,
Yet I fhould kill thee with much cherifhing:
Good night,good night.
    Rom. Parting is fuch fweete forrow,
That I fhall fay goodnight,till it be morrow.
    Iul. Sleepe dwell vpon thine eyes, peace in thy breft.
    Rom. Would I were fleepe and peace fo fweet to reft,
The gray ey'd morne fmiles on the frowning night,
Checking the Eafterne Clouds with ftreakes of light,
And darkneffe fleckel'd like a drunkard reeles,
From forth dayes pathway,made by *Titans* wheeles.
Hence will I to my ghoftly Fries clofe Cell,
His helpe to craue,and my deare hap to tell.   *Exit.*

Enter Frier alone with a basket.

    Fri. The gray ey'd morne fmiles on the frowning night,
Checkring the Eafterne Cloudes with ftreaks of light:
And fleckled darkneffe like a drunkard reeles,
From forth daies path,and *Titans* burning wheeles :
Now ere the Sun aduance his burning eye,
The day to cheere,and nights danke dew to dry,
I muft vpfill this Ofier Cage of ours,
With balefull weedes,and precious Iuiced flowers,
The earth that's Natures mother, is her Tombe,
What is her burying graue that is her wombe :
And from her wombe children of diuers kind

                                                   We

PLATE 6   Duplicate lines in Shakespeare's *Romeo and Juliet*.

*Caſ.*This did I feare, but thought he had no weapon :
For he was great of heart.

Lod. Oh Sparton Dogge:
More fell then Anguiſh, Hunger, or the Sea :
Looke on the Tragicke Loading of this bed :
This is thy worke :
The Obiect poyſons Sight,

Let it be hid. *Gratiano,*keepe the houſe,
And ſeize vpon the Fortunes of the Moore,
For they ſucceede on you. To you, Lord Gouernor,
Remaines th eCenſure of this helliſh villaine :
The Time, the Place, the Torture, oh inforce it :
My ſelfe will ſtraight aboord, and to the State,
This heauie Act, with heauie heart relate. *Exeunt.*

FINIS.

The Names of the Actors.
(:*.*:)

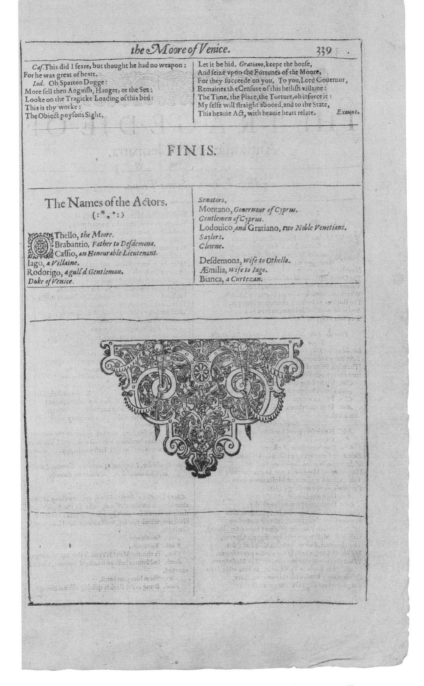

Thello, *the Moore.*
Brabantio, *Father to Deſdemona.*
Caſſio, *an Honourable Lieutenant.*
Iago, *a Villaine.*
Rodorigo, *a gull'd Gentleman.*
Duke of Venice.

Senators.
Montano, *Gonernour of Cyprus.*
Gentlemen of Cyprus.
Lodouico, *and* Gratiano, *two Noble Venetians.*
Saylors.
Clowne.

Deſdemona, *wife to Othello.*
Æmilia, *wife to Iago.*
Bianca, *a Curtezan.*

PLATE 7 *Othello*'s character list is evaluative rather than neutrally descriptive.

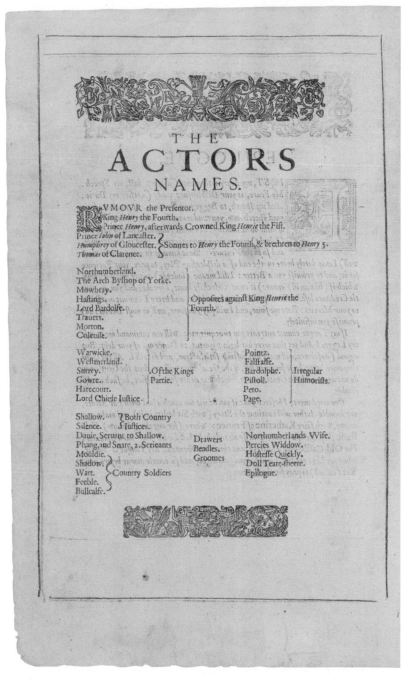

PLATE 8 This full page list of the characters in *Henry IV Part 2* is partly to fill out an otherwise spare page: it also works to codify the play's different factions.

PLATE 9 The indoor Sam Wanamaker Theatre at Shakespeare's Globe draws inspiration from Blackfriars. © *The Shakespeare Globe Trust*.

PLATE 10 Shakespeare's statue in Poets' Corner (1740) shows him pointing to a scroll with words from *The Tempest*. © *Dean and Chapter of Westminster.*

A Tragi-
Coomodie, Called
the
Witch.

long since Actted by his Maties Servants
at the Black-Friers.

Written by. Tho. Middleton.

The Sceane Rauenna.

The Persons.		The Persons	
Duke		Duchesse.	
L. Gouerno.^r		Isabella } Neice to ye Gouerno.^r	
Sebastian } Contracted to Isabella.		Francisca } Antonio's Sister	
Fernando } his Frend.		Amoretta } ye Duchess-woman.	
Antonio } Husband to Isabella.		Florida } a Curtezan.	
Abberzanes } a Gent. neither honest, wise, nor valiant.		Heccat } ye cheif Witch	
Almachildes } a fantasticall Gentleman.		Stadlin } witches	
Gaspero & } Servants to		Hoppo }	
Hermio } Antonio			
Fire-stone } y.^e Clowne & Heccats Son.		other Witches } Mutts. & Servants }	

G.STEEVENS

PLATE 11 Thomas Middleton's play *The Witch* was prepared by
the theatrical scribe Ralph Crane, who worked on the First Folio.
Bodleian Library, MS. Malone 12.

PLATE 12 Pork butcher? Shakespeare's monument in Holy Trinity Church in Stratford-upon-Avon. *Photograph by Richard Wheeler.*

Labels visible in image: S PAULES CHURCH, Hamsted Mills, Hamsted, the Water house, S:Brides, Quene-hyche, Three Cranes, The Eell Schipes, The Galley fuste, THAMESIS, The Bear Gardne, The Globe

PLATE 13   Detail from Claes Visscher's panorama of London, 1616, showing the prominence of St Paul's Church in the city. *Bodleian Library, Douce Prints a.53 (2)*.

PLATE 14 A sermon at St Paul's Cross, by John Gipkyn, 1616.
© Society of Antiquaries of London, UK/Bridgeman Images.

Thif. If hee come not, then the play is mar'd. It goes not forward, doth it?

Quin. It is not possible: you haue not a man in all *Athens*, able to discharge *Piramus* but hee.

Thif. No, hee hath simply the best wit of any handy-craft man in *Athens*.

Quin. Yea, and the best person too, and hee is a very *Paramour*, for a sweet voyce.

Thif. You must say, Paragon. A Paramour is (God blesse vs) a thing of nought.

Enter Snug the Ioyner.

Snug. Masters, the Duke is comming from the Temple, and there is two or three Lords & Ladies more married. If our sport had gone forward, we had all bin made men.

Thif. O sweet bully *Bottome*: thus hath he lost sixe-pence a day, during his life; he could not haue scaped sixe-pence a day. And the Duke had not giuen him sixpence a day for playing *Piramus*, Ile be hang'd. He would haue deserued it. Sixpence a day in *Piramus*, or nothing.

Enter Bottome.

Bot. Where are these Lads? Where are these hearts?

Quin. *Bottome*, ô most couragious day! O most happie houre!

Bot. Masters, I am to discourse wonders; but ask me not what. For if I tell you, I am no true *Athenian*. I will tell you euery thing as it fell out.

Qu. Let vs heare, sweet *Bottome.*

Bot. Not a word of me: all that I will tell you, is, that the Duke hath dined. Get your apparell together, good strings to your beards, new ribbands to your pumps, meete presently at the Palace, euery man looke ore his part: for the short and the long is, our play is preferred: In any case let *Thisby* haue cleane linnen: and let not him that playes the Lion, paire his nailes, for they shall hang out for the Lions clawes. And most deare Actors, eate no Onions, nor Garlicke; for wee are to vtter sweete breath, and I doe not doubt but to heare them say, it is a sweet Comedy. No more words: away, go away.

Exeunt.

Actus Quintus.

Enter Theseus, Hippolita, Egeus and his Lords.

Hip. Tis strange my *Theseus*, y these louers speake of.

The. More strange then true. I neuer may beleeue These anticke fables, nor these Fairy toyes, Louers and mad men haue such seething braines, Such shaping phantasies, that apprehend more Then coole reason euer comprehends. The Lunaticke, the Louer, and the Poet, Are of imagination all compact. One sees more diuels then vaste hell can hold; That is the mad man. The Louer, all as franticke, Sees *Helens* beauty in a brow of *Egipt*. The Poets eye in a fine frenzy rolling, doth glance From heauen to earth, from earth to heauen. And as imagination bodies forth the forms of things Vnknowne; the Poets pen turnes them to shapes, And giues to aire nothing, a locall habitation, And a name. Such tricks hath strong imagination,

That if it would but apprehend some ioy, It comprehends some bringer of that ioy. Or in the night, imagining some feare, How easie is a bush suppos'd a Beare?

Hip. But all the storie of the night told ouer, And all their minds transfigur'd so together, More witnesseth than fancies images, And growes to something of great constancie; But howsoeuer, strange, and admirable.

Enter louers, Lysander, Demetrius, Hermia, and Helena.

The. Heere come the louers, full of ioy and mirth: Ioy, gentle friends, ioy and fresh dayes Of loue accompany your hearts.

Lyf. More then to vs, waite in your royall walkes, your boord, your bed.

The. Come now, what maskes, what dances shall we haue, To weare away this long age of three houres, Between our after supper, and bed-time? Where is our vsuall manager of mirth? What Reuels are in hand? Is there no play, To ease the anguish of a torturing houre? Call *Egeus.*

Ege. Heere mighty *Theseus.*

The. Say, what abridgement haue you for this euening? What maske? What musicke? How shall we beguile The lazie time, if not with some delight?

Ege. There is a breefe how many sports are rife: Make choise of which your Highnesse will see first.

Lyf. The battell with the Centaurs to be sung By an Athenian Eunuch, to the Harpe.

The. Wee'l none of that. That haue I told my Loue In glory of my kinsman Hercules.

Lyf. The riot of the tipsie Bachanals, Tearing the Thracian singer, in their rage?

The. That is an old deuice, and it was plaid When I from *Thebes* came last a Conqueror.

Lyf. The thrice three Muses, mourning for the death of learning, late deceast in beggerie.

The. That is some Satire keene and criticall, Not sorting with a nuptiall ceremonie.

Lyf. A tedious breefe Scene of yong *Piramus*, And his loue *Thisby*; very tragicall mirth.

The. Merry and tragicall? Tedious, and briefe? That is, hot ice, and wondrous strange snow. How shall wee finde the concord of this discord?

Ege. A play there is, my Lord, some ten words long, Which is as breefe, as I haue knowne a play; But by ten words, my Lord, it is too long: Which makes it tedious. For in all the play, There is not one word apt, one Player fitted. And tragicall my noble Lord it is: for *Piramus* Therein doth kill himselfe. Which when I saw Rehearst, I must confesse, made mine eyes water: But more merrie teares, the passion of loud laughter Neuer shed.

Thef. What are they that do play it?

Ege. Hard handed men, that worke in Athens heere, Which neuer labour'd in their mindes till now; And now haue toyled their vnbreathed memories With this same play, against your nuptiall.

The. And we will heare it.

O 2 *Phil.*

PLATE 15   Inky fingerprints from Jaggard's workshop on a copy of the First Folio that later belonged to Edmond Malone. *Bodleian Library, Arch. G c.8*

PLATE 16 The monument to the First Folio at St Mary Aldermanbury, the London church attended by John Heminge and Henry Condell. © *Kiev.Victor/Shutterstock.*

to 1623). Among the plays, histories seem to be the best sellers. Over the same period there are six editions of *Henry IV* (the play called 'Part I' in the Folio but not marked in this way in its quarto publications) and five editions each of *Richard II* and *Richard III*. These plays continued to be printed as individual editions after the Folio, too, with *Henry IV* appearing in 1632 and 1639, *Richard III* in 1629 and 1634, and *Richard II* in 1634.

The majority of Shakespeare's plays in print in this period had more than one edition. Two plays exist in substantially different editions: *Romeo and Juliet* and *Hamlet*. *The True Tragedy of Richard Duke of York* (printed in 1595 and retitled in the Folio as *3 Henry VI*), *Love's Labour's Lost* (1598) and *Much Ado About Nothing* (1600) were all single-edition plays that were not reprinted, and therefore may not have been especially popular. A fourth example of a single-edition Shakespeare play from this period is *2 Henry IV*: strikingly, the sequel to the best-selling Part I did not capture anything like the same market approval (as is often the case with sequels right up to the modern period). We might look, for the sake of comparison, at the reprint figures for two best-selling non-Shakespearean plays of the same period. Thomas Kyd's *The Spanish Tragedy* had nine editions to 1623, the anonymous play *Mucedorus* had eight. Of Shakespeare's plays written before 1600, only *1 Henry VI*, *The Two Gentlemen of Verona*, *The Comedy of Errors* and *As You Like It* remained unprinted until the Folio in 1623. So early Shakespeare seems to have been a valuable print commodity. Lukas Erne, in an extensive study of Shakespeare's position in the early modern book trade, sees him as 'a surprisingly prominent man-in-print' with 'a commanding bibliographic presence among the dramatists of his time'.[2]

For the plays written by Shakespeare in the seventeenth century, the picture is a bit different. The majority of these plays were not printed until the First Folio. Only *King Lear* (1608), *Pericles* (1609, and not in the Folio), *Troilus and Cressida* (1609) and, belatedly, *Othello* (1622) were published. Apart from *Pericles*, the others each had only a single edition. That leaves *Twelfth Night*, *Measure for Measure*, *All's Well that Ends Well*, *Antony and Cleopatra*, *Timon of Athens*, *Macbeth*, *The Winter's Tale*, *The Tempest*, *Cymbeline* and *Henry VIII* as stage plays from the second half of Shakespeare's career that, for whatever reason, were not translated into printed book form before 1623. It's tricky to interpret this evidence, since scholars sometimes argue that a play entered print when it was no longer an active part of the performance repertoire, so that not being printed might be a paradoxical sign of popularity (on stage) rather than its opposite. But we can see that while Shakespeare's earlier plays continued to be reprinted into the seventeenth century, the overall presence of Shakespeare – and perhaps therefore his popularity with readers – seems to have been decreasing.

Dividing Shakespeare's career into two halves suggests his earlier work was more popular in print than his later. Let's look at the picture a different way. If we divide the years between the first Shakespeare publication in 1593 and the First Folio in 1623 into three ten-year periods, we can see that in the first, 1593–1602, there are thirty-three individual editions of Shakespeare's works (including the poems). In the second, 1603–12, there are only two-thirds as many: nineteen. And in the third, 1613–22, the number decreases again, to sixteen (and six of those are in a single year, 1619, and will be discussed below as a separate group, the Pavier quartos). So the number of editions published in the first ten-year period is almost equal to that of the next twenty years.

What, then, are we to conclude from this attempt to chart Shakespeare's popularity through the metric of plays printed and number of individual editions? It is hard to know quite how to interpret the evidence, and certainly any suggestion that Shakespeare becomes less popular in the early seventeenth century has tended to feel counter-intuitive. Nevertheless, it seems on the face of it to suggest a Shakespeare whose early work is more saleable in book form than his later, and whose work is at peak print popularity in the first decade of his writing career. Writing on the four-hundredth anniversary of Shakespeare's fortieth birthday, the outspoken Shakespearean Gary Taylor didn't pull his punches: 'Like millions of other men when they hit that midlife speed-bump, [Shakespeare] felt a little old, a little anxious about the younger, faster, more fashionable men lining up to replace him.' (Taylor was then working on the collected edition of Thomas Middleton, so he may have felt the new man particularly acutely.) Although Taylor's view of the midlife crisis is articulated round twenty-first century First World ideas of the average lifespan (most of Shakespeare's writing contemporaries, including Thomas Kyd, Christopher Marlowe, Robert Greene and Thomas Nashe, didn't reach forty, never mind encounter it as a speed-bump), his point is a compelling one, precisely because it doesn't fit the usual narrative. Taylor argues that Shakespeare collaborated with Thomas Middleton and with John Fletcher (as discussed in Chapter 3), and, on *Pericles*, with George Wilkins, because 'they had the juice. He didn't'. While this unflinching narrative of decline is deliberately extreme, the history of Shakespeare in print is heavily weighted towards his Elizabethan rather than later works.[3]

Shakespeare's reputation in the theatre

How about Shakespeare in the theatre? Shakespeare's plays had been an important part of the King's Men's repertoire since their foundation as the Chamberlain's Men in 1594. Most years he had produced two plays for performance – an average of 45,000 words. However, this was only a minor proportion of the number of plays performed in a year. Given that most plays in this period probably had between five and ten performances, and that there were performances six days a week for the majority of the year except in the season of Lent, we can see that, even if Shakespeare's plays were an artistically or commercially significant part of the repertoire, they were a relatively small numerical proportion of it.

Other important and successful playwrights were also supplying the King's Men. Thomas Middleton's *The Revenger's Tragedy* (1608) drew on and overleaped *Hamlet*, audaciously short-circuiting the prince's reflective delay by beginning with the earlier play's most iconic moment: its hero nose to nose with a skull and thence with mortality. Middleton's alienated protagonist Vindice is a version of Hamlet – mordant, misogynistic, passionate – but tainted by a darker, more compromised world. Ben Jonson's urban comedies *Volpone* (1606) and *The Alchemist* (1610) also registered a different, more cynical world-view from Shakespeare's preferred romantic structures in escapist settings. If Shakespeare's comic protagonists are heading towards marriage, Jonson's are heading towards jail, as they plot and prey on the venality of their fellows. John Webster, whose *The Duchess of Malfi* (1613) was printed in the same year as the Folio with a cast list of King's Men actors including Richard Burbage and Henry Condell who had performed it, tailored his dark moral vision to the chiaroscuro lighting effects of the new indoor theatre at Blackfriars. These writers all did things Shake-speare didn't.

The portmanteau playwrights Beaumont and Fletcher were the real challenge to Shakespeare's immediate legacy, however, even as their plays were strongly influenced by Shakespearean plots and themes. Their collaborative plays and those now thought to be by Fletcher alone (the myth of their writing partnership was so strong in the early modern period that plays were attributed to the double act even after Beaumont's death in 1616, or when in fact they appear to have been by Fletcher) combined romance, politics and the fashionably Italianate form of tragicomedy in 'ironic, emotionally flamboyant' plays.[4] By 1620 their plays dominated the King's Men repertoire, as an analysis of extant records of court performances indicates.

At the court season of 1612–13 from Christmas to the spring, the King's Men presented a repertoire of eighteen plays, of which seven, plus the now lost *Cardenio*, a Shakespeare–Fletcher collaboration, were Shakespeare's. Four were by Beaumont and Fletcher; one by each of Ben Jonson, Cyril Tourneur and John Ford; the authorship of the others is uncertain. Ten years later the court season appears to have included only one Shakespeare play, *Twelfth Night*.[5] The same is true in 1630, where, out of a repertoire of twenty (half of them by Beaumont and Fletcher), only one Shakespeare play was included, *A Midsummer Night's Dream*. Shakespeare is being eclipsed as the King's Men embrace a new dramatic aesthetic. The evidence we have of revivals in the professional theatre during the seventeenth century may also suggest that some of Shakespeare's works were looking old-fashioned and dropping out of the repertoire. Perhaps theatre, like most of the popular entertainment industry now, was a young man's game. By the 1610s, as Andrew Gurr points out, the King's Men had moved away from the Shakespeare plays so strongly associated with their outdoor theatre, the Globe, and towards a more sophisticated Blackfriars clientele who wanted different entertainment: 'the King's Men were beginning to be characterized as the company supplying Beaumont and Fletcher's plays to the gentry.'[6] The closure of the Globe for twelve months after a fire in 1613 (caused by cannon fire during a performance of *Henry VIII*) may have exacerbated the reorientation of the company towards the particular aesthetics and audience expectation of Blackfriars and thus away from the space most strongly associated with Shakespearean dramaturgy.

The Oscar-winning film *Shakespeare in Love* (dir. John Madden, 1998) has a memorable cameo of the street urchin John Webster, feeding a cat mice with placid sadism, expressing his admiration for Shakespeare's gory *Titus Andronicus*. It's poetic licence: an in-joke for audiences who know that this boy will grow up to be a playwright whose work is characterised by macabre and sensational violence. But when the real John Webster, introducing his play *The White Devil* to readers in 1612, reviewed his dramatic peers, Shakespeare was no longer his sole reference point:

> I have ever truly cherished my good opinion of other men's
> worthy labours, especially of that full and heightened style
> of Master Chapman; the laboured and understanding works
> of Master Jonson; the no less worthy composures of the both wor-
> thily excellent Master Beaumont and Master Fletcher; and lastly
> (without wrong last to be named) the right happy and copious
> industry of Master Shakespeare, Master Dekker, and Master
> Heywood, wishing what I write may be read by their light...[7]

At this point at the end of his career, then, Shakespeare is not pre-eminent among his fellow writers, nor the single writer a man a generation younger would look up to. He is one of a group of theatrical worthies, all of them younger than him, characterised by 'right happy and copious industry' (it's not even clear Webster means this as a compliment, since earlier in the same preface he defends himself against the charge of being a slow writer with the suggestion that the man who writes quickly will also be forgotten quickly). We might compare this rather faint praise with what Francis Meres had written enthusiastically about Shakespeare fourteen years earlier, in 1598:

> As Plautus and Seneca are accounted the best for Comedy and
> Tragedy among the Latins: so Shakespeare among the English
> is the most excellent in both kinds for the stage; for Comedy,
> witness his *Gentlemen of Verona*, his *Errors*, his *Love labours lost*,
> his *Love labours won*, his *Midsummer night dream*, & his *Merchant*

of Venice: for Tragedy his *Richard the 2, Richard the 3, Henry the 4, King John, Titus Andronicus* and his *Romeo and Juliet*.[8]

'Most excellent' versus 'right happy and copious industry': the terms of praise seem qualitatively different. Taken collectively, this evidence of Shakespeare's declining print presence, of the increasing sidelining of his plays in the King's Men repertoire at the showpiece of their year at court, and of references to him as one among many other playwrights of equal estimation, suggests his reputation was waning. He had retired from active theatre writing in around 1613 (and died in his home town of Stratford-upon-Avon, two days' travel from London). 'Why did Shakespeare retire to Stratford?' taunts the merciless Gary Taylor. 'Maybe because he was no longer wanted in London.'

Shakespeare's death in April 1616 was greeted by the London literati with – silence. The outpouring of elegies that would be written for the actor Richard Burbage on his death in 1619 had no equivalent for Shakespeare, who went unmemorialised until publication of the Folio seven years later. Shakespeare was not buried in Westminster Abbey, as was Francis Beaumont, who died the same year, or as Ben Jonson would be on his death in 1637. His monument in Holy Trinity Church Stratford (PLATE 12) was probably completed within a couple of years of his death, but it commemorates Shakespeare as a local man rather than a playwright (indeed, commentators have often felt that its figure is disappointingly unintellectual or unartistic: the critic John Dover Wilson's observation that the bust has the look of a 'self-satisfied pork butcher' has been much quoted).[9] Shakespeare the poet, Shakespeare the dramatist, seems to have been almost immediately forgotten.

And, further, Shakespeare had been dead for just a few years when active preparation of the First Folio began. The publisher of the quarto edition of *Troilus and Cressida* of 1609 had urged customers to buy now: 'believe this, that when he is gone and his comedies out of sale, you will scramble for them'.[10] But the publishing history of Shakespeare does not suggest a sudden nostalgic boom in sales after 1616. Rather, the years immediately after death might be seen as the most difficult period for an artistic reputation: neither classic nor current, neither vintage nor fashionable, but in a kind of post-popular doldrum, like the stock of The Beatles in the 1970s, or of Jane Austen in the 1840s. So why were his works picked up for the expensive and elaborate folio treatment? Why did the publishers, or the actors, or both, think this was the moment to bring out a collected edition of Shakespeare's plays?

The Pavier quartos

We can begin to answer this question by looking at a tantalising and complex publishing phenomenon that appears in 1619 and is known to scholars under the term 'the Pavier quartos'. When we looked above at the pattern of publication of Shakespeare's plays, the last of the three decades, from 1613 to 1622, saw sixteen editions printed. But the pattern year by year has one notable blip: 1613, one edition; 1614, none; 1615, one; 1616, one; 1617, one; 1618, none; 1619, six; 1620, one; 1621, none; 1622, four. The bumper year is 1619. Those six editions – of the first and second parts of *The Contention* and *Pericles* (three plays printed together as one edition), *The Merchant of Venice*, *The Merry Wives of Windsor*, *A Midsummer Night's Dream*, *Henry V* and *King Lear* – are all attributable to one stationer, Thomas Pavier.

Pavier was a London publisher much involved in the printing of quarto play texts and of other low-end publications, including ballads and chapbooks. He also held the rights to some previously printed Shakespeare plays, and had published a second edition quarto of *Henry V* (1602). Pavier had often worked with the Folio printer, William Jaggard, and in 1619 they collaborated again to

publish ten quarto titles, all attributed to Shakespeare. The first
of these was an edition of three plays, each with separate title
pages but with continuous signatures (the symbols at the bottom
of the printed page that serve something of the function of page
numbers for those collating or binding the pages) suggesting they
were intended to be bound together as a single work. The edition
comprised the early history plays, which would be retitled as *2*
and *3 Henry VI: 'The Whole Contention between the two famous houses,
Lancaster and York. With the tragical ends of the good Duke Humfrey,
Richard Duke of York, and King Henry the sixth. Divided into two parts,
and newly corrected and enlarged. Written by William Shakespeare,
Gent. Printed at London for T.P.* Together with these works was
the seafaring romance *Pericles*, now generally considered to be a
collaboration with George Wilkins. With these three titles, Pavier
thus did something that had never been done before but now
seems completely standard: he combined works by Shakespeare
into a multi-play volume. Next Pavier printed a fourth play, *A
Yorkshire Tragedy*. This short work is based on the true crime
story of Walter Calverley of Yorkshire, who murdered his two
children and attempted to murder his wife in 1605, a Jacobean
scandal which prompted a pamphlet, a ballad and another play
by Wilkins. *A Yorkshire Tragedy* had been printed in 1608 with
an attribution to Shakespeare (FIGURE I), although the scholarly
consensus now is that it is not by him, and that the most likely
author is Thomas Middleton.

Pavier, still in partnership with Jaggard, then went on to publish
editions of *The Merchant of Venice*, *The Merry Wives of Windsor*, *King
Lear*, *Henry V* and *A Midsummer Night's Dream*. He also included
a play titled *Sir John Oldcastle*, which was a sort of stand-in for
Shakespeare's *Henry IV* plays. *Sir John Oldcastle* is of unknown
authorship, but it appears to have been a riposte by the rival
company the Admiral's Men to the impudence of Shakespeare's

depiction of Falstaff. Falstaff's original designation in the play was Oldcastle, after a historical knight in Henry's army, but the influential Elizabethan descendants of the man objected to his audacious representation and the name was changed (we can see its vestigial traces in the banter about the 'old lad of the castle' (*1 Henry IV* 1.2.41–2) and in a few lines where the metre is irregular because of the substitution of the two-syllable 'Falstaff' for the longer original). But this second group of Pavier plays was printed in such a way as to disguise the fact that they were new editions. Instead they were given false imprints, with title pages copied from the first edition to pass them off as old stock. Something had obviously happened to derail the original plan.

Pavier may have originally intended to publish all of these plays – and perhaps others too – with continuous signatures for binding together as an anthology. In this he pre-empts the Folio in the ambition to produce a collected, if not a complete, Shakespeare. He was still publishing in the smaller quarto format rather than aspiring to the status of folio printing. And while Pavier's criteria for including or reprinting the plays is obviously very different from that of the First Folio (hence his inclusion of *Pericles* and *A Yorkshire Tragedy*, for instance), he too is gathering a compilation of plays organised around their putatively shared author. What happened to interrupt his plans may well have been the intervention of the King's Men. A letter from William Herbert, the Lord Chamberlain, was lodged in the Stationers' Company records in 1619: 'It is thought fit and so ordered that no plays that his Majesty's players do play shall be printed without consent of some of them.'[11] Herbert's intervention may well be first among the 'favours' that Heminge and Condell mentioned but did not enumerate when they dedicated the First Folio to him and his brother Philip. The precise reasons for his letter are unknown, but he obviously intervened to protect the King's Men's dramatic repertoire, either for their exclusive performance, or because they had their own plans for publication: the First Folio.

Earlier in this chapter we traced a narrative of decline in Shakespeare's print and theatrical presence during the second decade of the seventeenth century. But Pavier's entry into the market with ten Shakespearean plays (neither *Sir John Oldcastle* nor *A Yorkshire Tragedy* would now be attributed to Shakespeare, and we don't know whether Pavier himself believed his own attribution) is an important counterweight to that argument. Pavier seems to have felt that there was a market for Shakespeare's plays, and, further, that there was a market for publishing related plays with continuous signatures for binding as a collection. It may be that Pavier's publishing project encroached on the plan for the First Folio, or it may be that this radical publishing move galvanised the King's Men into preparing their own volume. Either of these scenarios might explain the intervention of William Herbert on their behalf to stop further publication. So Pavier may have been inadvertently testing the market, or creating that market. The fact that Jaggard – but not Pavier – is so prominent among the publication team of the Folio suggests that their efforts to republish Shakespeare in 1619 were not entirely unwelcome to the King's Men, even as they were prevented from completing the series as originally planned. Pavier's publishing project used to be seen as a piratical attempt to capitalise on Shakespeare's reputation; perhaps it should rather be seen as an important milestone in testing the posthumous market for the playwright's work. Pavier's ultimate Shakespearean legacy, then, can be seen to be the First Folio itself.[12]

'Grown from Quarto into Folio'

Writing after the publication of the second edition of the Folio in 1632 – but in a comment that may well have had in mind its predecessor of 1623 – the lawyer and controversialist William

Prynne noted with disapproval that 'some play books are grown from Quarto into Folio'. Prynne's anti-theatrical agenda is clear from the long title of his book *Histriomastix, The players' scourge or actors' tragedy ... wherein it is largely evidenced ... that popular stage-plays ... are sinful, heathenish, lewd, ungodly spectacles and most pernicious corruptions...* He observes that whereas before his playbook enemies were pygmies (the small format quartos), they are become 'giantlike' adversaries in their new folio incarnations. Prynne singles out for particular marginal comment that 'Shakespeare's plays are printed in the best crown paper, far better than most Bibles.'[13] Size matters. And presentation confers value on contents.

The word 'folio' refers to a size of book in which a standard piece of paper is folded once to make two printed pages on each side (see Chapter 4). Because paper sizes were not in fact entirely standard it's hard to give an absolute size for the resulting book, but it is roughly equivalent to modern foolscap paper. In our own period, it is often the format for so-called coffee-table books: art catalogues, high-end illustrated books of photography, expensive reference works such as atlases – books to be looked at rather than to be read. The dominant association of such books, then as now, is luxury. The quality of images and overall production in them commands a high purchase price; they are not usually essential or utilitarian, so they suggest their buyers have spare money to spend on extravagances; they are too big to consult on the go, and so suggest the leisure to sit and browse. Shakespeare's world had equivalent associations of the folio format. This kind of publication was usually reserved for works of conspicuous seriousness: Bibles and works of theology, law, topography, heraldry, genealogy and history. By buying them you were making a statement about yourself: about your wealth, your library, your intellectual concerns, your part in scholarly conversations. To publish plays – the fodder of the Bankside theatres – in this high-status format was to set

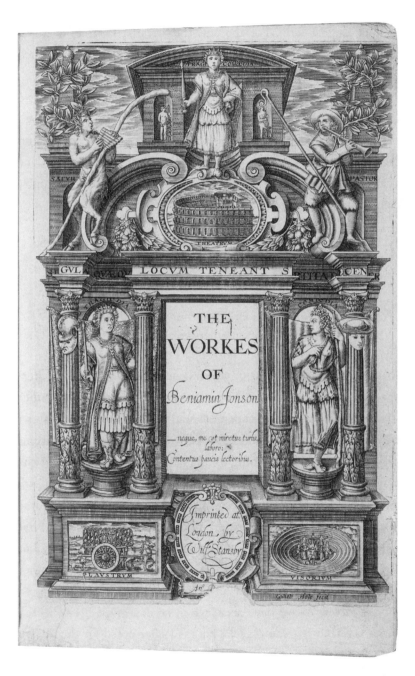

FIGURE 4 Jonson's *Workes* (1616) is presented as a highbrow volume in the classical tradition. *Bodleian Library*, *Arch. A d.*28.

content against form. For the anti-theatricalist Prynne, it was a sign of cultural depravity to suggest that plays were worth such publishing treatment.

Only one volume of plays from the professional theatres had been published in folio format before Shakespeare's. Ben Jonson's plays – partly covered with the cultural figleaf of his poetry and his court masques under the title *Workes* – appeared in 1616, the year of Shakespeare's death (FIGURE 4). Jonson's grandiose ambition earned some scoffs:

> *To Mr. Ben Jonson demanding the reason why he called his plays works.*
> Pray tell me, Ben, where does the mystery lurk,
> What others call a play you call a work.
> *Thus answered by a friend in Mr. Jonson's defense.*
> The author's friend thus for the author says,
> Ben's plays are works, when others' works are plays.[14]

At stake here is the extent to which drama could be a serious literary form – a work, with its associations of labour and effort, rather than a play, with associations of triviality and leisure. Publishing plays in the high-status folio format was part of the intermittent progress towards establishing drama's literary credentials, but the market could not apparently support many of these books. Jonson's folio of 1616 was not reprinted until 1640, and a second volume planned in 1631 foundered before publication; Shakespeare's First Folio of 1623 was reprinted nine years later in 1632; the Beaumont and Fletcher folio volume appeared in 1647. There were no other similar collections: no Thomas Dekker, no Thomas Middleton, no John Webster. As we have seen, when he conceived his collected series of Shakespearean plays, Thomas Pavier opted for the quarto format, and this continued to be the standard for play books for decades. Edward Blount's collection of John Lyly's plays in 1632, which, like Pavier's, had continuous signatures and separate title pages, opted for the pocket-size duodecimo format. The Shakespeare collection wasn't, then, part of a major trend in the book trade.

Publishing the plays in the Folio was a significant statement about the value of the book's contents, and about its cultural aspirations, pitching the plays towards a more elite audience than could have been imagined at their first outings in the public theatres. But there were practical considerations about the format too. Ben Jonson's 1616 folio is self-evidently a luxury volume, with a single column of text surrounded by ample margins, and with interleaving title pages with details of performance. The text of Jonson's literary works could have been neatly fitted into just half the space, and thus it is an ostentatious 'waste' of paper – the most expensive part of book production, as discussed in Chapter 4. Jonson's book bespeaks extravagance: a kind of conspicuous consumption or bookish bling.

When we compare this to the Shakespeare Folio, there are some revealing differences. The prefatory verses to the 1623 book mirror the layout of Jonson's exactly – a single, centred column of italic verse. The introduction to the volume gives that same impression of luxury and ease cultivated by Jonson. But once the Shakespeare Folio begins presenting its plays, the layout becomes immediately much more cramped. As Kevin J. Donovan estimates, two columns of pica type versus one column of English type in the Jonson means that every page of the Shakespeare Folio contains almost twice as much type as its folio predecessor.[15] The folio format was the one publishers would choose if there was such a lot of material to be printed that it was actually cheaper to do it at this larger scale. Steven Galbraith has worked out that it was actually cheaper – in terms of paper use – to publish Shakespeare's plays in folio than in quarto. The eighteen plays previously published as quartos required 177 sheets of paper; in the Folio they took just 115 sheets. Galbraith calls this the bibliographic economics of 'necessity' or of 'economy', and argues that the Shakespeare Folio may have been published in that format less to aggrandise its contents and more to keep costs under control.[16] We might add to that list of modern large-format books (the coffee-table books discussed above) a distinctly downmarket publication that is rapidly becoming extinct: the telephone directory. That is published in a similar large format not to be aspirational or luxurious – far from it – but to cram in a lot of information in the most cost-efficient way possible.

Economics

Costs and purchasers were clearly prominent in the minds of Heminge and Condell when they signed the prefatory letter 'to the great Variety of Readers'. The humour of their immediate acknowledgement that 'the fate of all books depends upon your capacities, and not of your heads alone but of your purses' introduces an anxiety which never leaves their prose. Their injunction to read the book is always coupled with a further imperative, to 'buy it first'. As discussed in Chapter 1, they stress the inadequacy and imperfection of previously printed Shakespeare plays: 'before, you were abused with diverse stolen and surreptitious copies'. This may well be a marketing technique: an attempt to encourage those play-book readers who have already purchased some of these plays in individual editions to cough up the money for the collection by denigrating the copies previously on sale. The hard-headed emphasis on money here can come as a shock to modern readers expecting a more poetic or abstract rationale for the first collected edition of Shakespeare.

But the men who transformed rags to paper, lampblack and oil into ink, and handwritten sheaves into typeset pages, all needed to be paid. There had to be some profit at every stage in the production chain, from the making of the raw materials to the retailing of the printed book. So how much of an investment were the publishers making in this book, and how likely were they to recover it?

Peter Blayney is the expert on these figures. Following his analysis, if we take the cost of an unbound copy of the Folio as 15*s* (the price is often stated to have been a pound, but that appears to have included some form of binding), then 5*s* of that was probably the profit for the retail bookseller, who would have bought his copies wholesale at 10*s*. Since the publisher had probably paid the printers about 3*s* 4*d* for their work and about the same again for paper and the rights to the plays, that means his profit was about a third of the wholesale cost, 3*s* 4*d*. The 227 sheets needed for each copy of the First Folio probably cost around 2*s* 3*d* – a cost met by the publisher. It's interesting that in this case the large amount of text to be set and the relative complexities of the two-column format seem to have made print-shop labour costs higher than the cost of paper, rather than, as is usual in book production of this period, the other way around. The printers paid out for the compositors and other pressmen in their workshop and added 50 per cent for their overheads and profit, which suggests that they were earning a shilling or so on each copy.[17]

It is not possible to be certain how many copies of the First Folio were printed. The publishers needed to balance the risk of paying out large sums for paper, and the burden of storing unsold books, against the wish to make a profit and to spread fixed costs effectively. There were Stationers' Company regulations to limit the number of copies of any single edition, and known print runs in the period rarely exceeded 1,200 copies. A conservative estimate of the number of copies of this large book to be printed is 700. That would mean that Jaggard's print shop received a payment of around £35 on this job. Theirs is the safest place to be in the economic chain, since they were paid in advance and were not dependent on the speed or volume of subsequent sales. By contrast, any profit for both the publisher/wholesaler (Blount and Isaac Jaggard, with smaller shares for the other stationers in their consortium) and the retail bookseller was directly dependent on sales. Booksellers would probably not want to overcommit to copies of the Folio before they had tested the market, and therefore the cashflow for the publishers, Blount and Jaggard, was uncertain. If, say, they had paid out around £78 for paper (based on 2s 3d per copy and 700 copies) and £116 for printing (3s 4d per copy), then they would need to have passed on more than half the print run wholesale before they recovered their initial costs and started to make any profit.

So we know how the price of each copy might break down, and how profit might be distributed across the production and supply chain. But how should we conceptualise these sums of money? Economic historians tend to understand the changing value of money in relation to fixed staples – such as loaves of bread, pints of ale, or sheep. But it might be more precise to tag the sums of money involved in the production of the Folio to the account books of its first recorded purchaser, the Kentish gentleman Sir Edward Dering. Dering, like many fashionable young men in this period, spent the season of Michaelmas Term (the autumn legal season when the courts were in sitting) in London where, on 6 December 1623, he bought both the Jonson folio and the Shakespeare one. Dering was wealthy and enjoyed shopping, especially for clothes and accessories and books, and the ledger of his expenditure gives an exactly contemporaneous sense of what other things cost relative to the First Folio. In 1623 Dering records payment of 11s for a pair of boots and 2s each for a pair of spurs and gloves, threepence for some lemons, twopence for conveying a letter, sixpence for 'going by water' and 1s to see a play, a pound for 'a copy of my mother's picture', 12s for fishing rods and equipment, £4 for 'a gilt sword', £1 12s for 'a pair of pearl colour stockings'. It cost him 16s for 'a fortnight's use of a chamber', 4*s* 6*d* for coral tooth powder, 6*s* to hire a coach for an afternoon, sixpence for a wax candle, and £1 10*s* per fortnight for the stabling of two horses.[18]

Dering's lifestyle was clearly an affluent one, but within his patterns of expenditure, the cost of the First Folio was not out of line with other luxury items. It cost significantly less than one of his fashionable suits, for instance: he paid out more than £4 for black velvet to make breeches, and some of his suits cost £10 or more once all the lavish fabric, decoration and tailoring is totted up. For Dering, then, the Folio was affordable. His yearly expenses for 1623 are recorded as £323. But some of his other payments make clear the amount of money on which other Londoners survived: he pays 4*s* to a porter for four days' work, for instance, and sixpence to the barber and a shilling to the laundress. Back on his Kent estate he pays a labourer called Thomas Hamms 8*d* a day for ploughing. A schoolmaster in Shakespeare's hometown of Stratford earned £5 per year in 1629, probably in addition to accommodation; an equivalent post in neighbouring Oxfordshire carried a salary of £13 6*s*.[19] Even for these educated men in relatively desirable employment, then, buying a book for 15*s* would have been a stretch. It would have taken a working man – Bottom the weaver, say, or Snug the joiner from *A Midsummer Night's Dream* – the best part of a month to earn the purchase price of the First Folio.

The Folio's major investors Edward Blount and Isaac Jaggard had to be patient: their initial investment must have taken many years to make a return. Discussing quarto editions earlier in this chapter, we made the reasonable assumption that stocks of a printed edition must have all been sold out if a second or subsequent edition was published. If the same is true of the First Folio, then its copies did not run out until the early 1630s: a second edition was printed in 1632. For some scholars, this nine-year period has seemed a very short time, and for others rather a long one.

It might help to compare the Folio with the market fate of other contemporary folios that share a publisher or printer with Shakespeare. In 1622, for example, Edward Blount published a translation of the Spanish picaresque romance *The Rogue, or the Life of Guzman de Alfarache*, a 400-page folio volume. It was reprinted in 1623, 1630 and 1634, suggesting much quicker sales than the Shakespeare. On the other hand, two folio works of genealogy and heraldry printed alongside Shakespeare in Jaggard's printshop, William Burton's *The Description of Leicestershire* (1622) and André Favyn's *The Theater of Honour and Knighthood* (1623) were never reprinted. Most of the men directly involved in publishing the First Folio were dead by the time of the Second, so we can't know whether Isaac Jaggard or Edward Blount would have been willing to reinvest in a second edition. Blount had, in any case, sold his rights in Shakespeare on to his fellow stationer Robert Allot in 1630. Allot was the main investor behind the second edition in 1632. It's also interesting to note that there was not much other Shakespeare publication during the 1620s: those staples of Shakespeare in print, his narrative poems *Venus and Adonis* and *The Rape of Lucrece* continued to be issued in new editions, but the fact that the Folio publishers had bought up most of the rights to his plays had the effect of suppressing the quarto market. Ben Jonson wrote of his bookseller in an epigram, that he 'call'st a book good or bad, as it doth sell';[20] whether, by this analysis, the First Folio was 'good' or 'bad' is difficult to weigh up. If the evidence of the success of the First Folio in economic terms is mixed, it is nevertheless hard to make the case that it flew immediately off the shelves or that it was a huge money-spinner for its investors.

Autumn 1623

Let's take this book back to that first appearance, at the end of 1623, in Blount's shop, to try to understand the world into which it was born and how that might have shaped its contents. Edward Blount, the Folio's major publisher, had his retail premises in the heart of the London book trade, which was centred around St Paul's Church in London. Claes Visscher's contemporary panorama of the city, engraved in 1616, the year of Shakespeare's death, shows a view of St Paul's, with its tower as the dominant landmark (PLATE 13). Looking north from the South Bank over the polygonal structures of the Bear Garden and Globe theatres in Southwark, the church is at the heart of the composition, and is first in the accompanying key to prominent city buildings.

But for those who might imagine a churchyard to be quiet and contemplative, the busy economic and political centre that surrounded St Paul's is rather a surprise. The Churchyard contained a score of bookseller shops and stalls, as well as the city's most famous outdoor pulpit, Paul's Cross (PLATE 14), where preachers included poet and divine John Donne, the controversial Archbishop William Laud, and Thomas Adams, dubbed by Robert Southey 'the Shakespeare of the Puritans'.[21] Because the area around the church was one of the few open spaces in a crowded city, it became the favoured place of assembly and news exchange. Thomas Carlyle would later describe it as 'a kind of *Times* newspaper'.[22] It was a place to hear gossip as well as official news, to meet friends, to cut business deals, to look fashionable and well connected, and to find out from other Londoners what was going on. Later in the seventeenth century there was a term for these fashionable gossip-mongers: a Paul's walker. Even the church itself was hardly a hushed or sanctified space: a boys' company performed plays in a theatre as part of the precinct, and the aisles of St Paul's were an important place for London gallants to show off. A bishop's description at the end of the sixteenth century noted that the church was 'very noisomely kept by reason of certain heaps of dirt and other filthy thing in many corners', and it was clearly common to drink, smoke

FIGURE 5 Engraving of Paul's Walk, after Wenceslaus Hollar. *Bodleian Library*, 247124 *f*.4.

the newly fashionable tobacco or gamble during services. Off the south–north aisle of St Paul's business was conducted, and it was the place to go to consult schoolmasters, bookbinders, stationers, glaziers, carpenters, joiners, mercers, hosiers, and other tradesmen who had shops in the church.[23]

Thomas Dekker, writing a satirical instruction manual for the would-be man of fashion, indicated the required behaviour inside the church with a fine eye for the necessary gestures:

> bend your course directly in the middle line, that the whole body of the Church may appear to be yours, where, in view of all, you may publish your suit in what manner you affect most, either with the slide of your cloak from the one shoulder, and then you must (as 'twere in anger) suddenly snatch at the middle of the inside (if it be taffeta at the least) and so by the means your costly lining is betrayed, or else by the pretty advantage of Compliment.

Dekker goes on with some tips for looking well-connected: 'if by chance you either encounter, or aloof, off throw your inquisitive eye upon any knight or Squire, being your familiar, salute him not by his name of Sir such a one, or so, but call him Ned or Jack etc. This will set off your estimation with great men'.[24] Other chapters in Dekker's book usefully collocate the space of St Paul's with other arenas for the aspirant Londoner, as he details appropriate behaviour in playhouses, ordinaries (public houses where meals were served), taverns, and the city at night. St Paul's takes its place in a cultural geography of publicly visible and fashionable behaviour: it's in this spirit that the bookshops of the Churchyard like Blount's have been dubbed 'performance spaces'.[25]

Even the regular sermons at the outdoor pulpit at Paul's Cross were not merely religious (early modern religion was always also politics, and also, to an extent, public performance). Trying to find out more about Prince Charles's visit to Spain in February 1623, for example, the habitual Paul's walker John Chamberlain took himself to Paul's Cross, on the assumption that 'it may be the preacher hath order to say somewhat in this business':[26] preachers did sometimes use this space to deliver official messages about matters of current politics. Anniversaries of important events, such as the accession of the monarch or the failed Gunpowder Plot of 1605, were also marked by Paul's Cross sermons and attended by large, heterogeneous crowds including courtiers, ambassadors, civic and ecclesiastical dignitaries as well as tourists, pickpockets and various godly sermon-gadders. On occasion the sovereign attended sermons there: James had in 1620 attended a sermon to launch a campaign to rebuild the cathedral.

So the book trade was located within the most topical and vibrant public space in the city, and unsurprisingly its own products tended to align themselves with the priorities of the Paul's yard clientele. The book trade was an intrinsic part of the bustle of what King Lear calls 'who's in, who's out' (5.3.15), and its customers were characterised by their interest in the heady Paul's mix of gossip, politics, fashion and ideas. New books were a particular draw: the playwright John Webster dismisses 'those ignorant asses (who visiting stationers' shops their use is not to enquire for good books but new books)'.[27] Writing in 1603 Thomas Jackson remarked that 'the first question at every stationers' shop is, what new thing?'[28] Samuel Rowlands's satirical *'Tis Merry When Gossips Meet* (1602, often reprinted) opens with a prefatory conversation, beginning when the bookseller's apprentice calls out 'What lack you, gentleman? See a new book, new come forth sir; buy a new book, sir.' After a long conversation about his reading tastes, the gentleman is persuaded to buy a book of 'excellent quality and rare operation'; in a nicely postmodern twist he has in fact bought the very book in which he appears and which he and the reader, similarly eager for new material, go on to read.[29] All the discussion of Paul's Churchyard constructs it as a space of exclusively male sociability and consumption. If women read this or other books – and we know from signatures dating from the later seventeenth century in copies of the First Folio that they did – they probably did not go to the booksellers themselves to buy them.

Gary Taylor points out that of the 500 individual works published in 1623, more than two-thirds were new titles not previously published, and about a fifth were directly topical works such as news books or almanacs.[30] Regular customers to Blount's shop in November 1623 would thus have been particularly interested in the new arrival of the Shakespeare Folio, and perhaps Blount drew their attention particularly to the previously unpublished material it contained. The First Folio would have been jostling for attention in Blount's shop amid his fashionably cosmopolitan literary stock, and in Paul's Churchyard amid the gossip and chatter of the day.

The Spanish Match

What might that chatter have been in late 1623 and early 1624? The big political issue was the ongoing uncertainty over the so-called 'Spanish Match' – the proposed marriage between Prince Charles, heir to the English throne, and the Spanish Infanta, Maria Anna, daughter to Philip III of Spain. The political mood of the period seems, from surviving letters and accounts, to have been rather wearied by this prospective alliance. John Chamberlain wrote to a correspondent in November that 'we do not know what to judge of the match, but that it goes on like the Spanish pavanne [dance] backward and forward'.[31] Charles, with the royal favourite George Villiers, the Duke of Buckingham, had gone unannounced to Madrid in February 1623 to try to seize the initiative in the courtship. But Anglo-Spanish diplomatic relations were more complicated than

Charles had understood, and the issue of his proposed conversion to Catholicism became crucial to the marriage negotiations. Charles seems to have agreed to this, although, since he felt himself to be virtually a prisoner in the Spanish court, it was probably a concession to facilitate his return home. He returned, still unmarried, from Spain in October 1623, and began to extricate himself from any promise to marry the Infanta.

His return to England was a cause of national celebration, focused around St Paul's. The poet John Taylor reported in his *Prince Charles His Welcome from Spaine* (1623) how 'the joyful news of his happy return filled the whole kingdom with excessive joy' and described celebratory bonfires at St Paul's. A broadside ballad with the title 'Prince Charles his welcome to the court, or a true subjects love for his happy returne from Spaine' echoed this rejoicing at 'Long lookt for *Charles* thou doublest our delight / Long lookt for Prince, we now attain thy sight'.[32]

Elsewhere there was little cause for revelry and the mood was altogether less celebratory. The autumn weather was unremittingly wet, and the London streets were thick with mud. John Chamberlain, keeping up his regular correspondence with Dudley Carleton, a diplomat friend posted abroad, felt that 'we are so daily (as it were) called upon and visited with new disasters'. He cited several doleful instances: the deaths of numerous Catholics in the Blackfriars district when the floor of an upper room where they were listening to a Jesuit preacher gave way; a London fire in which a nobleman had lost goods 'at least to the value of £10,000'; the death of the antiquary William Camden; and the continued, and in Chamberlain's view dangerous, influence of the Spanish ambassador at court. A couple of weeks later he reported to his correspondent an outbreak of 'a contagious spotted or purple fever that reigns much which together with the smallpox hath taken away many of good sort as well as meaner people', and sighed that the ongoing possibility of dynastic union with Catholic Spain meant that 'the truth is that priests and Jesuits swarm here extraordinarily, and are grown so bold that if any of quality men or women fall sick and have any friends or kindred that way affected, under that colour they will find access to them and use persuasion which whether it prevail or no, if the party die, they will find means though they be past sense to anoint and cross them with such other ceremonies'.[33] Catholicism, a thorn in the side of the English establishment throughout Elizabeth's reign, was again high on the national agenda as the First Folio emerged into print.

People have argued for centuries about Shakespeare's own doctrinal affiliations, but those of the First Folio itself have not been considered. Can a book have a politics? Can a book of secular plays be allied to a particular religion? Perhaps we should look more closely at the way the First Folio, emerging into a heightened atmosphere of doctrinal tension because of religious and nationalistic opposition to the proposed Spanish match, is shaped by that religio-political controversy.

In the autumn of 1623 the newly published First Folio entered a distinctly Hispanophile context: the bookshop of the cosmopolitan publisher Edward Blount in Paul's Churchyard. Blount's shop would have been full of Spanish literary material: it was one of his particular publishing specialities. He had printed the first English translation of the Spanish mock-romance *Don Quixote*, and a folio text of Matteo Aleman's picaresque prose narrative *Guzman de Alfarache* was published at about the same time as the Shakespeare edition. Blount's European-inflected publishing list also included a dictionary of Spanish, as well as of Latin and Italian, and a wide range of translated works from European languages, including Montaigne's *Essays*, which we know Shakespeare read. The petty nationalism of late 1623 London was unlikely to be favourable to Blount's refined literary brand.

The first play in the Shakespeare First Folio presents a dynastic Mediterranean marriage between old enemies (the marriage of Prospero's daughter Miranda to Ferdinand, son of his rival King Alonso, in *The Tempest*). The closing play depicts plucky Britain both beating and paying tribute to an imperial power (the final reconciliation with Rome which ends *Cymbeline*). It has been suggested that this order was deliberately organised to coincide with, and to echo, an anticipated successful conclusion to the Spanish match negotiations.[34] Perhaps in expectation of this political outcome, Blount involved his Hispanist contacts James Mabbe and Leonard Digges in the eulogies to Shakespeare which preface the First Folio (see Chapter 1 on the eulogies, and Chapter 3 for more details on Mabbe and Digges). If their Spanish connections are not significant, then it is rather hard to see why Blount – or Heminge and Condell – picked these particular men to write for the Folio: they were not previously connected with drama, or with Shakespeare, in any obvious way.

But Blount seems to have been spreading his bets. The Folio's dedicatees are prominent members of the anti-Spanish faction in James's court. Perhaps the Pembroke brothers had always been intended as the book's patrons.[35] Or perhaps this was a late substitution to reflect the change in the political wind in 1623. We know from the pioneering detailed work undertaken by Charlton Hinman that the preliminaries were the penultimate part of the book to be printed (see Chapter 4), probably not until October of 1623, so there was time to make a change. Either way, the strongly anti-Spanish mood of that autumn must have been a difficult one for Blount and his literary network, whose intellectual affiliations were so markedly internationalist compared with the jingoism of the times. The author most associated by later ages with the idea of Englishness thus emerged from a distinctly cosmopolitan literary stable, and the Folio registers some contradictory contemporary allusions that have been lost in the construction of Shakespeare's plays as timeless classics.

'Buy it first': the book's buyers

What sort of book buyer might enter Blount's shop and browse, or even buy this new collection of plays? Blount's premises in Paul's Churchyard had a total floor area of between 522 and 542 square feet, and a frontage 13 feet 3 inches wide: it's the size of a small convenience store, but probably only part of it was used for retail sales.[36] Blount would also have had to store his wholesale books somewhere; since the church precinct was also the centre for the wholesale trade, it would make sense if they were on hand. Descriptions of bookshop culture in this period suggest that there was as much talking and smoking as there was actual buying of books, so Blount's shop must have had space for his customers, like Edward Dering, to look at his stock, to ask about new titles, and make their selection. In an epigram titled 'To my Bookseller', Ben Jonson asked the addressee 'be thou my book's intelligencer, note / What each man says of it';[37] obviously, book selling was a sociable and conversational business.

The men who bought the early copies of the First Folio are mostly invisible to history, but a few instances, such as that of Edward Dering, stand out. Anthony West, in the most extensive survey of ownership patterns, identifies that the earliest owners, like Dering, 'were noblemen and commoners of standing', and lists an earl, two bishops, a baron, a herald of arms, a mayor, a gentleman, and 'possibly' a lawyer.[38] Two early owners of the Folio are discussed in more detail in the Coda. Thus, the immediate demographic suggests that the address to that 'great Variety of Readers' was rhetorical rather than literal, at least in the marketplace of the 1620s. In contrast to the previous individual play quartos by which Shakespeare had been known during his lifetime, the Folio's target audience was elite. Jaggard and Blount aimed it squarely at the gallants who gathered in Paul's Churchyard to collect news and gossip, to conduct business, and to show off. These human stories intersected in the publication of the First Folio, where men with technical, creative, dramatic and economic expertise met to produce the book.

THREE

Team Shakespeare:
The Backers

HE TITLE PAGE of the First Folio stresses singularity. We get the image of a person – the engraving of Shakespeare – and his name, in large capitals, heads the book's title: 'Mr William Shakespeares Comedies, Histories, & Tragedies'. The First Folio is presented to us as a monument to, or even a literary biography of, a single individual.

But this impression of solo genius is immediately undermined: Shakespeare's is by no means the only name in the book. The title page engraving is signed by Martin Droeshout. Visible in the opening pages are the names of fellow writers, including Ben Jonson, Hugh Holland, Leonard Digges and 'I.M.' (probably James Mabbe). Jonson's poem names other writers as Shakespeare's peers: Chaucer, Spenser, Beaumont, Kyd, Marlowe and Lyly, as well as the classical dramatists Aeschylus, Euripides, Sophocles, Aristophanes, Terence and Plautus, and the sovereigns 'Eliza and our James'; Digges adds 'Naso' (the Roman poet Ovid). In addition to this literary company, there are other people involved. The title page names the men who led the publishing: Isaac Jaggard and Edward Blount. The colophon (publishing information) at the end of the book adds William Jaggard and a consortium of other stationers, John Smithweeke (elsewhere usually spelt Smethwick) and William Aspley. William Earl of Pembroke and his brother Philip Earl of Montgomery are named as dedicatees. The King's Men actors John

Heminge and Henry Condell sign their names to the introductory epistles. Two columns of 'the names of the principal actors in all these plays' number twenty-five individual players, including the celebrity actors Will Kemp and Richard Burbage in addition to Shakespeare himself. And that is before we begin to count up the hundreds of dramatic characters in the plays, from the first speaker, the ship's Master calling out to another member of his crew, 'Boatswain', in *The Tempest*, to the last, Cymbeline king of ancient Britain, proclaiming 'such a peace' (5.6.486).

There are other people who are not named in the book but whose contribution can be uncovered and reinstated. On one page of *A Midsummer Night's Dream* in a copy of the Folio now in the Bodleian Library in Oxford, three black inky fingerprints are clearly visible (PLATE 15): these are almost certainly the individual and inadvertent marks of one of Jaggard's print-shop workers, handling the damp, newly printed page with work-stained hands. We don't know who these workers were – apart from the cack-handed apprentice John Leason whose work, particularly in setting the type for the tragedies, needed to be checked and corrected by his more experienced print-shop colleagues – but we can distinguish them by their habits of spelling and punctuation. We also know from similarities with his other work that the theatrical scribe Ralph Crane provided the neat copy for half a dozen or more plays. There are other playwrights whose presence can be traced even if they are not named: Thomas Middleton, who co-authored *Timon of Athens* and provided additional material for a revival of *Macbeth* and *Measure for Measure*; John Fletcher, co-author of *Henry VIII*, and perhaps others too. Some scholars have speculated that, in an age when the majority of plays were collaboratively authored, other playwrights may have contributed to the plays included here as Shakespeare's: the names of Thomas Nashe and George Peele hover in the air, perhaps for contributions to *1 Henry VI* and *Titus Andronicus* respectively. Rights for previously published plays needed to be negotiated from other stationers, whose own print shops had left their mark in different ways on the texts, which were then reset for the Folio, and who thus also stand in the expanding troupe of writers, financiers and artisans who are behind this book.

The point of this catalogue of agents is to point out that the First Folio depends on, and registers, a network of human interactions across technical, artistic and commercial boundaries. It has come to seem the work of a single genius – in fact, perhaps, to be the very definition of genius[1] – whereas in fact it is the product of many different people with different amounts of agency and investment – personal, intellectual and economic – in the project. It's a commonplace to describe theatre – the activity underpinning the very existence of this book – as a collaborative art form in which the author's words are shaped, embodied and adapted by actors, directors, producers, designers, musicians and, above all, audiences. Understanding the many and various people behind the First Folio helps us to see that just as the performance of drama requires teamwork, so too does its publication. This chapter aims to animate these individual biographies and chart their interactions, to humanise this monumental book as a product of people and their creative, artisanal and economic energies. Let's try to bring its recorded and unrecorded contributors to life.

The dedicatory poets: Shakespeare's 'friends'

A number of writers besides Shakespeare make their way into his First Folio, by their contribution to the plays attributed to him, and by their poems in praise of him. Chief among those 'friends' whose verses commend the plays to readers is Ben Jonson (1572–1637). Jonson, born in London and 'brought up poorly' (his bricklayer step-father was the occasion of jokes against him), attended Westminster School under the influential antiquary William Camden, to whom

Jonson was to dedicate his own 1616 *Workes* in 'profession of my thankfulness'.² Jonson may, like Shakespeare, have been an actor as well as, or before he was, a playwright: tradition has it he played the memorably histrionic grieving father Hieronimo in Thomas Kyd's blockbuster hit of the early 1590s, *The Spanish Tragedy*, a play that stayed with him throughout his career just as it did with Shakespeare (he mentions it in *The Taming of the Shrew* in the phrase 'Go by, Saint Jeronimy!' (Induction 1.7), and his *Hamlet* draws on and reworks its intense themes of blood, vengeance and memory). Jonson's elegy in the First Folio compares Shakespeare to 'industrious Kyd', along with Christopher Marlowe and John Lyly, long-dead fellow playwrights from the early 1590s. Jonson's earliest surviving play, *The Case is Altered*, dates from around 1597, and was followed by a string of popular hits, including his 'humours' dramas *Every Man In His Humour* and *Every Man Out of His Humour*. Probably a number of his plays from this period, written collaboratively with other dramatists, have not survived. At the end of the sixteenth century he was involved in an energetic 'war of the theatres', dramatising aesthetic antagonisms with other writers in his *The Poetaster*.

Unlike Shakespeare, who wrote exclusively for the Chamberlain's Men, in which he was a shareholder from 1594, Jonson's plays were performed by different companies, including the Chamberlain's Men and the Children of Her Majesty's Chapel. He was a larger-than-life figure – literally: in one poem, Falstaff-like, Jonson jokes that he 'doth hardly approach / His friends, but to break chairs, or crack a coach' and elsewhere he apostrophises his 'mountain belly'.³ Branded on the thumb as a convicted felon for the murder of the actor Gabriel Spencer in a duel in 1598, Jonson converted to Catholicism in prison, and he was an acquaintance of some of the Gunpowder plotters. He was in prison again in 1605, this time for, in his own words, 'writing something against the Scots' in the collaborative play *Eastward Hoe*.[4] Ever paradoxical, during the reign of King James, Jonson worked to ingratiate himself at court. He wrote masques – elaborate, proto-operatic spectacles commissioned and performed by different court factions – and, in a sometimes fractious partnership with the designer Inigo Jones, developed the visual and verbal sophistication of the form. Jonson was also active in writing commissions for other noble patrons, many of whom he addressed in his poetry. Comedies such as *Volpone*, *The Alchemist* and *Bartholomew Fair* consolidated his reputation in the public theatre, although success in writing tragedies eluded him. In 1616 he published nine of his plays, along with masque texts and poetry, in a folio volume he called *Workes*: the direct model for the publication of Shakespeare's collected works (see Chapter 2). By the early 1620s Jonson's star was waning somewhat and he was marginalised from the jockeying for influence at court around the vexed question of the Spanish match. He continued writing, however, right up until his death in 1637.[5]

Jonson knew Shakespeare, probably quite well: early modern London and its literary community were relatively small, and the two men were actively involved in the theatre industry for fifteen or so shared years. Along with Heminge and Condell and other members of the Chamberlain's Men, Shakespeare is listed as one of the 'Principal comedians' performing in *Every Man in His Humour* in 1598: his name heads the list. He also performed in the Roman tragedy *Sejanus* (1603), which was not a stage success. The revised printed text of the play which has survived does not make clear why it aroused such strong responses, nor why Jonson himself ended up before the Privy Council on charges that the play included 'popery and treason':[6] Jonson tells his readers the play 'is not the same with that which was acted on the public stage, wherein a second pen had good share' – it has been suggested that this 'second pen' might have been Shakespeare's.[7] If that's

true – and it is not uncontentious – it would be the only time
the two men collaborated.

But Jonson's and Shakespeare's work was intertwined in any
case – and not always harmoniously. In the report of Jonson's table
talk published by his Scottish friend William Drummond of Haw-
thornden, we learn his opinion 'that Shakespeare wanted [lacked]
art'.[8] He points out that Bohemia, the land in *The Winter's Tale*
on which Antigonus is shipwrecked with the baby Perdita shortly
before his memorable 'Exit, pursued by a bear', had 'no sea near
by some one hundred miles'.[9] Some of Jonson's views which do not
directly concern Shakespeare nevertheless stress their artistic and
dramaturgical differences: Jonson explains he never wrote his version
of Plautus' famous twin-play *Amphitrio* because 'he could never find
two so like others that he persuade the spectators they were one'.[10]
This never stopped Shakespeare in *The Comedy of Errors* or *Twelfth
Night*. Jonson was also scornful of history plays, probably pointedly
Shakespeare's, which he dismissed as 'three rusty swords' who 'fight
over York and Lancaster's long jars' (prologue to *Every Man in His
Humour*): we can hear Shakespeare's reply in the mock-humility of
the Chorus in *Henry V*, which apologises for the 'four or five most
vile and ragged foils, / Right ill-disposed in brawl ridiculous' that
will 'disgrace ... The name of Agincourt' (4.0.49–52).

In his *Discoveries*, Jonson recalls the suggestion from the letter
'To the great Variety of Readers' by Heminge and Condell in the
First Folio that Shakespeare 'never blotted out line' and replies,
'Would he had blotted a thousand'. Jonson maintains that he is
publicising his comment because of 'their ignorance, who choose
that circumstance to commend their friend by, wherein he most
faulted'. But Jonson goes on:

I loved the man, and do honour his memory, on this side
idolatry, as much as any. He was, indeed, honest, and of an

open and free nature; had an excellent fantasy, brave notions,
and gentle expressions; wherein he flowed with that facility
that sometime it was necessary he should be stopped.[11]

Jonson cites evidence of this absurd over-fluency, 'as when he said
in the person of Caesar, one speaking to him, "Caesar, thou dost
me wrong", he replied, "Caesar never did wrong, but with just
cause"; and such like: which were ridiculous.'[12] It's hard to quite
recover what was so specifically ridiculous about that particular
example, but what's more significant is that no line quite like this
actually appears in the Folio *Julius Caesar*, which reads 'Know,
Cesar doth no wrong, nor without cause / Will he be satisfied'
(Folio 3.1.47–8).[13] It's tantalising to wonder whether Jonson mis-
remembered or misquoted in his disapproval, or whether Shakespeare was sufficiently stung by the remark that he, or someone
else, altered the speech to mitigate the criticism.

This background gives a context to Jonson's poems in the prefatory pages of the First Folio, and gives his praise an undercurrent
of paradox. He certainly had strong and long-standing connections
to Shakespeare – although, as a tireless freelancer, he was also the
most prolific contributor of eulogistic verse in print in the period.
Some of these other poems crown now rather forgotten poets with
laurels somewhat similar to those he places on Shakespeare's head
– for instance, predicting that the work of the eccentric traveller
Thomas Coryate will survive 'unto all ages' (it hasn't), or telling
Sir John Beaumont, author of a sycophantic account of the Tudor
accession which argued that of course King James was the true
heir to Elizabeth, 'this book will live' (nor has this). Writing to
John Selden, Jonson admitted rather ruefully:

... I confess (as every Muse hath err'd,
And mine not least) I have too oft preferr'd
Men past their terms, and prais'd some Names too much[14]

This early modern rent-a-quote thus vows to be more circumspect in his celebrity endorsements – but contradicts himself by voicing his regret within a eulogistic poem of the very kind he vowed to avoid in future. In fact, attaching himself to a prestigious literary production like the First Folio – and giving it his imprimatur on the very first page – may have been beneficial to Jonson at this point, given that he was rather on the outside of the great events of the early 1620s. Eulogies, as Shakespeare's own sonnets know, enhance both praised and praiser.

Jonson's praise of Shakespeare in the First Folio is interesting. He suggests something readers have long wanted to believe, that Shakespeare's writing is revelatory of the man himself:

> Look how the father's face
> Lives in his issue, even so, the race
> Of Shakespeare's mind, and manners brightly shines
> In his well-turned, and true-filed lines

He connects Shakespeare to the literary greats of the classical past, despite the fact of his 'small Latin and less Greek' (as an autodidact who did not attend university, Jonson's own substantial classical learning was important to him, and his description of Shakespeare's is all relative: we know that Shakespeare was proficient in Latin, and some scholars believe he may have had knowledge of Greek). Perhaps pointedly he does not compare Shakespeare to any contemporary poets: Marlowe, Kyd and Lyly are all poets of two generations ago. There is no mention of John Fletcher, for instance, who had taken over from Shakespeare as the King's Men's chief dramatist and who in the early 1620s was at the height of his solo writing career. Nor of the prolific Thomas Heywood, who claimed in 1633 to have had 'an entire hand or at least a main finger in two hundred and twenty plays'.[15] Nor of Thomas Middleton, whose topical play *A Game at Chesse* was to be the box-office hit of the decade the following year, and who had worked on Shakespeare's scripts for the King's Men, as will be discussed below. Shakespeare is memorialised as a figure from the literary past, rather than its present. Even the apparent honorific of 'gentle Shakespeare' is slightly barbed. During the late 1590s Shakespeare and his father, John, worked hard to acquire a coat of arms (it involved bribing the College of Arms to discover – that is, invent – a genealogy of past greatness), and they eventually got the title and the pointed motto *Non Sanz Droict* (Not without right) in 1596. A couple of years later a comic upstart in a Jonson play has the satirical motto 'Not without mustard'.[16]

Others of the eulogists to the First Folio are less well known. Hugh Holland was a fellow Westminster School pupil with Jonson, and was linked with him and with Philip Sidney, Edmund Spenser and Michael Drayton by William Camden, their old headmaster, as 'the most pregnant wits of these our times'. Much of Holland's poetic work, including his sonnet in the First Folio, 'Upon the Lines and Life of the Famous Scenic Poet, Master William Shakespeare', is memorialising: he wrote elegies on the death of Queen Elizabeth, of the chivalric young heir to the Stuart throne Prince Henry and, in 1625, of King James. He also wrote dedicatory poems for literary works in his social network, including for Jonson's *Sejanus* and works by Thomas Coryate. He was a Catholic for a time; was under the patronage of the Duke of Buckingham; on his death in 1633 he was buried in Westminster Abbey.

The initials I.M. are generally associated with James Mabbe, translator and poet, who was connected with the Folio publisher Edward Blount. The two collaborated to publish the Spanish romance *The Rogue* (for which Jonson wrote a dedicatory poem), which was dedicated, like the Shakespeare Folio, to the Herbert brothers William, Earl of Pembroke and Philip, Earl of Montgomery. Mabbe is known to have admired Shakespeare: he sent an

Oxford friend a copy of poems by the Spanish writer Lope de Vega with a handwritten inscription comparing them to Shakespeare's sonnets. We do not know whether they knew each other personally. Also connected with matters Spanish is the final dedicatory poet, Leonard Digges. We know that Mabbe and Digges knew each other and that they operated in the same literary networks. Digges translated a Spanish work with the mouth-watering title *Gerardo, the Unfortunate Spaniard, or a Pattern for Lascivious Lovers* (1622), which he dedicated to the Herberts. We don't know the extent of his knowledge of Shakespeare, although Digges does provide another dedicatory poem for the 1640 edition of Shakespeare's poems.

'The principal actors in all these plays': Shakespeare's fellow players

Shakespeare wrote for actors. He wrote with knowledge of the particular skills, physical characteristics, and even speech patterns of the men – only men, of course, could act on the early modern stage – who formed the Chamberlain's, later the King's, Men.[17] The First Folio includes the names of the entire company from its beginning in the 1590s through to its then current membership. Twenty-six men, including Shakespeare, are listed under 'The Names of the Principal Actors in all these Plays'.

Two of these names have a particular and direct responsibility for the First Folio: John Heminge and Henry Condell. Heminge and Condell, signatories to the letters to the Herbert brothers and to the 'great Variety of Readers' at the beginning of the First Folio, also appear in Shakespeare's will: they, along with Richard Burbage, are each given money to buy mourning rings. For the eighteen plays that had not previously been printed, the publishers needed to negotiate with the King's Men, who held the manuscript copies among their other company properties, probably at the Globe or the Blackfriars theatre. It seems likely that these two men were the liaison point between the worlds of theatre and publishing.

John Heminge was the last of the original group of shareholders who had come together to form the playing company the Chamberlain's Men in 1594. He was two years younger than Shakespeare (he was baptised in 1566), and came to London from Droitwich in Worcestershire. He was apprenticed to a grocer near London's Guildhall at the age of 12, and in his will more than forty years later he still identified as 'citizen and grocer'.[18] At some point he turned to the theatre, and is named as a player in Jonson plays, including *Every Man In His Humour* and *Every Man Out of His Humour, Sejanus, The Alchemist* and *Catiline*. A late manuscript addition to a Jonson play suggests he played one of the avaricious old men, Corbaccio, in *Volpone*. (Jonson plays feature heavily in our account of actors not because they dominated the early modern repertoire but because they are unique in routinely recording the names of their performers, although not linked to specific roles.) In the second decade of the seventeenth century Heminge seems to have become more involved in the administration and management of the company: Andrew Gurr calls him the company's 'controller of finances'.[19] In 1618 he represented the players to the Master of the Revels who licensed all scripts for performance, and he was the payee for court performances. Heminge continued to apprentice boy actors with the King's Men to the Grocers' Company. A contemporary ballad describing the fire at the Globe Theatre mocks 'old stuttering Heminge' 'with swollen eyes' and 'distressed': the attribution of a stutter is suggestive, but it may be less an accurate description of the man than a pun on 'hemming', or hesitating in speech. Heminge kept a taphouse selling beer and ale in property adjacent to the theatre – in effect, running an early theatre bar.[20]

Henry Condell was another actor with the Chamberlain's Men who joined in the later 1590s. His name appears in a number of cast lists for plays from 1598 onwards, including Jonson's *Every Man In His Humour* (performed 1598) and *Every Man Out of His Humour* (1599), *Sejanus* (1603) and *Catiline* (1611). More specifically, we know he played Mosca the parasite in *Volpone* (1605) and Surly in *The Alchemist* (1610). In a metatheatrical induction scene to John Marston's play *The Malcontent* he appears as himself, along with Burbage, Lowin, Sly and Sincklo, also listed in the Folio. He is also named as the corrupt Cardinal, brother to Ferdinand and the Duchess in Webster's *The Duchess of Malfi* (1613). Born in East Anglia, probably in 1576, Condell was another migrant to the rapidly growing metropolis, where he spent his theatrical career: perhaps this shared experience of migration helped form a particular bond with Heminge and with the Stratford-born Shakespeare when they were young men together trying to make it in the big city. He married Elizabeth Smart at the church of St Laurence Poutney near London Bridge, and was a churchwarden at St Mary Aldermanbury alongside Heminge – a memorial monument was raised to them and the Folio in the churchyard at the end of the nineteenth century (PLATE 16). Nine Condell children, of whom only three survived infancy, were baptised in the church between 1599 and 1611. Like Heminge, Condell seems to have gathered valuable administrative skills and may have moved from acting to more managerial responsibilities in the company. In addition he was named as executor of a number of playhouse wills. He also gathered property, purchasing a house in Fulham. He died in 1627.

Clearly Heminge and Condell were vitally important to the First Folio project since they were the connection between the publication and the theatre: without them, there was no access to the unpublished material. As long-standing sharers in the company, they presumably had access to play scripts and the authority to negotiate their publication. However, the extent of their involvement in the book needs some investigation. They are almost always described as 'editors' of the First Folio, but the associations of careful preparatory work that title now carries are not necessarily relevant to the form of this book. There are, as modern editors have revealed in great detail and as discussed in Chapter 1, any number of misprints, misreadings and lapses in presentational consistency that are not compatible with 'editing' in the sense we might understand it now.

To be fair to Heminge and Condell, they never themselves claim to be editors – and nor does the word itself, and thus the concept of the activity, exist in the sense of preparing literary work for accurate publication until the eighteenth century. Nor is it evident that they have any particular interest in or experience of play publication or of literature more generally. There are no books listed among the household stuff Condell apportions out in his will; Heminge bequeaths embroidered cushions and pictures, but the only mention of books is those that attest to the 'good yearly profit' he has gained from his theatre shares – so account books.[21] Their own description of their labours is as a combination of memorial and collation. 'We have but collected' his plays, they claim in the epistle to the Herberts, 'and done an office to the dead, to procure his orphans, guardians'. Not for 'self-profit', they add, but 'only to keep the memory of so worthy a friend and fellow alive, as was our Shakespeare'. Addressing their readers they repeat the language: they are 'friends' who have taken 'care and pain to have collected and published' the works. They only 'gather his works and give them to you'; it is for others to praise him.

As signatories to two prefatory epistles and as self-appointed curators of Shakespeare's memory, John Heminge and Henry Condell are the most prominent members of the King's Men in the First Folio. But the list of twenty-six actors offers a composite record of the changing personnel of the company from its earliest foundation up to the 1620s. They appear to be listed in the order of their association with the Chamberlain's Men. The first seven names – Shakespeare, Burbage, Heminge, Augustine Phillips, William Kemp, Thomas Pope and George Bryan – were the original sharers, or shareholders, in the company under the patronage first of Henry Carey and then of his son George. It's thought that Henry Condell, next in the list, replaced Bryan early in the company's history. The eighth sharer was probably the next named, William Sly.

We can piece together something of the other actors and of their role in Shakespeare's dramatic success. Almost uniquely in the organisation of the early modern theatre world, Shakespeare wrote throughout his career for a single company with a relatively settled personnel: he wrote for actors whose professional history and strengths he knew. He even knew their physical appearances, and some of the relatively rare references in the plays to characters' appearance may be in-jokes about particular actors. The actors shaped Shakespeare's writing and its development. The contours of his writing career give us some clues about them. Early plays, such as the *Henry VI* plays, and comedies, including *The Taming of the Shrew* and *The Comedy of Errors*, tend to distribute parts fairly evenly across the company, suggesting that the Chamberlain's Men began with an ensemble style. *Richard III* is the first experiment in developing a lengthy role for a star actor – Richard Burbage – and this pattern becomes the norm at the turn of the seventeenth century. One scholar suggests that this changing distribution of roles is related to the changing financial organisation of the company: as the power balance and the number of shares became focused in a smaller number of hands towards the end of the 1590s, so too the number of lines in Shakespeare's plays became more narrowly distributed.[22] It seems also likely, for example, that during the 1590s the company had two young male actors who could both play young women equally well, thus the pairings of Helena and Hermia in *A Midsummer Night's Dream*, or Julia and Sylvia in *The*

Two Gentleman of Verona, or Rosalind and Celia in *As You Like It*. Further, in the first decade of the seventeenth century Shakespeare apparently felt new confidence that the King's Men employed an actor who could convincingly play a mature and powerful woman, and thus he wrote the parts of Lady Macbeth, Volumnia, the redoubtable mother of Coriolanus, and Cleopatra.

We also have some scattered clues about individual actors. Like Heminge, Condell and Shakespeare, Augustine Phillips is also in the Jonson cast lists for *Every Man In His Humour* and *Every Man Out of His Humour* and for *Sejanus*. He comes most to prominence in the records when the company are involved in the political fallout after the ill-fated rebellion by Robert Devereux, the Earl of Essex, against the Queen in 1601. Essex's supporters had paid the company 40 shillings to perform at the Globe what was described as a play of the 'deposing and killing of King Richard the second'. Most scholars believe this to have been Shakespeare's *Richard II*, a play about the deposition of an unpopular king by his kinsman Bolingbroke. Phillips seems to have acted as the spokesman for the company in the subsequent investigation by the Privy Council. When questioned Phillips maintained the company's ignorance about any wider implication of the performance, even suggesting that they would have 'determined to play some other play, holding that of King Richard as being so old and so long out of use that they should have a small company at it'.[23] It's striking that at no point does Shakespeare (or any other putative author) seem to have been drawn directly into the issue, and, in any case, the Privy Council turned its attention to the play's sponsors rather than its actors. Phillips was also a musician, like many actors; he left musical instruments to his sons in his will on his death in 1605. He also left bequests to other members of the King's Men – including a gold piece to Shakespeare and to Condell, and a silver bowl to his executors, Heminge and Richard Burbage.

Little is known of George Bryan, who was not listed with the others in the Jonson cast lists and so may have left the company before 1598, to be replaced by Henry Condell. Thomas Pope, stepbrother of Augustine Phillips, did act in the Jonson plays and was probably known for comic parts. In a satiric poem of 1599 Samuel Rowlands calls him 'Pope the clown'. The best-known comedian in the Chamberlain's Men was, however, William Kemp (FIGURE 6). With Burbage, Kemp was the company's celebrity actor: the two men are mentioned together in an extended skit on metropolitan literary culture written and performed by Cambridge students at the beginning of the seventeenth century. Where Burbage developed his reputation in tragedy, Kemp did so in comedy. He is so intrinsic to the roles Shakespeare wrote for him that on occasion in the text of the First Folio his name replaces that of his character. In *Much Ado About Nothing* the malevolent melancholic Don John plots to destroy his brother's friend Claudio by falsely suggesting Claudio's bride Hero has been unfaithful to him. It is down to the Watch, a haplessly amateur neighbourhood patrol, to reveal the truth. Their constable, the pompous ignoramus Dogberry, attempts to speak in an elevated Latinate diction that constantly trips him up, making his attempts to drill his recruits comically malapropistic: disloyalty becomes 'allegiance', deserving 'desertless', sensible 'senseless', and apprehend 'comprehend' (3.3). Dogberry's great rhetorical triumph comes when he repeats and thus jubilantly perpetuates the slur on him by one of his prisoners: 'remember that I am an ass' (4.2.74). The text of the First Folio, however, ascribes this not to the character Dogberry but to the actor Kemp, in dialogue with another specific actor, Richard Cowley (PLATE 17).

We can speculate about the other roles that Kemp played too. His must have been the comic tour de force of Lance in *The Two Gentlemen of Verona*, the humorous servant who, contrary to the

FIGURE 6 Will Kemp, the clown. © *National Portrait Gallery, London.*

actors' lore that advises against working with children or animals, has as his straight man a wonderfully inexpressive dog, Crab, 'the sourest-natured dog that lives', which hears a tale of terrible woe and 'sheds not a tear nor speaks a word' (2.3.5–6, 30–31). He probably played the clown, Lancelot Gobbo, in *The Merchant of Venice*. He would have stolen the show in *A Midsummer Night's Dream* as the irrepressible Bottom, the weaver-cum-actor-cum-ass (maybe this last role is what Dogberry also refers to when repeating that he is an ass – Shakespeare's characters sometimes do refer to their roles in other plays in a sort of in-joke for regular theatregoers, for example when Polonius in *Hamlet* recalls playing the role of Caesar in the recent performances of *Julius Caesar*). Bottom wants to play all the parts in the mechanicals' play for Duke Theseus of 'Pyramus and Thisbe', and on the stage this comic role is always threatening to run away with the audience's affections. The fairy queen Titania needs to have magic juice on her eyelids in order to fall in love with him, but generations of audiences have needed no such chemical manipulation.

It's sometimes suggested that Hamlet's advice to the visiting players who come to Elsinore and perform at his instigation the pointed political melodrama 'The Murder of Gonzago' before the court has something to do with Shakespeare's impatience at the improvisatory genius of Kemp: 'let those that play your clowns speak no more than is set down for them; for there be of them that will themselves laugh to set on some quantity of barren spectators to laugh too, though in the mean time some necessary question of the play be then to be considered' (3.2.38–43). Clowns, Hamlet seems to say here, have a habit of stealing the limelight and diverting attention from what's important in the play.

Nowhere is this more obvious in Shakespeare's work than in the character of Falstaff, another Kemp creation. Playing against type – Kemp's trademark athleticism must have been trammelled somewhat by the early modern equivalent of a fat-suit to play that 'stuffed cloak-bag of guts' (*1 Henry IV* 2.5.456–7) – Kemp created a dynamically comic dramatic focus forever pulling audiences, as well as Prince Hal, heir to the throne, away from the 'necessary question' of political government. In *1 Henry IV* the king is beset by rebels who wish to take his throne and partition his kingdom, but the more pressing theatrical threat is the all-consuming figure of Falstaff, who pushes Henry IV right out of the dramatic spotlight. Shakespeare's writing of the character, plus Kemp's embodiment of it, created an early modern phenomenon. There are more references to Falstaff in early modern culture than to all the other characters of Shakespeare put together. This had a great theatrical pay-off, and many critics assume that the sequel, *Henry IV Part 2*, is shaped to meet the public demand for more

Falstaff. Nevertheless, Falstaff's very popularity creates a moral dilemma. The overarching structure of the *Henry IV* plays is that of the biblical parable of the prodigal son: as in the gospel story, the prince must set aside his tavern jests and step into the serious public role for which he is destined. The sign of this transformation must be his separation from Falstaff, 'That villainous, abominable misleader of youth' (2.5.467–8). The moral trajectory of the play (get rid of Falstaff!) is thus on a collision course with its theatrical one (more Falstaff!).

It may be that these diversionary comic character successes created a rift in the company. At the end of the 1590s, Falstaff was more famous than Shakespeare or anyone else in the company. For whatever reason, Kemp left the Chamberlain's Men in 1599, and danced from London to Norwich in an eccentric and energetic adventure described in his book *Kemp's Nine Days' Wonder* (1600). *Henry V*, performed in 1599, can only tease us with the promise that Falstaff/Kemp is still around: he dies, offstage and without ever appearing, in Act 2.

Following his departure, the clown role was taken over by the more mordant, cerebral Robert Armin, also listed in the Folio, who replaced Kemp's physicality with musical ability and a way of deflecting a humorous commentary onto other characters (PLATE 18). The figure of Feste in *Twelfth Night* shows us Armin's gifts as a singer, as well as his particular brand of ironic rather than slapstick humour, as in this exchange with his mistress, Olivia, who is in mourning for her dead brother:

FESTE Good madonna, why mournest thou?
OLIVIA Good fool, for my brother's death.
FESTE I think his soul is in hell, madonna.
OLIVIA I know his soul is in heaven, fool.
FESTE The more fool, madonna, to mourn for your brother's soul, being in heaven. (1.5.62–7)

Armin's cleverness turns Olivia's piety against her, and also subtly prepares us for the play's comic trajectory: that Olivia must be brought out of her excessive grief and back into the world of the living, by falling violently in love. Armin would also have played the philosophical, enigmatic Fool who accompanies the dispossessed king for much of *King Lear*: indeed, this character shares a line with Feste. It's often argued that the peculiar distribution of this role in the tragedy – the Fool is absent from the opening court scene where we might expect him, and then disappears after the enigmatic line 'And I'll go to bed at noon' (3.6.43) – reflects the fact that the part was doubled with that of Cordelia, whose own patchy presence in the play is its mirror opposite. Lear's line as he bears in the body of his favoured youngest daughter, 'And my poor fool is hanged' (5.3.281), confirms their interconnectedness. If it's true that the two roles were doubled, it also means that Armin could play a convincing female role, since Cordelia is the play's nearest thing to a heroine.

Most crucial of all to Shakespeare's playwriting was the partnership with Richard Burbage (PLATE 19). Burbage was born into a theatrical family: when he was just 8 years old his father James, a joiner-turned-actor, opened The Theatre, a playhouse in Shoreditch, and both Richard and his brother Cuthbert followed his inspiration into early modern showbusiness. Richard was born in 1568 and so was four years younger than Shakespeare. After an apprentice period with other theatrical companies, he joined the newly founded Lord Chamberlain's Men in 1594 and became a sharer. At that point he and Shakespeare became colleagues, a relationship which would last until Shakespeare's death two decades later, but they may have met earlier, even as children: James Burbage's company toured to Warwickshire, including Stratford, in the 1570s when Shakespeare was in his teens. Richard Burbage became the Chamberlain's Men's lead player, and by the first decade of the seventeenth century he had come to dominate the company's repertoire. An early joke in the diary of a London law student tells us something about a comic rivalry between playwright and lead actor, fresh from the success of Burbage's show-stopping Richard III:

> Upon a time when Burbage played Richard III there was a citizen grew so far in liking with him that before she went from the play she appointed him to come that night unto her by the name of Richard III. Shakespeare, overhearing their conclusion, went before, was entertained at his game ere Burbage came. Then message being brought that Richard III was at the door, Shakespeare caused return to be made that William the Conqueror was before Richard III.[24]

He and Shakespeare also worked together in other artistic pursuits: Burbage was an accomplished painter, and he and the dramatist designed an impresa (a decorative heraldic device combining a symbol and a motto) for the Earl of Rutland.

Burbage's exceptional talent transformed Shakespeare's writing, and the parts of Hamlet, Lear, Othello, Coriolanus, Brutus, Antony and Prospero were almost certainly all written for him. He was particularly accomplished at the presentation of grief: a contemporary appreciation noted 'no man can act so well / This point of sorrow, for none him can draw / So truly to the life this map of woe'.[25] The roles written for him place questions of personality and motivation at the heart of their plays: when we think about Hamlet's vacillation, or Othello's jealousy, or Coriolanus' pride, these are all attributes imagined for, and embodied by, Burbage.

Burbage's acting was characterised by its realism, particularly by contrast with previous acting styles. A later account describes him almost as we might perceive a method actor of the twentieth century who got into role and stayed there: 'a delightful Proteus, so wholly transforming himself into his part, and putting off himself with his clothes, as he never (not so much as in the tiring-house) assumed himself again until the play was done'.[26] This realism was clearly distinct from the more histrionic and stylised presentation of earlier great actors such as the rival Admiral's Men's Edward Alleyn, who played the bombastic overreaching heroes of Marlowe's plays, including Tamburlaine and Faustus. By contrast, Burbage's was a more interior style, and more convincing. When Hamlet, played by Burbage, encounters the travelling players at Elsinore, this seems like the meeting of two distinct theatrical traditions: the modern Shakespeare–Burbage one, and the older, more stylised, Marlowe–Alleyn one. Hamlet asks for a speech from an old play about the fall of Troy – and the speech sounds like something from Marlowe, perhaps his early play *Dido, Queen of Carthage*, in which the Troy-survivor Aeneas recounts the horrors of the city's sack. Burbage as Hamlet pays homage to the power of that earlier tradition, but confidently eclipses it in his emotional range. His believability was almost proverbial: a contemporary court lady's questionable defence of her own conduct was judged so believable by the Paul's-walker John Chamberlain that 'diverse said Burbage could not have acted better'.[27]

Burbage was thus Shakespeare's partner and collaborator in many of his greatest plays, and it is clear that the playwright wrote with the developing talent of his leading actor in mind. For contemporaries, the roles were seen to be inseparable from their instantiation in the performance of Burbage himself. Indeed, an elegy on Burbage's death in 1619 suggested that only now had these tragic characters truly perished:

He's gone, and with him what a world is dead. ...
No more: young Hamlet, old Hieronimo,
Kind Lear, the grieved Moor, and more beside
That lived in him have now forever died.

Burbage's death was widely commemorated – more so, as some contemporaries noted, than the death of James's queen, Anne, only a couple of weeks earlier. The Earl of Pembroke, one of the dedicatees of the First Folio, professed himself, in a letter to James Hay, unable to 'endure' a play after the 'loss of my old acquaintance Burbage'.[28]

The 'incomparable pair of brethren': the book's patrons

William, Earl of Pembroke, and his brother, Philip, Earl of Montgomery, also appear as 'the most noble and incomparable pair of brethren' to whom the First Folio is dedicated. Heminge and Condell's letter of dedication addresses them as gods accepting the gift of 'the remains of your servant Shakespeare'. Noting that 'no man … come near your Lordships but with a kind of religious address', the actors seem almost to mock their patrons in the guise of pagan gods of the new world (the reference seems to be to Pliny's *Natural History*): 'many nations (we have heard) that had not gums and incense, obtained their requests with a leavened cake. It was no fault to approach their gods by what means they could.' The actors draw on the history of their association with these patrons and 'for the many favours we have received from your Lordships'. These favours included Pembroke's writing in May 1619 to the Stationers' Company apparently to put a stop to the stationer Thomas Pavier's plans to publish a sequence of Shakespeare plays (see Chapter 2). We don't know whether this acquaintance included direct contact with Shakespeare, although the dedicatory letter reminds the Herberts that they have 'prosecuted [the plays] and their author living, with so much favour'. Some scholars have believed that the dedication of Shakespeare's Sonnets to 'Mr W.H., the only begetter' refers to William Herbert, although the patron of Shakespeare's narrative poems *Venus and Adonis* and *The Rape of Lucrece*, Henry Wriothesley Earl of Southampton, is more often assumed.

The Herberts were indeed powerful allies for the King's Men. William Herbert (1580–1630) had inherited his father's extensive Welsh estates in 1601 (PLATE 20). He had assiduously cultivated a career as a courtier but decisively lost Elizabeth's favour when his affair with Mary Fitton, one of her gentlewomen, ended in pregnancy. He and his brother Philip began again currying favour with the new king: like many ambitious courtiers they travelled northward to meet the new king as he progressed towards London in 1603. They were rewarded: both became, as they are acknowledged in the First Folio, knights of the garter. William's close relationship with James was marked and furthered by extravagant gifts, including a New Year present of a jewel reputed to be worth £40,000. The well-connected Earl of Pembroke, who was so adept at cultivating the king's patronage, was in turn sought after as a patron himself, and was an active sponsor of literary and artistic culture. Pembroke gave Ben Jonson an annual grant and was the dedicatee of *Sejanus*; he helped Jonson when he was imprisoned for the *Eastward Hoe* affair, and Jonson wrote an epigram describing his patron's 'one true posture' in a vicious world.[29] He supported his distant relative, the poet George Herbert, and commissioned pictures from Marcus Gheeraerts the Younger and Nicholas Hilliard, and music from John Dowland. He was the dedicatee of books produced by Folio publisher Edward Blount, including works by Samuel Daniel and the Italian John Florio, and a translation by Leonard Digges from the Spanish. In 1617 he became Chancellor of Oxford University. He and his brother were known as prominent investors in the Virginia Company, a Jacobean joint-stock company aiming to develop profitable settlements in the New World, so may have been interested in the fact that Shakespeare's most colonial play, *The Tempest*, comes first in the Folio. William Herbert's increasing opposition to the Spanish match was well known. Michael Brennan, who has undertaken the most extensive study of Pembroke's patronage, suggests that as 'anti-Spanish and anti-Catholic tracts continued to flood onto the market between 1623 and 1625 ... Pembroke was addressed as a patron who was known to be openly sympathetic to such views.'[30] His presence as the patron of the Shakespeare Folio may therefore have resonated in the immediate context of Charles's return from Spain in autumn 1623.

Philip, Earl of Montgomery (1584–1650) was less obviously interested in the literary arts than his bookish older brother William, although he too was a sought-after patron by aspiring writers, of whom he particularly favoured his kinsmen George Herbert and the playwright Philip Massinger (PLATE 21). John Aubrey's account that Philip's 'chief delight was in hunting and hawking' corresponds with another later assessment: 'he pretended to no other qualifications than to understand horses and dogs very well.'[31] Unlike William, he seemed to have little political ambition, but threw himself into the masques, entertainments and other diversions of court leisure, gaining a reputation for rough and violent behaviour, often over gambling disagreements. He succeeded his brother as the 4th Earl of Pembroke in 1630, and at Wilton House, their seat near Salisbury, he developed a fine collection of paintings, especially by Van Dyck. Philip also commissioned the architect Inigo Jones to transform the Tudor manor house in his innovative introduction of Palladian architecture.

The dedication to the Herberts is followed, as is common in printed books of this period, by another dedication: to its readers. In this succession, we can see an older patronage system of literary publication overlapping with the modern, commercial one, in which it is readers – or, as the First Folio makes clear, buyers – whose endorsement is the ultimate marker of success. Nobody has suggested that the Herberts gave the book any financial subsidy: this book needed to stand on its own two feet in the literary marketplace of Paul's Churchyard. 'The great Variety of Readers', that potentially heterogeneous group of economic patrons who are also implicitly a part of the creation of the First Folio, are discussed in this book's Coda.

Printers and publishers

If the personnel of the playhouse have left their mark on Shakespeare's plays, so too have the men of the printing shop. We do not know what contact Shakespeare had during his lifetime with the publishing industry. Scholars disagree about whether, and if so how much, Shakespeare engaged with the publication of his own work during his lifetime. We do know that he was connected to one London printer, Richard Field, a fellow Stratford émigré whose family were acquainted with the Shakespeares in Warwickshire. Field was responsible for publishing some of the books by other writers who were most influential on Shakespeare: the translation of Plutarch's *Lives of the Noble Grecians and Romans* that he used for his Roman plays, including *Julius Caesar* and *Antony and Cleopatra*, for instance, and the source for the English history plays, Holinshed's *Chronicles*. Field was also the first publisher of Shakespeare's narrative poems *Venus and Adonis* and *The Rape of Lucrece*, and there seems to be a private joke about him in *Cymbeline* in an otherwise random reference to a 'Richard du Champ' (a Frenchified version of Field's name). Had Shakespeare been directly involved in finding publishers for his plays, we might have expected him to approach his trusted colleague Richard Field.

But Field did not publish any of the plays, and there is no direct evidence of Shakespeare's involvement with those publishers who did. He might just have come into contact with William Jaggard, the Folio's printer, because from the middle of the first decade of the seventeenth century the Jaggard print shop printed the playbills by which the King's Men advertised their performances.[32] There must have been regular traffic between the Globe Theatre and Jaggard's print shop over the river. Whether or not the two men were personally acquainted, Jaggard certainly knew of Shakespeare. Further, he seems to have long considered his name to be a powerful publishing commodity.

William Jaggard had built up a profitable print business since becoming a freeman of the Stationers' Company at the end of his apprenticeship in 1591. He first appears in print on the title page of a 1594 sermon by John Dove. He opened a print shop in the Barbican, and soon expanded by taking over another printer's business. He became printer to the City of London in 1610. In 1599 he published *The Passionate Pilgrim*, an anthology of poems inscribed on the title page to 'W. Shakespeare': the book contained a couple of Shakespeare's unpublished sonnets, and some extracts from his play *Love's Labour's Lost*, but the majority of the unattributed material was by other writers, including Richard Barnfield and Walter Raleigh. The collection seems to have been successful, as it was immediately reprinted. In 1612 a third edition added some poems on the classical theme of Helen of Troy by Thomas Heywood, who had previously published them with Jaggard in 1609. Heywood does not seem to have been pleased by his printer cannibalising his works unacknowledged within a book attributed to another writer, and in his *An Apology for Actors* of 1612 he reported that Shakespeare wasn't pleased either: 'the author I know much offended with M. Jaggard (that altogether unknown to him) presumed to make so bold with his name'.[33] Presumably stung by this charge, Jaggard printed a replacement title page for unsold copies of the third edition which no longer included the attribution to Shakespeare.

Even if, as Heywood suggests, Jaggard did not know Shakespeare, he continued to take an interest in his work. In 1619, in association with the stationer Thomas Pavier, with whom he had worked on a number of previous titles, Jaggard began to print a quarto collection of plays attributed to Shakespeare: the Pavier quartos discussed in Chapter 2. After four volumes had appeared it seems that the King's Men were able to prevent any further publication thanks to the intervention of the Lord Chamberlain, later a dedicatee of the First Folio. The remaining plays were printed despite this injunction, disguised with false dates so as to look like earlier editions. Jaggard's professional work thus had elements of subterfuge, and he was often embroiled in disputes with his authors about the quality of his work. Heywood complained that his work was so mangled in the press that he wanted the printer to include a list of errata, but that Jaggard refused to 'publish his own disworkmanship'.[34] Another author, Ralph Brooke, who published a book of heraldry with Jaggard's print shop in 1619, also accused him of poor workmanship. Brooke advertised a second edition (by another printer in 1622) as 'with amendment of divers faults, committed by the Printer, in the time of the Author's sickness'. Jaggard mounted his own defence, publishing a third volume on heraldry, this time by Augustine Vincent. In this volume Jaggard signs an extended vindication of his professional practice, sarcastically mocking Brooke's claim that 'his sickness, confining him to his chamber, and absenting him from the Press, then was the time, that the Printer took to bring in that Trojan horse of Barbarisms, and literal errors, which overrun the whole volume of his Catalogue.'[35]

Against this repeated charge of poor work must be set the self-evident quality of some of Jaggard's output. His work also includes complicatedly illustrated and decorative books such as Edward Topsell's natural history book *The History of Four-footed Beasts* (1607). Jaggard's Topsell features scores of beautiful, and beautifully placed, woodcuts (PLATE 22), including the German engraver Albrecht Dürer's famous image of an apparently armour-plated rhinoceros (Dürer was working from a written description and had never seen one of these beasts). The Topsell edition demonstrates that Jaggard's business could produce the highest-quality books. Jaggard's print shop seems always to have been busy, and clearly his work was in demand. During the process of printing the Shakespeare collection, for instance, there seem to have been at least two other books in production at his Barbican print shop at any one time, as well as official printing associated with the City printer role, playbills, and other printing jobs of an occasional nature (see Chapter 4). Jaggard clearly felt the playbill work was highly important to his business, and he complained successfully to parliament in 1620 when he temporarily lost the monopoly when the king arbitrarily granted rights 'for the sole printing of paper or parchment on the one side', whatever the content, to two other stationers.[36]

Jaggard's final – and most authoritative – encounter with Shakespeare's works was his involvement in the First Folio. His name appears separately from that of his son, Isaac, suggesting that each man had a specific role in the publication of the book. Perhaps William Jaggard's task was to manage the business of printing, whereas Isaac took on some of the other duties associated with publishing. Jaggard had gone blind in 1612, probably as a result of syphilis. In the exchange of blame with Brooke about responsibility for errors in the heraldry publication, he defended himself with dignity: 'howsoever it hath pleased God to make me and him [Brooke] to style me a blind-printer, though I could tell him by the way, that it is no right conclusion in schools, that because Homer was blind and a poet therefore he was a blind-poet':[37] the proud assertion that the adjective is less important than the noun resounds unexpectedly with much more modern attitudes to physical ability and disability. Jaggard was proud of his work, noting that 'it touches a Printer as much to maintain his reputation in the art he lives by, as a herald [like Ralph Brooke] in his profession'. Just as the very book which would secure that reputation and commend him to posterity was being completed in his printing shop, William Jaggard died. The signature on his will, dated March 1623, indicates his decline: the script is wayward, trailing off the page. His son Isaac was appointed to the post of City printer in place of 'his late father deceased' on 4 November 1623; the fellow stationer and Shakespeare publisher Thomas Pavier was appointed to oversee William's estate.

William Jaggard's successful printing business passed to his son. Isaac, born in 1595, had grown into manhood just as his father's blindness advanced, and he must have been effectively a partner in the business since his teens, when other men might expect still to be apprentices. He was admitted as freeman of the Stationers' Company in 1613 when he was just 18, probably because of his father's incapacity. His first appearance in print is on the title page of a pocket-sized book: an octavo of George Chapman's translation of Musaeus in 1616 states 'Printed by Isaac Jaggard'. Thereafter the majority of Jaggard publications continue to appear under William's name, but some are attributed to Isaac, suggesting that they had a degree of professional independence. Isaac's titles include Heywood's *A Woman Killed with Kindness* (1617) and a translation of Boccaccio's *The Decameron* (1620). His is the single name associated with the Folio project from the beginning. When the book was advertised in the English-language section of the Frankfurt Book Fair materials for 1622, it was described thus: 'Playes, written by M. William Shakespeare, all in one volume, printed by Isaac Jaggard, in fol.'[38] Here, Isaac seems to be in the role of sole publisher. Perhaps Edward Blount came in on the project later as co-publisher when the investment costs of this big undertaking became clear: their two names are on the Folio's title page. It's easy to imagine the young Isaac's ambition to develop the print business into a publishing business too, and further to speculate that the large scale of the Shakespeare book may well have seemed an exciting challenge to a young man with new ideas to develop for the family firm. At some point, though, it apparently became economically prudent to split the risk and take on publishing partners: Blount, Smithweeke and Aspley. Isaac Jaggard outlived his father by only four years, and on his death in 1627 the business was sold off.

Partner with the Jaggards in the publication was the stationer Edward Blount (1562–*c*.1632). Blount had a good grammar-school education at the Merchant Taylors' School, where he would have been taught by one of the age's most influential humanist educationalists, Richard Mulcaster. The Merchant Taylors' curriculum included Latin, Italian and French, and this cosmopolitanism may have been a formative influence on the man who went on to publish such a sophisticatedly European literary list. Blount may have overlapped with fellow pupils Thomas Lodge and Thomas Kyd. Like them, he pursued a literary career, but in a different key.

Blount was apprenticed to the foremost literary publisher of the Elizabethan age, William Ponsonby, from 1578 to 1588. He then built up his own business in the 1590s, operating from Paul's Churchyard, the centre of the London book trade, where he took on the shop at the sign of the Black Bear in 1609. His first publications give a sense of his interests: a translation from the French poet Josuah Sylvester, a book of French and Italian songs, and the English–Italian dictionary by the Italian writer John Florio, with whom he retained a strong connection throughout his life. Blount's publishing priorities were in translations of continental literature. He published Florio's landmark translation of the philosopher Montaigne, and a translation of the new Spanish mock-romance *Don Quixote*. He also published travel books, dictionaries and other translations. His was the first edition of Marlowe's *Hero and Leander* and of Shakespeare's enigmatic poem 'The Phoenix and Turtle'. Blount's cultural interests spread beyond books: he is associated with the import of art objects as well as seeds and exotic foodstuffs, and also was a factor for manuscripts and certain banned books from continental Europe for trusted clients.[39]

All this makes Blount a significant player in the world of European literary fiction, philosophy and travel publication in London. It doesn't quite explain his willingness to invest in the Shakespeare First Folio. In 1623 Blount had almost no track record of publishing drama, other than highbrow closet, Latinate or occasional drama by Samuel Daniels, Ben Jonson and William Alexander; he did go on, right at the end of his career, to publish a collection of plays by John Lyly in 1632. On occasion he appears to have bought the rights to plays but sold them on without publishing them. When he and Isaac Jaggard entered their claim in the Stationers' Register to the eighteen Shakespeare plays not previously printed, a search of the register revealed that Blount himself owned, but presumably had forgotten, the rights to the unpublished *Antony and Cleopatra* (entered in the register in 1608, shortly after the play's performance). But perhaps Blount was more interested in the monumental quality of the collected works than in small quarto publications. Perhaps he saw the collected Shakespeare as the English equivalent of Cervantes or Montaigne: something to publish on grounds of cultural significance and literary worth rather than mere commercial viability. As he wrote in an epistle 'To the Reader' in a book of essays published in 1620, 'I take not upon me to write either in the praise or discommendation of this book; it belongs not unto me, but now it is abroad, must wholly be submitted to your judgement and censure.' But Blount anticipated his readers would share his own judgement: 'if the book please you, come home to my shop, you shall have it bound ready to your hand, where in the mean time I expect you'.[40] Blount

suggests that his shop in Paul's Churchyard also served as a binders' workshop, selling books ready bound. He seems to have been
increasingly apt to appear in his own books, signing a prefatory
letter or humbly presenting a list of errata. Neither appears in the
First Folio. In his dedication of the posthumous publication of *Hero
and Leander* to Marlowe's friend Sir Thomas Walsingham – cousin
to the Elizabethan spymaster Sir Francis Walsingham – Blount
talks of the 'further obsequies due unto the deceased' once the
body is buried. Blount appoints himself 'executor to the unhappy
deceased author of this poem'.[41] We do not know whether he knew
Shakespeare and felt any similar personal obligation in taking on
the investment in the First Folio.

Blount's business after the publication of the Folio seems to have
dipped. Gary Taylor has identified that between 1603 and 1623
Blount published a regular average of 3.4 books per year, whereas
between the end of 1623 and the summer of 1628 he published
nothing at all.[42] It may be that this is related to the economic
strain of underwriting the Shakespeare project, or it may be that
other personal financial factors are more relevant: although our
priorities might assume that the Shakespeare Folio was the most
important thing in Blount's life, there were doubtless many other
aspects to his balance sheet. Whatever the facts of his finances, his
death in 1632 meant that he was not involved in the publication
of the second edition in that year.

Two other publishers, William Aspley and John Smithweeke,
are named at the end of the First Folio in the colophon. These
men were probably brought in relatively late in the publication
schedule because they owned the rights to previously published
plays, and preferred to be recompensed by a share in the Folio
profits rather than a single transfer fee (negotiations with other
stationers seem to have concluded with the sale of their interest
in individual plays). Aspley, whose shop at the sign of the Parrot

was adjacent to Blount's in Paul's Churchyard, owned two plays: *2 Henry IV* and *Much Ado About Nothing*. Each had been published only once: the history play must have been a marked commercial disappointment to Aspley as a sequel to the much reprinted *Part I*. Smithwecke joined the syndicate on the basis of his ownership of the rights to *Romeo and Juliet*, *Hamlet*, *Love's Labour's Lost* and the play that appears to be a version of *The Taming of the Shrew* but differs from it in lots of particulars, *The Taming of a Shrew*. Having retained his rights, he published some of these plays as individual quartos in the Caroline period. The colophon at the end of the book, 'Printed at the Charges of W. Jaggard, Ed. Blount, J. Smithweeke, and W. Aspley, 1623', indicates that all four men had a financial stake in its publication.

The Jaggards and Blount were well-established businessmen with money to invest in a speculative and more long-term commercial project. Working for them were a range of craftsmen and artisans who were variously expert in the printing processes described in Chapter 4: individuals who fetched paper and dampened it ready for printing, mixed ink, estimated the amount of space each page of manuscript would take in the Folio page format and divided the task between the compositors, prepared and operated the printing press, checked printed pages for corrections, dried, folded, assembled and stitched the printed pages together. Much of their work cannot be traced, but we can discern a category of distinct people involved in the process of typesetting: print-shop workers known as compositors.

Compositors worked from manuscript copy to set lines of individual type into composing sticks, before transferring them to the forme. It was a skilled job requiring manual dexterity as well as a level of understanding of the manuscript copy. Writing later in the century about the task of the compositor, Joseph Moxon admitted that

Yet, by mine honor, I will deale in this,
As secretly and iustlie, as your soule
Should with your bodie.

Leon. Being that I flow in greefe,
The smallest twine may lead me.

Frier. 'Tis well consented, presently away,
For to strange sores, strangely they straine the cure,
Come Lady, die to liue, this wedding day
Perhaps is but prolong'd, haue patience & endure. *Exit.*

Bene. Lady *Beatrice*, haue you wept all this while?

Beat. Yea, and I will weepe a while longer.

Bene. I will not desire that.

Beat. You haue no reason, I doe it freely.

Bene. Surelie I doe beleeue your fair cosin is wrong'd.

Beat. Ah, how much might the man deserue of mee
that would right her!

Bene. Is there any way to shew such friendship?

Beat. A verie euen way, but no such friend.

Bene. May a man doe it?

Beat. It is a mans office, but not yours.

Bene. I doe loue nothing in the world so well as you,
is not that strange?

Beat. As strange as the thing I know not, it were as
possible for me to say, I loued nothing so well as you, but
beleeue me not, and yet I lie not, I confesse nothing, nor
I deny nothing, I am sorry for my cousin.

Bene. By my sword *Beatrice* thou lou'st me.

Beat. Doe not sweare by it and eat it.

Bene. I will sweare by it that you loue mee, and I will
make him eat it that sayes I loue not you.

Beat. Will you not eat your word?

Bene. With no sawce that can be deuised to it, I protest I loue thee.

Beat. Why then God forgiue me.

Bene. What offence sweet Beatrice?

Beat. You haue stayed me in a happy howre, I was a-
bout to protest I loued you.

Bene. And doe it with all thy heart.

Beat. I loue you with so much of my heart, that none
is left to protest.

Bened. Come, bid me doe any thing for thee.

Beat. Kill *Claudio.*

Bene. Ha, not for the wide world.

Beat. You kill me to denie, farewell.

Bene. Tarrie sweet *Beatrice.*

Beat. I am gone, though I am heere, there is no loue
in you, nay I pray you let me goe.

Bene. Beatrice.

Beat. Infaith I will goe.

Bene. Wee'll be friends first.

Beat. You dare easier be friends with mee, than fight
with mine enemy.

Bene. Is *Claudio* thine enemie?

Beat. Is a not approued in the height a villaine, that
hath slandered, scorned, dishonoured my kinswoman? O
that I were a man! what, beare her in hand vntill they
come to take hands, and then with publike accusation
vncouered slander, vnmittigated rancour? O God that I
were a man! I would eat his heart in the market-place.

Bene. Heare me Beatrice.

Beat. Talke with a man out at a window, a proper
saying.

Bene. Nay but *Beatrice.*

Beat. Sweet *Hero*, she is wrong'd, shee is slandered,
she is vndone.

Bene. Beat?

Beat. Princes and Counties! surelie a Princely testi-
monie, a goodly Count, Comfect, a sweet Gallant surelie, O that I were a man for his sake! or that I had any
friend would be a man for my sake! But manhood is mel-
ted into curfies, valour into complement, and men are
onelie turned into tongue, and trim ones too: he is now
as valiant as *Hercules*, that only tells a lie, and sweares it:
I cannot be a man with wishing, therfore I will die a woman with grieuing.

Bene. Tarry good *Beatrice*, by this hand I loue thee.

Beat. Vse it for my loue some other way then swea-
ring by it.

Bened. Thinke you in your soule the Count *Claudio*
hath wrong'd *Hero?*

Beat. Yea, as sure as I haue a thought, or a soule.

Bene. Enough, I am engagde, I will challenge him, I
will kisse your hand, and so leaue you: by this hand *Claudio* shall render me a deere account: as you heare of me,
so thinke of me: goe comfort your coosin, I must say she
is dead, and so farewell.

*Enter the Constables, Borachio, and the Towne Clerke
in gownes.*

Keeper. Is our whole dissembly appeard?

Cowley. O a stoole and a cushion for the Sexton.

Sexton. Which be the malefactors?

Andrew. Marry that am I, and my partner.

Cowley. Nay that's certaine, wee haue the exhibition
to examine.

Sexton. But which are the offenders that are to be ex-
amined, let them come before master Constable.

Kemp. Yea marry, let them come before mee, what is
your name, friend?

Bor. Borachio.

Kem. Pray write downe *Borachio.* Yours sirra.

Con. I am a Gentleman sir, and my name is *Conrade.*

Kee. Write downe Master gentleman *Conrade:* maisters, doe you serue God: maisters, it is proued alreadie
that you are little better than false knaues, and it will goe
neere to be thought so shortly, how answer you for your
selues?

Con. Marry sir, we say we are none.

Kemp. A maruellous witty fellow I assure you, but I
will goe about with him: come you hither sirra, a word
in your eare sir, I say to you, it is thought you are false
knaues.

Bor. Sir, I say to you, we are none.

Kemp. Well, stand aside, fore God they are both in
a tale: haue you writ downe that they are none?

Sext. Master Constable, you goe not the way to examine, you must call forth the watch that are their ac-
cusers.

Kemp. Yea marry, that's the eftest way, let the watch
come forth: masters, I charge you in the Princes name,
accuse these men.

Watch 1. This man said sir, that *Don Iohn* the Princes
brother was a villaine.

Kemp. Write downe, Prince *Iohn* a villaine: why this
is flat periurie, to call a Princes brother villaine.

Bora. Master Constable.

Kemp. Pray thee fellow peace, I do not like thy looke
I promise thee.

Sexton. What heard you him say else?

Watch 2. Mary that he had receiued a thousand Du-
kates of *Don Iohn*, for accusing the Lady *Hero* wrong-
fully.

Kem.

PLATE 17   Speech prefixes showing the names of actors – Kemp and Cowley – rather than characters.

THE $\mathcal{B}$

History of the two Maids of More-clacke,

VVith the life and simple maner of I o h n
in the Hospitall.

Played by the Children of the Kings
Maiesties Reuels.

VVritten by Robert Armin, seruant to the Kings
most excellent Maiestie.

LONDON,
Printed by *N. O.* for *Thomas Archer*, and is to be sold at his
shop in Popes-head Pallace, 1 6 0 9.

PLATE 18 Robert Armin's particular talents as an actor were showcased
in the musical and melancholic aspects of Feste in *Twelfth Night* or the Fool
in *King Lear*. Portrait from *The History of the Two Maids of More-clacke*, 1609.
Bodleian Library, Mal. 201 ②.

PLATE 19 The first Hamlet – and Othello, Richard III, and many others:
Richard Burbage. *By permission of the Trustees of the Dulwich Picture Gallery.*

PLATE 20 William Herbert, Earl of Pembroke, one of the two dedicatees of the First Folio. © *National Portrait Gallery, London.*

PLATE 21 Philip Herbert, Earl of Montgomery, one of the two dedicatees of the First Folio. © *National Portrait Gallery, London.*

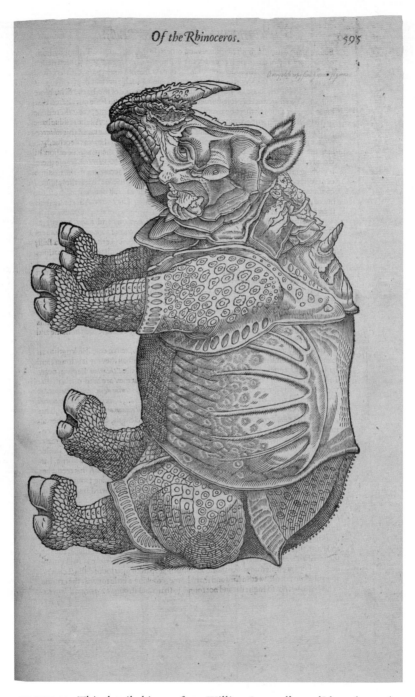

PLATE 22 This detailed image from William Jaggard's workshop shows that it could produce high quality printing. From Topsell, *The History of Four-footed Beasts*, first published in 1607. *Bodleian Library, Douce T subt.* 15 (1).

Euans. O'man, art thou Lunaties ? Haſt thou vnderſtandings for thy Caſes, & the numbers of the Genders? Thou art as fooliſh Chriſtian creatures, as I would deſires.

Mi.Page. Pre'thee hold thy peace.

Eu. Shew me now (*william*) ſome declenſions of your Pronounes.

Will. Forſooth, I haue forgot.

Eu. It is *Qui, que, quod* : if you forget your *Quies,* your *Ques,* and your *Quods,* you muſt be preeches: Goe your waies and play, go.

M.Page. He is a better ſcholler then I thought he was.

Eu. He is a good ſprag-memory: Farewel *Mis.Page.*

Miſ.Page. Adieu good Sir *Hugh* :

Get you home boy, Come we ſtay too long.   *Exeunt.*

Scena Secunda.

Enter Falſtoffe, Miſt.Ford, Miſt. Page, Seruants,Ford,
Page,Caius,Euans, Shallow.

Fal. Mi.Ford, Your ſorrow hath eaten vp my ſufferance; I ſee you are obſequious in your loue, and I profeſſe requitall to a haires bredth, not onely Miſt. *Ford,* in the ſimple office of loue, but in all the accuſtrement, complement, and ceremony of it : But are you ſure of your husband now?

Miſ.Ford. Hee's a birding (ſweet Sir *Iohn.*)

Miſ.Ford. What hoa, goſſip *Ford* : what hoa.

Miſ.Ford. Step into th'chamber, Sir *Iohn.*

Miſ.Page. How now (ſweete heart) whoſe at home beſides your ſelfe?

Miſ Ford Why none but mine owne people.

Miſ Page. Indeed?

Miſ Ford. No certainly : Speake louder.

Miſt.Pag. Truly, I am ſo glad you haue no body here.

Miſt.Ford. Why?

Miſ Page. Why woman, your husband is in his olde lines againe : he ſo takes on yonder with my husband, ſo railes againſt all married mankinde ; ſo curſes all *Eues* daughters, of what complexion ſoeuer ; and ſo buffettes himſelfe on the for-head : crying peere-out, peere-out, that any madneſſe I euer yet beheld, ſeem'd but tameneſſe, ciuility, and patience to this his diſtemper he is in now : I am glad the fat Knight is not heere.

Miſ.Ford: Why, do's he talke of him?

Miſ.Page. Of none but him, and ſweares he was caried out the laſt time hee ſearch'd for him, in a Basket: Proteſts to my husband he is now heere, & hath drawne him and the reſt of their company from their ſport, to make another experiment of his ſuſpition : But I am glad the Knight is not heere; now he ſhall ſee his owne foolerie.

Miſt.Ford. How neere is he Miſtris *Page?*

Miſ.Pag. Hard by, at ſtreet end ; he wil be here anon.

Miſt.Ford. I am vndone, the Knight is heere.

Miſt.Page. Why then you are vtterly ſham'd, & hee's but a dead man. What a woman are you ? Away with him, away with him : Better ſhame, then murther.

Miſt.Ford. Which way ſhould he go ? How ſhould I beſtow him ? Shall I put him into the basket againe?

Fal. No, Ile come no more i'th Basket:

May I not go out ere he come?

Miſt.Page. Alas : three of Mr.*Fords* brothers watch the doore with Piſtols, that none ſhall iſſue out : otherwiſe you might ſlip away ere hee came : But what make you heere?

Fal. What ſhall I do ? Ile creepe vp into the chimney.

Miſt.Ford. There they alwaes vſe to diſcharge their Birding-peeces : creepe into the Kill-hole.

Fal. Where is it?

Miſt.Ford. He will ſeeke there on my word : Neyther Preſſe, Coffer, Cheſt, Trunke, Well, Vault, but he hath an abſtract for the remembrance of ſuch places, and goes to them by his Note : There is no hiding you in the house.

Fal. Ile go out then.

Miſt.Ford. If you goe out in your owne ſemblance, you die Sir *Iohn,* vnleſſe you go out diſguis'd.

Miſt.Ford. How might we diſguile him?

Miſt.Page. Alas the day I know not, there is no womans gowne bigge enough for him : otherwiſe he might put on a hat, a muffler, and a kerchiefe, and ſo eſcape.

Fal. Good hearts, deuiſe something : any extremitie, rather then a miſchiefe.

Miſt.Ford. My Maids Aunt the fat woman of *Brainford,* has a gowne aboue.

Miſt.Page. On my word it will ſerue him : ſhee's as big as he is : and there's her thrum'd hat, and her muffler too : run vp Sir *Iohn.*

Miſt.Ford. Go, go, ſweet Sir *Iohn: Miſtris Page* and I will looke ſome linnen for your head.

Miſt.Page. Quicke, quicke, wee'le come dreſſe you ſtraight : put on the gowne the while.

Miſt.Ford. I would my husband would meete him in this ſhape : he cannot abide the old woman of Brainford ; he ſweares ſhe's a witch, forbad her my houſe, and hath threatned to beate her.

Miſt.Page. Heauen guide him to thy husbands cudgell : and the diuell guide his cudgell afterwards.

Miſt.Ford. But is my husband comming?

Miſt.Page. I in good ſadneſſe is he, and talkes of the basket too, howſoeuer he hath had intelligence.

Miſt.Ford. Wee'l try that: for Ile appoint my men to carry the basket againe, to meete him at the doore with it, as they did laſt time.

Miſt.Page. Nay, but hee'l be heere preſently:let's go dreſſe him like the witch of *Brainford.*

Miſt.Ford. Ile firſt direct direct my men, what they ſhall doe with the basket: Goe vp, Ile bring linnen for him ſtraight.

Miſt.Page. Hang him diſhoneſt Varlet,

We cannot miſuſe enough:

We'll leaue a proofe by that which we will doo,

Wiues may be merry, and yet honeſt too :

We do not acte that often, ieſt, and laugh,

'Tis old, but true, Still Swine eats all the draugh.

Miſt.Page. Go Sirs, take the basket againe on your ſhoulders : your Maſter is hard at doore : if hee bid you ſet it downe, obey him : quickly, diſpatch.

1 *Ser.* Come, come, take it vp.

2 *Ser.* Pray heauen it be not full of Knight againe.

1 *Ser.* I hope not, I had liefe as beare ſo much lead.

Ford. I, but if it proue true (Mr. *Page*) haue you any way then to vnſoole me againe. Set downe the basket villaine : ſome body call my wife : Youth in a basket : Oh you Panderly Raſcals, there's a knot : a gin, a packe, a conſpiracie againſt me? Now ſhall the diuel ſham'd, What wife I ſay: Come, come forth : behold what ho-

next

PLATE 23   A 'massed entry' in *The Merry Wives of Windsor* lists at the beginning of the scene all those characters who will enter during it: a hallmark of the scribe Ralph Crane.

Scena Tertia.

Enter Alonso, Sebastian, Anthonio, Gonzallo,
Adrian, Francisco, &c.

Gon. By'r lakin, I can goe no further, Sir,
My old bones akes : here's a maze trod indeede
Through fourth' rights, & Meanders : by your patience,
I needes must rest me.

Al. Old Lord, I cannot blame thee,
Who, am my selfe attach'd with wearinesse
To th'dulling of my spirits : Sit downe, and rest :
Euen here I will put off my hope, and keepe it
No longer for my Flatterer : he is dround
Whom thus we stray to finde, and the Sea mocks
Our frustrate search on land : well, let him goe.

Ant. I am right glad, that he's so out of hope :
Doe not for one repulse forgoe the purpose
That you resolu'd t'effect.

Seb. The next aduantage will we take throughly.

Ant. Let it be to night,
For now they are opprest'd with trauaile, they
Will not, nor cannot vse such vigilance
As when they are fresh.

Solemne and strange Musicke : and Prosper on the top (inui-
sible.) Enter seuerall strange shapes, bringing in a Banket ;
and dance about it with gentle actions of salutations, and
inuiting the King, &c. to eate, they depart.

Seb. I say to night : no more.

Al. What harmony is this ? my good friends, harke.

Gon. Maruellous sweet Musicke.

Alo. Giue vs kind keepers, heauẽs : what were these ?

Seb. A liuing Drolerie : now I will beleeue
That there are Vnicornes : that in Arabia
There is one Tree, the Phœnix throne, one Phœnix
At this houre reigning there.

Ant. Ile beleeue both :
And what do's else want credit, come to me
And Ile besworne 'tis true : Trauellers nere did lye,
Though fooles at home condemne 'em.

Gon. If in Naples
I should report this now, would they beleeue me ?
If I should say I saw such Islands ;
(For certes, these are people of the Island)
Who though they are of monstrous shape, yet note
Their manners are more gentle, kinde, then of
Our humaine generation you shall finde
Many, nay almost any.

Pro. Honest Lord,
Thou hast said well : for some of you there present ;
Are worse then diuels.

Al. I cannot too much muse
Such shapes, such gesture, and such sound expressing
(Although they want the vse of tongue) a kinde
Of excellent dumbe discourse.

Pro. Praise in departing.

Fr. They vanish'd strangely.

Seb. No matter, since (macks.
They haue left their Viands behinde ; for wee haue sto-
Wilt please you taste of what is here?

Alo. Not I.

Gon. Faith Sir, you neede not feare : when wee were (Boyes
Who would beleeue that there were Mountayneeres,
Dew-lapt, like Buls, whose throats had hanging at'em
Wallets of flesh ? or that there were such men

Whose heads stood in their brests ? which now we finde
Each putter out of fiue for one, will bring vs
Good warrant of.

Al. I will stand to, and feede,
Although my last, no matter, since I feele
The best is past : brother : my Lord, the Duke,
Stand too, and doe as we.

Thunder and Lightning. Enter Ariell (like a Harpey) claps
his wings vpon the Table, and with a quient deuice the
Banquet vanishes.

Ar. You are three men of sinne, whom destiny
That hath to instrument this lower world,
And what is in't : the neuer surfeited Sea,
Hath caus'd to belch vp you ; and on this Island,
Where man doth not inhabit, you 'mongst men,
Being most vnfit to liue : I haue made you mad ;
And euen with such like valour, men hang and drowne
Their proper selues : you fooles, I and my fellowe
Are ministers of Fate, the Elements
Of whom your swords are temper'd, may as well
Wound the loud windes, or with bemockt-at-Stabs
Kill the still closing waters, as diminish
One dowle that's in my plumbe : My fellow ministers
Are like-invulnerable : if you could hurt,
Your swords are now too massie for your strengths,
And will not be vplifted : But remember
(For that's my businesse to you) that you three
From Millaine did supplant good Prospero,
Expos'd vnto the Sea (which hath requit it)
Him, and his innocent childe : for which foule deed,
The Powres, delaying (not forgetting) haue
Incens'd the Seas, and Shores ; yea, all the Creatures
Against your peace : Thee of thy Sonne, Alonso
They haue bereft ; and doe pronounce by me
Lingring perdition (worse then any death
Can be at once) shall step, by step attend
You, and your wayes, whose wraths to guard you from,
Which here, in this most desolate Isle, else fils
Vpon your heads, is nothing but hearts-sorrow,
And a cleere life ensuing.

He vanishes in Thunder : then (to soft Musicke,) Enter the
shapes againe, and daunce (with mockes and mowes) and
carrying out the Table.

Pro. Brauely the figure of this Harpie, hast thou
Perform'd (my Ariell) a grace it had deuouring :
Of my Instruction, hast thou nothing bated
In what thou had'st to say ; so with good life,
And obseruation strange, my meaner ministers
Their seuerall kindes haue done : my high charmes work,
And these (mine enemies) are all knit vp
In their distractions : they now are in my powre ;
And in these fits, I leaue them, while I visit
Yong Ferdinand (whom they suppose is droun'd)
And his, and mine lou'd darling.

Gon. I'th name of something holy, Sir, why stand you
In this strange stare ?

Al. O, it is monstrous : monstrous :
Me thought the billowes spoke, and told me of it,
The windes did sing it to me : and the Thunder
(That deepe and dreadfull Organ-Pipe) pronounc'd
The name of Prosper : it did base my Trespasse,
Therefore my Sonne i'th Ooze is bedded ; and
I'le seeke him deeper then ere plummet sounded,
And with him there lye mudded. *Exit.*

Seb. But one feend at a time,
Ile fight their Legions ore.

B   *Ant.*

PLATE 24 Ralph Crane's hand in the text of *The Tempest*, shown in his typical brackets and hyphens.

Roger Jackson — Entred for his Copie under the hands
of mr Pledowarden A Boole called
A Daylie exercise of Pietie devided into
4 parts viz Confession of Sinnes Thanks-
giuing of prayers ... written in
latine by John Gerard and translated into
English prouided he brings further authority
before it be printed

12° Feb 1629 — mr mr Dr ... should it to the Booke
of mr Jacksons

Mr Blount
Isaak Jaggard — Entred for their Copie under the hands
of mr Dr Worrall and mr Cole
warden mr William Shakspeers Comedyes
Histories & Tragedyes soe manie of the
said Copies as are not formerly Entred to
other men viz

        G.s. The Tempest
            The two gentlemen of Verona
            Measure for Measure
            The Comedy of Errors
Comedyes: As you like it
            All's well that ends well
            Twelfe night
            The winters tale
Histories: The thirde parte of Henry ye sixt
            Henry the eight
            Coriolanus
            Timon of Athens
Tragedies: Julius Cæsar
            Macbeth
            Anthonie & Cleopatra
            Cymbeline

        11° Nouembris

Nath. Newberie — Entred for his Copie under the hands of
mr Dr Featlie and mr Cole warden A
Boole called A sweet posie for gods saints
to smell on conteyninge manie wittie and
choise flowers

Nath. Butter — Entred for his Copie under the hands of
mr Cottington and mr Cole warden A
Boole called The Wonderfull resignation
of Mustapha and the advauncinge of Amurath
a yonger Brother of the latter ... Ottman

        14° Nouember

Mr Jackson — Entred for his Copie under the hands of
mr Dr ... and mr ... warden
A Boole called An exposition upon the Ten
Comandem[ents] by mr Peter Barker minister
at Storegrave in Yorkshire

PLATE 25 The entry in the Stationers' Register marking Edward Blount
and Isaac Jaggard's rights to previously unpublished Shakespeare plays.
*Reproduced with the permission of the Worshipful Company of Stationers and
Newspaper Makers.*

Then this for whom we rendred vp this woe. *Exeunt.*
Enter Leonato, Bene. Marg. Vrsula, old man, Frier, Hero.
Frier. Did I not tell you she was innocent?
Leo. So are the *Prince* and *Claudio* who accus'd her,
Vpon the errour that you heard debated:
But *Margaret* was in some fault for this,
Although against her will as it appeares,
In the true course of all the question.
Old. Well, I am glad that all things sort so well.
Bene. And so am I, being else by faith enforc'd
To call young *Claudio* to a reckoning for it.
Leo. Well daughter, and you gentlewomen all,
Withdraw into a chamber by your selues,
And when I send for you, come hither mask'd:
The *Prince* and *Claudio* promis'd by this howre
To visit me, you know your office Brother,
You must be father to your brothers daughter,
And giue her to young *Claudio*.   *Exeunt Ladies.*
Old. Which I will doe with confirm'd countenance.
Bene. Frier, I must intreat your paines, I thinke.
Frier. To doe what Signior?
Bene. To binde me, or vndoe me, one of them:
Signior *Leonato*, truth it is good Signior,
Your neece regards me with an eye of fauour.
Leo. That eye my daughter lent her, 'tis most true.
Bene. And I doe with an eye of loue require her.
Leo. The sight whereof I thinke you had from me,
From *Claudio*, and the *Prince*, but what's your will?
Bened. Your answer sir is Enigmaticall,
But for my will, my will is, your good will
May stand with ours, this day to be conioyn'd,
In the state of honourable marriage,
In which (good Frier) I shall desire your helpe.
Leon. My heart is with your liking.
Frier. And my helpe.
     Enter Prince and Claudio, with attendants.
Prin. Good morrow to this faire assembly.
Leo. Good morrow *Prince*, good morrow *Claudio*:
We heere attend you, are you yet determin'd,
To day to marry with my brothers daughter?
Claud. Ile hold my minde were she an Ethiope.
Leo. Call her forth brother, heres the Frier ready.
Prin. Good morrow *Benedike*, why what's the matter?
That you haue such a Februarie face,
So full of frost, of storme, and clowdinesse.
Claud. I thinke he thinkes vpon the sauage bull:
Tush, feare not man, wee'll tip thy hornes with gold,
And all *Europa* shall reioyce at thee,
As once *Europa* did at lusty *Ioue*,
When he would play the noble beast in loue.
Ben. Bull *Ioue* sir, had an amiable low,
And some such strange bull leapt your fathers Cow,
A got a Calfe in that same noble feat,
Much like to you, for you haue iust his bleat.
     Enter brother, Hero, Beatrice, Margaret, Vrsula.
Cla. For this I owe you: here comes other recknings.
Which is the Lady I must seize vpon?
Leo. This same is she, and I doe giue you her.
Cla. Why then she's mine, sweet let me see your face.
Leon. No that you shal not, till you take her hand,
Before this Frier, and sweare to marry her.
Clau. Giue me your hand before this holy Frier,
I am your husband if you like of me.
Hero. And when I liu'd I was your other wife,
And when you lou'd, you were my other husband.
Clau. Another *Hero*?

Hero. Nothing certainer.
One *Hero* died, but I doe liue,
And surely as I liue, I am a maid.
Prin. The former *Hero*, *Hero* that is dead.
Leon. Shee died my Lord, but whiles her slander liu'd.
Frier. All this amazement can I qualifie,
When after that the holy rites are ended,
Ile tell you largely of faire *Heroes* death:
Meane time let wonder seeme familiar,
And to the chappell let vs presently.
Ben. Soft and faire Frier, which is *Beatrice*?
Beat. I answer to that name, what is your will?
Bene. Doe not you loue me?
Beat. Why no, no more then reason.
Bene. Why then your Vncle, and the Prince, & *Claudio*, haue beene deceiued, they swore you did.
Beat. Doe not you loue mee?
Bene. Troth no, no more then reason.
Beat. Why then my Cosin *Margaret* and *Vrsula*
Are much deceiu'd, for they did sweare you did.
Bene. They swore you were almost sicke for me.
Beat. They swore you were wel-nye dead for me.
Bene. 'Tis no matter, then you doe not loue me?
Beat. No truly, but in friendly recompence.
Leon. Come Cosin, I am sure you loue the gentlemã.
Clau. And Ile be sworne vpon't, that he loues her,
For heres a paper written in his hand,
A halting sonnet of his owne pure braine,
Fashioned to *Beatrice*.
Hero. And heeres another,
Writ in my cosins hand, stolne from her pocket,
Containing her affection vnto *Benedicke*.
Bene. A miracle, here's our owne hands against our
hearts: come I will haue thee, but by this light I take
thee for pittie.
Beat. I would not denie you, but by this good day, I
yeeld vpon great perswasion, & partly to saue your life,
for I was told, you were in a consumption.
Leon. Peace I will stop your mouth.
Prin. How dost thou *Benedicke* the married man?
Bene. Ile tell thee what Prince: a Colledge of witte-
crackers cannot flout mee out of my humour, dost thou
think I care for a Satyre or an Epigram? no, if a man will
be beaten with braines, a shall weare nothing handsome
about him: in briefe, since I do purpose to marry, I will
thinke nothing to any purpose that the world can say a-
gainst it, and therefore neuer flout at me, for I haue said
against it: for man is a giddy thing, and this is my conclusion: for thy part *Claudio*, I did thinke to haue beaten
thee, but in that thou art like to be my kinsman, liue vn-
bruis'd, and loue my cousin.
Cla. I had well hop'd y̆ wouldst haue denied *Beatrice*, y̆
I might haue cudgel'd thee out of thy single life, to make
thee a double dealer, which out of questiõ thou wilt be,
if my Cousin do not looke exceeding narrowly to thee.
Bene. Come, come, we are friends, let's haue a dance
ere we are married, that we may lighten our own hearts,
and our wiues heeles.
Leon. Wee'll haue dancing afterward.
Bene. First, of my vvord, therfore play musick. *Prince,*
thou art sad, get thee a vvife, get thee a vvife, there is no
staff more reuerend then one tipt with horn. *Enter, Mes.*
Messen. My Lord, your brother *Iohn* is tane in flight,
And brought with armed men backe to *Messina.*
Bene. Thinke not on him till to morrow, ile deuise
thee braue punishments for him: strike vp Pipers. *Dance.*

L   *F I N I S.*

PLATE 26 The cramped ending to *Much Ado About Nothing*, due to a miscalculation in the casting-off process.

To do that thing that eads all other deeds,
Which shackles accedents, and bolts vp change;
Which sleepes, and neuer pallates more the dung,
The beggers Nurse, and *Cæsars*.

Enter Proculeius.

Pro. *Cæsar* sends greeting to the Queene of Egypt,
And bids thee study on what faire demands
Thou mean'st to haue him grant thee.
Cleo. What's thy name?
Pro. My name is *Proculeius.*
Cleo. *Anthony*
Did tell me of you, bad me trust you, but
I do not greatly care to be deceiu'd
That haue no vse for trusting. If your Master
Would haue a Queene his begger, you must tell him,
That Maiesty to keepe *decorum*, must
No lesse begge then a Kingdome: If he please
To giue me conquer'd Egypt for my Sunne,
He giues me so much of mine owne, as I
Will kneele to him with thankes.
Pro. Be of good cheere:
Y'are falne into a Princely hand, feare nothing,
Make your full reference freely to my Lord,
Who is so full of Grace, that it flowes ouer
On all that neede. Let me report to him
Your sweet dependacie, and you shall finde
A Conqueror that will pray in ayde for kindnesse,
Where he for grace is kneel'd too.
Cleo. Pray you tell him,
I am his Fortunes Vassall, and I send him
The Greatnesse he has got. I hourely learne
A Doctrine of Obedience, and would gladly
Looke him i'th'Face.
Pro. This Ile report (deere Lady)
Haue comfort, for I know your plight is pittied
Of him that caus'd it.
Pro. You see how easily she may be surpriz'd:
Guard her till *Cæsar* come.
Iras. Royall Queene.
Char. Oh *Cleopatra*, thou art taken Queene.
Cleo. Quicke, quicke, good hands.
Pro. Hold worthy Lady, hold:
Doe not your selfe such wrong, who are in this
Releeu'd, but not betraid.
Cleo. What of death too that rids our dogs of languish
Pro. *Cleopatra*, do not abuse my Masters bounty, by
Th'vndoing of your selfe: Let the World see
His Noblenesse well acted, which your death
Will neuer let come forth.
Cleo. Where art thou Death?
Come hither come; Come, come, and take a Queene
Worth many Babes and Beggers.
Pro. Oh temperance Lady.
Cleo. Sir, I will eate no meate, Ile not drinke sir,
If idle talke will once be necessary,
Ile not sleepe neither. This mortall house Ile ruine,
Do *Cæsar* what he can. Know sir, that I
Will not waite pinnion'd at your Masters Court,
Nor once be chastic'd with the sober eye
Of dull *Octauia*. Shall they hoyst me vp,
And shew me to the showting Varlotarie
Of censuring Rome? Rather a ditch in Egypt.
Be gentle graue vnto me, rather on Nylus mudde
Lay me starke-nak'd, and let the water-Flies
Blow me into abhorring; rather make
My Countries high pyramides my Gibbet,

And hang me vp in Chaines.
Pro. You do extend
These thoughts of horror further then you shall
Finde cause in *Cæsar.*

Enter Dolabella.

Dol. *Proculeius*,
What thou hast done, thy Master *Cæsar* knowes,
And he hath sent for thee: for the Queene,
Ile take her to my Guard.
Pro. So *Dolabella*,
It shall content me best: Be gentle to her,
To *Cæsar* I will speake, what you shall please,
If you'l imploy me to him. *Exit Proculeius*
Cleo. Say, I would dye.
Dol. Most Noble Empresse, you haue heard of me.
Cleo. I cannot tell.
Dol. Assuredly you know me.
Cleo. No matter sir, what I haue heard or knowne:
You laugh when Boyes or Women tell their Dreames,
Is't not your tricke?
Dol. I vnderstand not, Madam.
Cleo. I dreampt there was an Emperor *Anthony.*
Oh such another sleepe, that I might see
But such another man.
Dol. If it might please ye.
Cleo. His face was as the Heau'ns, and therein stucke
A Sunne and Moone, which kept their course, & lighted
The little o'th'earth.
Dol. Most Soueraigne Creature.
Cleo. His legges bestrid the Ocean, his rear'd arme
Crested the world: His voyce was propertied
As all the tuned Spheres, and that to Friends:
But when he meant to quaile, and shake the Orbe,
He was as ratling Thunder. For his Bounty,
There was no winter in't. An *Anthony* it was,
That grew the more by reaping: His delights
Were Dolphin-like, they shew'd his backe aboue
The Element they liu'd in: In his Liuery
Walk'd Crownes and Crownets: Realms & Islands were
As plates dropt from his pocket.
Dol. *Cleopatra.*
Cleo. Thinke you there was, or might be such a man
As this I dreampt of?
Dol. Gentle Madam, no.
Cleo. You Lye vp to the hearing of the Gods:
But if there be, nor euer were one such
It's past the size of dreaming: Nature wants stuffe
To vie strange formes with fancie, yet t'imagine
An *Anthony* were Natures peece, 'gainst Fancie,
Condemning shadowes quite.
Dol. Heare me, good Madam:
Your losse is as your selfe, great; and you beare it
As answering to the waight, would I might neuer
Ore-take pursu'de successe: But I do feele
By the rebound of yours, a greefe that suites
My very heart at roote.
Cleo. I thanke you sir:
Know you what *Cæsar* meanes to do with me?
Dol. I am loath to tell you what, I would you knew.
Cleo. Nay pray you sir,
Dol. Though he be Honourable.
Cleo. Hee'l leade me then in Triumph.
Dol. Madam he will, I know't. *Flourish.*

*Enter Proculeius, Cæsar, Gallus, Mecenas,
and others of his Traine.*

All. Make way there *Cæsar.*

Cæs.

PLATE 27 What happens to Cleopatra? Perhaps a stage direction is missing from this key scene in *Antony and Cleopatra* because there wasn't enough room.

Deſeru'd much leſſe aduancement.

Lear. You? Did you?

Reg. I pray you Father being weake,ſeeme ſo,
If till the expiration of your Moneth
You will returne and ſoiourne with my Siſter,
Diſmiſſing halfe your traine, come then to me,
I am now from home,and out of that prouiſion
Which ſhall be needfull for your entertainement.

Lear. Returne to her? and fifty men diſmiſs'd?
No, rather I abiure all rooſes,and chuſe
To wage againſt the enmity oth'ayre,
To be a Comrade with the Wolfe,and Owle,
Neceſſities ſharpe pinch. Returne with her?
Why the hot-blooded *France*,that dowerleſſe tooke
Our yongeſt borne,I could as well be brought
To knee his Throne,and Squire-like penſion beg,
To keepe baſe life a foote; returne with her?
Perſwade me rather to be ſlaue and ſumpter
To this deteſted groome.

Gon. At your choice Sir.

Lear. I prythee Daughter do not make me mad,
I will not trouble thee my Child;farewell:
Wee'l no more meete,no more ſee one another.
But yet thou art my fleſh,my blood,my Daughter,
Or rather a diſeaſe that's in my fleſh,
Which I muſt needs call mine. Thou art a Byle,
A plague ſore,or emboſſed Carbuncle
In my corrupted blood. But Ile not chide thee,
Let ſhame come when it will,I do not call it,
I do not bid the Thunder-bearer ſhoote,
Nor tell tales of thee to high-iudging *Ioue*,
Mend when thou can'ſt,be better at thy leiſure,
I can be patient,I can ſtay with *Regan*,
I and my hundred Knights.

Reg. Not altogether ſo,
I look'd not for you yet,nor am prouided
For your fit welcome,giue eare Sir to my Siſter,
For thoſe that mingle reaſon with your paſſion,
Muſt be content to thinke you old,and ſo,
But ſhe knowes what ſhe doe's.

Lear. Is this well ſpoken?

Reg. I dare auouch it Sir,what fifty Followers?
Is it not well? What ſhould you need of more?
Yes,or ſo many? Sith that both charge and danger,
Speake 'gainſt ſo great a number? How in one houſe
Should many people,vnder two commands
Hold amity?'Tis hard,almoſt impoſſible.

Gon. Why might not you my Lord,receiue attendance
From thoſe that ſhe cals Seruants,or from mine?

Reg. Why not my Lord?
If then they chanc'd to ſlacke ye,
We could comptroll them; if you will come to me,
(For now I ſpie a danger)I entreate you
To bring but fiue and twentie,to no more
Will I giue place or notice.

Lear. I gaue you all.

Reg. And in good time you gaue it.

Lear. Made you my Guardians,my Depoſitaries,
But kept a reſeruation to be followed
With ſuch a number? What,muſt I come to you
With fiue and twenty? *Regan*,ſaid you ſo?

Reg. And ſpeak't againe my Lord, no more with me.

Lea. Thoſe wicked Creatures yet do look wel ſauor'd
When others are more wicked,not being the worſt
Stands in ſome ranke of praiſe,Ile go with thee,
Thy fifty yet doth double fiue and twenty,

And thou art twice her Loue.

Gon. Heare me my Lord;
What need you fiue and twenty? Ten? Or fiue?
To follow in a houſe,where twice ſo many
Haue a command to tend you?

Reg. What need one?

Lear. O reaſon not the need : our baſeſt Beggers
Are in the pooreſt thing ſuperfluous,
Allow not Nature,more then Nature needs:
Mans life is cheape as Beaſtes. Thou art a Lady;
If onely to go warme were gorgeous,
Why Nature needs not what thou gorgeous wear'ſt,
Which ſcarcely keepes thee warme,but for true need:
You Heauens,giue me that patience,patience I need,
You ſee me heere (you Gods)a poore old man,
As full of griefe as age,wretched in both,
If it be you that ſtirres theſe Daughters hearts
Againſt their Father,foole me not ſo much,
To beare it tamely:touch me with Noble anger,
And let not womens weapons,water drops,
Staine my mans cheekes. No you vnnaturall Hags,
I will haue ſuch reuenges on you both,
That all the world ſhall————I will do ſuch things,
What they are yet,I know not,but they ſhalbe
The terrors of the earth? you thinke Ile weepe,
No,Ile not weepe,I haue full cauſe of weeping,

Storme and Tempeſt.

But this heart ſhal break into a hundred thouſand flawes
Or ere Ile weepe; O Foole,I ſhall go mad.   *Exeunt.*

Corn. Let vs withdraw, 'twill be a Storme.

Reg. This houſe is little,the old man an'ds people,
Cannot be well beſtow'd.

Gon. 'Tis his owne blame hath put himſelfe from reſt,
And muſt needs taſte his folly.

Reg. For his particular,Ile receiue him gladly,
But not one follower.

Gon. So am I purpos'd,
Where is my Lord of *Gloſter*?

Enter Gloſter.

Corn. Followed the old man forth,he is return'd.

Glo. The King is in high rage.

Corn. Whether is he going?

Glo. He cals to Horſe,but will I know not whether.

Corn. 'Tis beſt to giue him way,he leads himſelfe.

Gon. My Lord,entreate him by no meanes to ſtay.

Glo. Alacke the night comes on,and the high windes
Do ſorely ruffle,for many Miles about
There's ſcarce a Buſh.

Reg. O Sir,to wilfull men,
The iniuries that they themſelues procure,
Muſt be their Schoole-Maſters: ſhut vp your doores,
He is attended with a deſperate traine,
And what they may incenſe him too,being apt,
To haue his eare abus'd,wiſedome bids feare.

Cor. Shut vp your doores my Lord, 'tis a wil'd night,
My *Regan* counſels well: come out oth'ſtorme.   *Exeunt.*

Actus Tertius. Scena Prima.

Storme ſtill. Enter Kent,and a Gentleman,ſeuerally.

Kent. Who's there beſides foule weather?

Gen. One minded like the weather,moſt vnquietly.

Kent.

PLATE 28 A marked-up sheet from *King Lear* showing how someone
in the printing house has identified errors to be corrected.
By permission of The Provost, Fellows and Scholars of The Queen's College, Oxford.

Deferu'd much leffe aduancement.

Lear. You? Did you?

Reg. I pray you Father being weake,feeme fo,
If till the expiration of your Moneth
You will returne and foiourne with my Sifter,
Difmiffing halfe your traine,come then to me,
I am now from home,and out of that prouifion
Which fhall be needfull for your entertainment.

Lear. Returne to her? and fifty men difmifs'd?
No, rather I abiure all roofes,and chufe
To wage againft the enmity oth'ayre,
To be a Comrade with the Wolfe,and Owle,
Neceffities fharpe pinch. Returne with her?
Why the hot-bloodied *France,*that dowerleffe tooke
Our yongeft borne,I could as well be brought
To knee his Throne,and Squire-like penfion beg,
To keepe bafe life a foote; returne with her?
Perfwade me rather to be flaue and fump ter
To this detefted groome.

Gon. At your choice Sir.

Lear. I prythee Daughter do not make me mad,
I will not trouble thee my Child;farewell:
Wee'l no more meete,no more fee one another,
But yet thou art my flefh,my blood,my Daughter,
Or rather a difeafe that's in my flefh,
Which I muft needs call mine. Thou art a Byle,
A plague fore,or imboffed Carbuncle
In my corrupted blood. But Ile not chide thee,
Let fhame come when it will,I do not call it,
I do not bid the Thunder-bearer fhoote,
Nor tell tales of thee to high-iudging *Ioue,*
Mend when thou can'ft,be better at thy leifure,
I can be patient,I can ftay with *Regan,*
I and my hundred Knights.

Reg. Not altogether fo,
I look'd not for you yet,nor am prouided
For your fit welcome,giue eare Sir to my Sifter,
For thofe that mingle reafon with your paffion,
Muft be content to thinke you old,and fo,
But fhe knowes what fhe doe's.

Lear. Is this well fpoken?

Reg. I dare auouch it Sir,what fifty Followers?
Is it not well? What fhould you need of more?
Yea,or fo many? Sith that both charge and danger,
Speake 'gainft fo great a number? How in one houfe
Should many people,vnder two commands
Hold amity? 'Tis hard,almoft impoffible.

Gon. Why might not you my Lord,receiue attendance
From thofe that fhe cals Seruants,or from mine?

Reg. Why not my Lord?
If then they chanc'd to flacke ye,
We could comptroll them; if you will come to me,
(For now I fpie a danger)I entreate you
To bring but fiue and twentie,to no more
Will I giue place or notice.

Lear. I gaue you all.

Reg. And in good time you gaue it.

Lear. Made you my Guardians,my Depofitaries,
But kept a referuation to be followed
With fuch a number? What,muft I come to you
With fiue and twenty? *Regan,*faid you fo?

Reg. And fpeak't againe my Lord, no more with me.

Ina. Thofe wicked Creatures yet do look wel fauor'd
When others are more wicked,not being the worft
Stands in fome ranke of praife,Ile go with thee,
Thy fifty yet doth double fiue and twenty,

And thou art twice her Loue.

Gon. Heare me my Lord;
What need you fiue and twenty? Ten? Or fiue?
To follow in a houfe,where twice fo many
Haue a command to tend you?

Reg. What need one?

Lear. O reafon not the need : our bafeft Beggers
Are in the pooreft thing fuperfluous,
Allow not Nature,more then Nature needs :
Mans life is cheape as Beaftes. Thou art a Lady;
If onely to go warme were gorgeous,
Why Nature needs not what thou gorgeous wear'ft,
Which fcarcely keepes thee warme,but for true need:
You Heauens,giue me that patience,patience I need,
You fee me heere (you Gods)a poore old man,
As full of griefe as age, wretched in both,
If it be you that ftirres thefe Daughters hearts
Againft their Father,foole me not fo much,
To beare it tamely:touch me with Noble anger,
And let not womens weapons,water drops,
Staine my mans cheekes. No you vnnaturall Hags,
I will haue fuch reuenges on you both,
That all the world fhall——I will do fuch things,
What they are yet,I know not,but they fhalbe
The terrors of the earth? you thinke Ile weepe,
No,Ile not weepe,I haue full caufe of weeping,

Storme and Tempeft.

But this heart fhal break into a hundred thoufand flawes
Or ere Ile weepe; O Foole,I fhall go mad, *Exeunt.*

Corn. Let vs withdraw, 'twill be a Storme.

Reg. This houfe is little,the old man an'ds people,
Cannot be well beftow'd.

Gon. 'Tis his owne blame hath put himfelfe from reft,
And muft needs tafte his folly.

Reg. For his particular,Ile receiue him gladly,
But not one follower.

Gon. So am I purpos'd,
Where is my Lord of *Glofter?*

Enter Glofter.

Corn. Followed the old man forth,he is return'd.

Glo. The King is in high rage.

Corn. Whether is he going?

Glo. He cals to Horfe,but will I know not whether.

Corn. 'Tis beft to giue him way,he leads himfelfe.

Gon. My Lord,entreate him by no meanes to ftay.

Glo. Alacke the night comes on,and the high windes
Do forely ruffle,for many Miles about
There's fcarce a Bufh.

Reg. O Sir,to wilfull men,
The iniuries that they themfelues procure,
Muft be their Schoole-Mafters: fhut vp your doores,
He is attended with a defperate traine,
And what they may incenfe him too,being apt,
To haue his eare abus'd,wifedome bids feare.

Cor. Shut vp your doores my Lord, 'tis a wil'd night,
My *Regan* counfels well: come out oth'ftorme. *Exeunt.*

Actus Tertius, Scena Prima.

Storme ftill. Enter Kent,and a Gentleman, feuerally.

Kent. Who's there befides foule weather?

Gen. One minded like the weather,moft vnquietly.

PLATE 29 The corrected – to an extent – *King Lear* page.

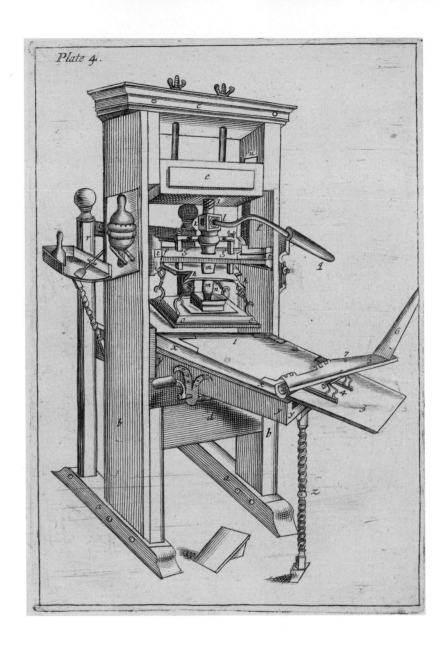

PLATE 30 Joseph Moxon's diagram of a printing press. Plate 4 from the
second volume of *Mechanick Exercises* by Joseph Moxon, 1683. *Bodleian
Library, 4° L 86 Th.*

The Workes of William Shakespeare,

containing all his Comedies, Histories, and
Tragedies: Truely set forth, according to their first
ORIGINALL.

The Names of the Principall Actors
in all these Playes.

William Shakespeare.

Richard Burbadge.

John Hemmings.

Augustine Phillips.

William Kempt.

Thomas Poope.

George Bryan.

Henry Condell.

William Slye.

Richard Cowly.

John Lowine.

Samuell Crosse.

Alexander Cooke.

Samuel Gilburne.

Robert Armin.

William Ostler.

Nathan Field.

John Underwood.

Nicholas Tooley.

William Ecclestone.

Joseph Taylor.

Robert Benfield.

Robert Goughe.

Richard Robinson.

Iohn Shancke.

Iohn Rice.

PLATE 31   An early hand, perhaps that of Lucius Cary, has annotated the
names of the acting company. *By permission of University of Glasgow Library,
Special Collections.*

Woman, commend me to her, I will not faile her.

Qui. Why, you say well : But I haue another messenger to your worship : Mistresse *Page* hath her heartie commendations to you to : and let mee tell you in your eare, shee's as fartuous a ciuill modest wife, and one (I tell you) that will not misse you morning nor euening prayer, as any is in *Windsor*, who ere bee the other : and shee bade me tell your worship, that her husband is seldome from home, but she hopes there will come a time. I neuer knew a woman so doate vpon a man ; surely I thinke you haue charmes, la : yes in truth.

Fal. Not I, I assure thee ; setting the attraction of my good parts aside, I haue no other charmes.

Qui. Blessing on your heart for't.

Fal. But I pray thee tell me this : has *Fords* wife, and *Pages* wife acquainted each other, how they loue me?

Qui. That were a iest indeed ; they haue not so little grace I hope, that were a tricke indeed : But Mistris *Page* would desire you to send her your little *Page* of al loues : her husband has a maruellous infectió to the little *Page* : and truely Master *Page* is an honest man : neuer a wife in *Windsor* leades a better life then she do's : doe what shee will, say what she will, take all, pay all, goe to bed when she list, rise when she list, all is as she will : and truly she deserues it ; for if there be a kinde woman in *Windsor*, she is one : you must send her your *Page*, no remedie.

Fal. Why, I will.

Qui. Nay, but doe so then, and looke you, hee may come and goe betweene you both : and in any case haue a nay-word, that you may know one anothers minde, and the Boy neuer neede to vnderstand any thing ; for 'tis not good that children should know any wickednes : olde folkes you know, haue discretion, as they say, and know the world.

Fal. Fare thee-well, commend mee to them both : there's my purse, I am yet thy debter : Boy, goe along with this woman, this newes distracts me.

Pist. This Puncke is one of *Cupids* Carriers, Clap on more sailes, pursue : vp with your fights : Giue fire : she is my prize, or Ocean whelme them all.

Fal. Saist thou so (old *Iacke*) go thy waies : Ile make more of thy olde body then I haue done : will they yet looke after thee? wilt thou after the expence of so much money, be now a gainer? good Body, I thanke thee : let them say 'tis grossely done, so it bee fairely done, no matter.

Bar. Sir *Iohn*, there's one Master *Broome* below would faine speake with you, and be acquainted with you ; and hath sent your worship a mornings draught of Sacke.

Fal. *Broome* is his name?

Bar. I Sir.

Fal. Call him in : such *Broomes* are welcome to mee, that ore'flowes such liquor : ah ha, Mistresse *Ford* and Mistresse *Page*, haue I encompass'd you? goe to, *via*.

Ford. 'Blesse you sir.

Fal. And you sir : would you speake with me?

Ford. I make bold, to presse, with so little preparation vpon you.

Fal. You'r welcome, what's your will? giue vs leaue Drawer.

Ford. Sir, I am a Gentleman that haue spent much, my name is *Broome*.

Fal. Good Master *Broome*, I desire more acquaintance of you.

Ford. Good Sir *Iohn*, I sue for yours : not to charge you, for I must let you vnderstand, I thinke my selfe in better plight for a Lender, then you are : the which hath something emboldned me to this vnseason'd intrusion : for they say, if money goe before, all waies doe lye open.

Fal. Money is a good Souldier (Sir) and will on.

Ford. Troth, and I haue a bag of money heere troubles me : if you will helpe to beare it (Sir *Iohn*) take all, or halfe, for easing me of the carriage.

Fal. Sir, I know not how I may deserue to bee your Porter.

Ford. I will tell you sir, if you will giue mee the hearing.

Fal. Speake (good Master *Broome*) I shall be glad to be your Seruant.

Ford. Sir, I heare you are a Scholler : (I will be briefe with you) and you haue been a man long knowne to me, though I had neuer so good means as desire, to make my selfe acquainted with you. I shall discouer a thing to you, wherein I must very much lay open mine owne imperfection : but (good Sir *Iohn*) as you haue one eye vpon my follies, as you heare them vnfolded, turne another into the Register of your owne, that I may passe with a reproofe the easier, sith you your selfe know how easie it is to be such an offender.

Fal. Very well Sir, proceed.

Ford. There is a Gentlewoman in this Towne, her husbands name is *Ford.*

Fal. Well Sir.

Ford. I haue long lou'd her, and I protest to you, bestowed much on her : followed her with a doating obseruance : Ingrost my opportunities to meete her : see deuery slight occasion that could but nigardly giue mee sight of her : not only bought many presents to giue her, but haue giuen largely to many, to know what shee would haue giuen : briefly, I haue pursu'd her, as Loue hath pursued mee, which hath beene on the wing of all occasions : But whatsoeuer I haue merited, either in my minde, or in my meanes, meede I am sure I haue : eceiued none, vnlesse Experience be a Iewell, that I haue purchased at an infinite rate, and that hath taught mee to say this,

    " *Loue like a shadow flies, when substance Loue pursues,*
    " *Pursuing that that flies, and flying what pursues.*

Fal. Haue you receiu'd no promise of satisfaction at her hands?

Ford. Neuer.

Fal. Haue you importun'd her to such a purpose?

Ford. Neuer.

Fal. Of what qualitie was your loue then?

Ford. Like a faire house, built on another mans ground, so that I haue lost my edifice, by mistaking the place, where I erected it.

Fal. To what purpose haue you vnfolded this to me?

For. When I haue told you that, I haue told you all : Some say, that though she appeare honest to mee, yet in other places shee enlargeth her mirth so farre, that there is shrewd construction made of her. Now (Sir *Iohn*) here is the heart of my purpose : you are a gentleman of excellent breeding, admirable discourse, of great admittance, authenticke in your place and person, generally allow'd for your many war-like, court-like, and learned preparations.

Fal. O Sir.

Ford. Beleeue it, for you know it : there is money, spend it, spend it, spend more ; spend all I haue, onely

giue

in a strict sense a good compositor need be no more than an English scholar, or indeed scarce so much; for if he knows but his letters and characters he shall meet with in his printed or written copy, and have otherwise a good natural capacity, he may be a better compositor than another man whose education has adorned him with Latin, Greek, Hebrew and other languages, and shall want a good natural genius.[43]

Moxon writes that the compositor is 'strictly to follow his copy, viz. To observe and do just so and no more than his copy will bear him out for, so that his copy is to be his rule and authority', but we know that in certain matters, compositors tended to import their own spelling and punctuation to the copy text. This is what makes them and their contribution visible in the printed book.

Neither spelling nor punctuation was standardised in this period. Even proper names were spelled in variant forms, and even by their owners: Shakespeare's six extant signatures are in the forms 'Willm Shakp', 'William Shaksper', 'Wm Shakspe', 'William Shakspere', 'Willm Shakspere' and 'William Shakspeare' (strikingly, none is exactly the form in which we have come to standardise his name: the medial 'e' is probably a function of print-shop type, in which the descenders of the 'k' and long-form 's' need a space between them). Nevertheless, individuals tended to favour particular spellings and word forms. Close analysis of the Folio's printed pages reveals the characteristic spelling and punctuation practices of at least five and perhaps as many as nine or ten distinct compositors, named by scholars as Compositors A, B, C, and so on. Some of the differences in these individuals' preferences can be sketched out.

For example, compositor A was responsible for work across all three genres in the Folio, and can be found because of his tendency to spell common words *doe*, *goe* and *here*. Generally judged to be the most accurate of the compositors, he is responsible for about a fifth of the book's printed pages. Compositor B, who did the majority of the typesetting, particularly on the tragedies, had different preferred spellings *do, go* and *heere*. These preferences can also be traced in other Jaggard books, so we know that Compositor B had been working there since at least 1619 and was evidently an experienced compositor. For this reason, it's likely that he was set to supervise a new recruit, the so-called compositor E, who has been identified as Jaggard's new apprentice John Leason.

Apprenticeships in the early modern period were contractual relationships between masters and apprentices, often regulated by guilds or other professional organisations. Apprentices were given food, clothing and accommodation by their masters in return for work. They were rarely paid – rather, the master tended to be paid to take them on – and were forbidden to marry, gamble or go to plays or taverns without their master's permission. The period of apprenticeship was at least seven years, and city regulations meant that apprentices were not to be freed before their twenty-fourth birthday. In return for this, the apprentice learned a trade and grew up to become a journeyman. In *Richard II*, Bolingbroke uses the imagery of apprenticeship to imagine his six-year period of banishment:

> Must I not serve a long apprenticehood
> To foreign passages, and in the end,
> Having my freedom, boast of nothing else
> But that I was a journeyman to grief?[44]

In the 1620s, Jaggard hadn't indentured a new apprentice for some years, so maybe he thought – erroneously, as it would seem – that another pair of hands, even unskilled ones, would help make the work on the Shakespeare Folio and concurrent projects easier. Or perhaps this was part of Isaac Jaggard's increasing influence in the family business. Young John Leason was from Hampshire and may well, like many other provincial apprentices, have never been to

London before he found himself indentured in Jaggard's noisy, inky print shop, bound to his new master in November 1622, when he was probably around 17 years old. His work on the Folio tragedies indicates to us that they were printed last, and, as discussed in Chapter 4, that work is also characterised by a high level of compositorial error (akin to what we would now call typos). We do not have any further records for him, so we do not know whether he continued in the printing trade – if so, we might expect to be able to trace him through the records of the Stationers' Company – or whether, like a high proportion of apprentice contracts in this period, Leason's indentures with Jaggard were broken early for some reason. Hence, even while it preserves and transmits Shakespeare's genius to future ages, so too the First Folio is the only surviving monument to Jaggard's teenage apprentice, whose work in the Barbican print shop at the beginning of the seventeenth century would otherwise leave no legible traces.

Leason's error-strewn presence in the First Folio gives us a rare insight into the work of an inexperienced print-shop worker and thus to something of the conditions of apprenticeship in seventeenth-century London. Rather nicely, it has also been ob-served that his work gradually becomes closer in form and general accuracy to that of Compositor B, his supervisor: the First Folio is a visible trace of his training. In a modern book on craftsmanship, Richard Sennett suggests that 10,000 hours of practice is needed to gain true expertise and skill:[45] if we imagine a twelve-hour working day and a six-day working week, that probably accounts for almost three years of apprentice training, not the mere few months John Leason had had at Jaggard's when he began to set the complex verse of Shakespeare's tragedies. And Leason's discrepant error rate indirectly shows us the level of skill that was expected of his long-serving colleagues, as they worked deftly and quickly to read their copy and then accurately pick out and place around

4 million individual pieces of type that make up the printed pages of the First Folio.

One final agent in the making of the book is the engraver Martin Droeshout. The portrait that, in Ben Jonson's words, 'was for gentle Shakespeare cut' on the Folio's title page is signed with his name in the left-hand corner. 'The graver' – 'engraver', but with a probable pun, in a memorial volume to a dead author – 'had a strife / With Nature, to out-do the life'. In fact the problems with the picture, which exists in three separate states, indicating two revisions, have led some scholars to believe that another inexperienced young man, Martin Droeshout the Younger (born in 1601), must have been responsible. It is perhaps more likely that the man commissioned by the Folio's publishers was Martin Droeshout the Elder (*c*.1565–*c*.1642; uncle to his young namesake), born to a Protestant Huguenot family who had moved to London as refugees from religious wars in the Low Countries in the late 1560s. Droeshout was born around 1565 and so was in his fifties when he undertook the Shakespeare portrait. Many scholars assume that the engraving was based, as was usual, on a painted portrait or miniature (now lost): so, like the plays it prefaces, Droeshout's engraving recalls a lost original even as it offers to reproduce it, 'according to the true original copies'. It may be that the problem of perspective in the engraving – the sense that the head and ruff are not securely or convincingly attached to the patterned doublet below – is because the original painting showed only the head.[46] Surviving records suggest that Droeshout was also, or perhaps primarily, a painter, so he may also have been responsible for any prior painting – although perhaps in that case we would not have the prominent claim next to his name of 'sculpsit', a word specifically denoting engraving.

A commentator in the early eighteenth century suggested Shakespeare had had his portrait painted by the Flemish immigrant painter Marcus Gheeraerts the Younger (1561/2–1636).[47] Gheeraerts was a royal painter at James's court. His head-and-shoulders portrait of the scholar William Camden (1620), itself predominantly composed of a head and a ruff over a dark, almost indistinguishable doublet, might give an indication of the kind of portrait he would have done of Shakespeare. If indeed he did, then that portrait has been lost. Charles Nicholls speculates, based on an analysis of the style of the ruff in the portrait and the apparent age of the sitter, that Shakespeare might have sat for an original painting around 1604, but we can't be sure of that, and, in any case, many painted portraits in this period were not taken from life. The Folio portrait has also been linked to the Chandos portrait, now in the National Portrait Gallery in London: that work, too, is the subject of controversy about the identity of both its painter and its sitter. Recently Katherine Duncan-Jones has suggested the Chandos portrait was painted by Joseph Taylor, one of the King's Men actors listed in the First Folio.[48] But, although there are similarities between the Chandos and Folio portraits, it does not seem likely that this painting is the lost original for the engraving.

We do not know for certain whether Droeshout ever met Shakespeare, although the playwright did lodge with the Mountjoys, French-born Huguenot migrants who worked as tire-makers (producing fashionable and elaborate headgear for wealthy women) in Silver Street. He became implicated there as a witness to a family dispute that ended up in court in 1612. The names of Charles Mountjoy and Martin Droeshout appear together in a list of denizens – foreign-born residents of England who have applied to the Crown for enhanced rights, particularly about the purchase, holding and bequeathing of property – in 1607. So it may be that through this connection, Droeshout and Shakespeare were known to one another, or it is possible that the actor Richard Burbage, himself a keen painter, might have had connections with Droeshout as a fellow artist. In any case, either Droeshout himself or the Folio publishers were dissatisfied with the details of the engraving, returning it twice to be retouched (see Chapter 4). We know little else about Droeshout's career, although there are a few surviving engravings by him. One, from 1623, is a full-length portrait of James, Marquess of Hamilton, but others which are closer in scale and composition to the Shakespeare portrait include oval pictures of the poet John Donne and the chronicler of martyrs John Foxe.

Invisible hands

As well as these identifiable individuals, there are some invisible hands, too. We know that some of the plays are printed from manuscripts by the pre-eminent theatrical scribe Ralph Crane. Little is known of Crane's life, although in the preface to his collection *The Workes of Mercy, both Corporall and Spiritual* (1621) – the only work written, as opposed to written out, by him – he describes being born in the City of London and trying 'the air of diverse noble countries' after his schooling. Crane identifies his 'one blest gift, a ready writer's pen' and describes his association with 'those civil, well-deserving men / That grace the stage with honour and delight': the King's Men.[49] Indeed, Crane is associated with a number of King's Men manuscripts, including the only extant copy of a masque by Ben Jonson performed before King James in 1618 titled *Pleasure Reconciled to Virtue*. He was particularly busy with theatrical work in the early 1620s, including work on plays by Thomas Middleton and by John Fletcher in collaboration with other writers. During 1624 he was at work on several copies of Middleton's anti-Spanish satire *A Game at Chesse*: this play, with its savage depiction of the Spanish ambassador Gondomar, was such a sensation that there was great demand for the script. Crane must, therefore, have been well known to Heminge and Condell and probably to the Folio's publishers also. It was customary for scribes in this period to copy works in their own style, making changes or emendations as they saw fit. The notion of the exact copy or replica was unfamiliar in the period, as manuscript copies of ostensibly the same poem or document vary in small and in larger ways: copying created a unique text. Crane is thus no mere mechanical copier, but rather an active agent in the appearance and organisation of the subsequent play texts.

Crane's extant manuscripts show a range of elements that we can also find in the First Folio, and thus attribute at least in part to his role in the text's transmission. He was interested to draw up neat columns of the characters in the play (as we can see in his transcript of Middleton's *The Witch*): examples of these are appended to five plays, including *The Tempest, The Two Gentlemen of Verona* and *The Winter's Tale*. He favoured so-called 'massed entries', a technique he had learned from work on Ben Jonson plays, in which all the characters for a scene are named at its head in classical style (this is evident in the printed copy of *The Duchess of Malfi* of 1623). We can see this in *The Merry Wives of Windsor* 4.2. Here, the opening Folio stage direction reads 'Enter Falstaff, Mistress Ford, Mistress Page, Servants, Ford, Page, Caius, Evans, Shallow', but the sense of the scene means the entrance of these characters needs to be staggered. At the beginning the merry wives of the title are bundling Falstaff into the linen basket, hiding him before Ford enters with the other characters. The opening stage direction is not an instruction for all the characters to come on stage together, but a list, in Crane's own style, of the personnel needed across the shape of the scene (PLATE 23).

Crane also made extensive use of parentheses to organise verse syntax. The example from *The Tempest* (PLATE 24) shows this preference, as well as having some of Crane's distinctive spellings and preferences for elisions. Some of the characteristic language of *The Tempest*, with its hyphenated compounds such as 'tempest-tossed', may have something to do with him. He was precise, perhaps even heavy-handed by modern standards, in punctuation. He tended to embellish stage directions in a more literary style. PLATE 24 shows a number of parentheses in a passage from *The Tempest* alongside one of his descriptive stage directions, perhaps drawing on his experience with the spectacular court masques of Ben Jonson. Trevor Howard-Hill, in the most extensive study of Crane's working practices, calls him the Folio's editor and certainly for those plays with which he is definitely (*The Tempest, The Two Gentlemen of Verona, The Merry Wives of Windsor, Measure for Measure, The Comedy of Errors, The Winter's Tale*) or more speculatively (*Othello, Timon of Athens, 2 Henry IV*) associated, he is a key figure in their transmission to us. It's noticeable that the Crane manuscripts are concentrated at the beginning of the Folio, and it has been speculated that the Folio publishers, or Heminge and Condell, intended to work more extensively with him as scribe. Perhaps pressures of other work, or the timing of the Folio production schedule, made this impossible.

Other playwrights

No other playwright is mentioned in the First Folio as a collaborator. No Shakespeare work before 1623 had been acknowledged in print as a collaboration. In fact the only early publication to list Shakespeare as a co-author in the entire period came later, in 1634: the first edition of *The Two Noble Kinsmen* was printed in 1634 (FIGURE 7) bearing the attribution: 'written by the memorable Worthies of their time Mr John Fletcher and Mr William Shakespeare, Gent.' The impression the Folio gives of Shakespeare solo could not be clearer, in the repetition of his name in the prefatory material and the commissioned portrait on the title page – and, as discussed in Chapter 1, the marginal place of collaborative work such as *Pericles* (omitted from the Folio) or *Timon of Athens* (apparently included as

THE
TWO
NOBLE
KINSMEN:
Prefented at the Blackfriers
by the Kings Maiefties fervants,
with great applaufe:

Written by the memorable Worthies
of their time;
$\lbrace$M^r. *John Fletcher*, and$\rbrace$ Gent.
$\lbrace$M^r. *William Shakfpeare.*$\rbrace$

Printed at *London* by *Tho. Cotes*, for *Iohn Waterfon:*
and are to be fold at the figne of the *Crowne*
in *Pauls* Church-yard. 1 6 3 4.

FIGURE 7 *The Two Noble Kinsmen*, co-written with John Fletcher
and not published until eleven years after the First Folio.
Bodleian Library Arch. G e.33 (3).

an afterthought substitute for a missing play). But we know that collaborative writing was the norm, not the exception, for the early modern theatre, and that it could take many different forms. The theatrical impresario Philip Henslowe records payments to teams of writers who seem to have divided up plays between them; some writers in the theatre business are constantly in work but never credited on a printed title page because their job is tidying or patching plays; we know of one dramatist, Robert Daborne, who subcontracted an act to another writer to meet a deadline; we think that sometimes a more senior writer might have paired with a more junior one in a kind of master–apprentice model; some plays seem to have had one writer for the main plot and another for a subplot (*The Changeling*, a sensational tragedy of adultery and violence performed by the King's Men in the 1620s, is a good example, in which Middleton seems to have been responsible for the tragic main plot and Rowley the comic subplot).

The idea that Shakespeare might have collaborated with other writers has been slow to take hold and contentious to argue. Debates about authorship and attribution still continue to be extremely heated ones. Something of a consensus, however, is emerging. Many scholars believe that John Fletcher also co-authored *Henry VIII*, that George Peele worked with Shakespeare on *Titus Andronicus*, that Thomas Nashe may have been involved in parts of *1 Henry VI*, and that Thomas Middleton was the co-author of *Timon of Athens*. So who were these men and how might they have collaborated with Shakespeare?

First, George Peele. Peele (1556–1596) was a Londoner who got a degree from the University of Oxford, and was part of a group sometimes called the University Wits: educated men from modest backgrounds who embraced print publication at the end of the sixteenth century, particularly in plays and prose fiction. Peele was involved in academic drama in Oxford, usually occasional plays designed for the visit of some dignitary, and he also wrote court drama and mayoral pageants, as well as poetry. Most significant for the collaboration with Shakespeare are his four plays for the professional theatre: *The Battle of Alcazar*, *Edward I*, *The Old Wives Tale* and *David and Bethsabe*, all written in the early 1590s. In these plays, Peele shows a predilection for grand symmetrical stage effects and for classical rhetorical patterning – both of these are evident in *Titus Andronicus* too. The play's opening stage direction is a good example of its bold large-scale choreography: 'Flourish. Enter the Tribunes and Senators aloft. And then enter Saturninus and his Followers at one door, and Bassianus and his Followers at the other, with drum and colours.'

Titus Andronicus is usually dated to 1591–92; it was printed in a quarto without any authorial name attached in 1594. The scholarly difficulty over Peele's possible contribution to the play is that questions of attribution can only be settled on internal evidence. Analysis of syntactic patterns, particularly the incidence of so-called 'feminine endings' (lines with an extra final unstressed syllable) has suggested that Act 1, and perhaps also 2.1 and 4.1, of *Titus* are non-Shakespearean; echoes of vocabulary have inclined some scholars to identify Peele, from his other extant writing, as the most likely collaborator. It may be that Shakespeare and Peele worked together or that Shakespeare took over and revised an old or unfinished Peele play: we do not have any other evidence of their contact. The apparently objective analysis, however, is intertwined with more evaluative judgement: put simply, many critics have wanted *Titus* to be collaborative to excuse its perceived inadequacies, or they have been willing to sacrifice the Shakespearean-ness of this particular play. The first suggestion that the play was not solely authored by Shakespeare was made by a Restoration reviser, Edward Ravenscroft, who brings co-authorship and literary quality together neatly:

I have been told by some anciently conversant with the stage, that it was not originally his, but brought by a private author to be acted, and he only gave some master-touches to one or two of the principal parts of characters; this I am apt to believe because tis the most incorrect and indigested piece in all his works, it seems rather a heap of rubbish than a structure.[50]

The question of value is also important in the argument over Thomas Nashe as a presence in *1 Henry VI*, a play also dated to the 1591–92 period. Thomas Nashe (1567–*c*.1601) was best known as a prose writer, a controversial satirist in print who often wrote under pseudonyms. His pugnacious style is lampooned in a Cambridge University comedy of 1601 where the writer 'Ingenioso' is described as a 'great schoolboy giving the world a bloody nose'.[51] He was imprisoned, along with his co-author Ben Jonson, for a controversial, now-lost comedy titled *The Isle of Dogs* (1597): a manuscript elegy by Jonson on Nashe's death emphasises the warmth of their relationship, as Jonson fears 'a general dearth of wit throughout this land' without its presiding genius, Nashe. Although Nashe was a master of print publication, some of his more risqué poems circulated in manuscript: the saucy theme of his 'Choice of Valentines' is clear from its alternative title, 'Nashe's dildo'. Nashe's works, and in particular his print quarrel with the Cambridge academic Gabriel Harvey, were singled out by the 1599 decrees of censorship issued by the Archbishop of Canterbury and the Bishop of London: the so-called Bishops' Ban. A book burning of prohibited titles probably included a number of Nashe's, and, although the injunction that 'none of their books be every printed hereafter' was not entirely observed, 1599 was an effective end to Nashe's fecund, gregarious, combative literary output.

Perhaps Nashe's best-known work for modern readers is the picaresque proto-novel *The Unfortunate Traveller* (published in 1594), in which the scapegrace hero Jack Wilton has various adventures across Europe, involving a motley, self-interested cast of prostitutes, Anabaptists, soldiers and poets. Nashe dedicated this work to the Earl of Southampton, in the same year that Shakespeare made him the dedicatee of his *Rape of Lucrece*. There are other, more concrete connections between the two writers: Shakespeare was influenced by a number of Nashe's inventive linguistic coinages. Nashe's play *Summer's Last Will and Testament*, about the refusal of a personified king Summer to cede power, influenced plays about deposition, including *Richard II* and *King Lear*, and his inventive jokes are key to the wordplay and banter between Falstaff and Prince Hal, especially in *1 Henry IV*. Some critics have also suggested that the page Moth in the highly literary and self-conscious comedy *Love's Labour's Lost* is a Shakespearean portrait of Nashe. One critic suggests that 'Nashe is so much a part of the fabric of Shakespeare's works that it is not too much to say that Shakespeare without Nashe and his works would not be Shakespeare.'[52] This ongoing influence therefore gives a context for potential collaboration early in Shakespeare's career. Analysing syntax and vocabulary in *1 Henry VI*, Gary Taylor has argued that Nashe's is the lion's share of this play, with Shakespeare very much the minor contributor: no wonder, then, that Nashe praised it so highly in one of his own pamphlets. Writing in 1592, Nashe defends drama, and in particular the stirring moral purpose of performed history:

> How would it have joyed brave Talbot (the terror of the French) to think that after he had lain two hundred years in his tomb, he should triumph again on the stage, and have his bones new embalmed with the tears of ten thousand spectators at least (at several times) who, in the tragedian that represents his person, imagine they behold him fresh bleeding.[53]

Talbot, the hero of *1 Henry VI*, here becomes the epitome of theatrical heroism.

Peele and Nashe have been associated with early Shakespearean plays. John Fletcher (1579–1625), by contrast, is associated with plays from the end of Shakespeare's writing career. Their collaboration *The Two Noble Kinsmen* was not included in the First Folio. Many scholars also see Fletcher's work in *Henry VIII*, a late play whose ironic subtitle, 'All is True', gives a sense of its knowing historical retrospection. Their lost joint play *Cardenio*, apparently based on *Don Quixote*, is known only from a few scattered allusions, although some scholars feel it underpins an extant eighteenth-century play titled *Double Falsehood*, and there have been some modern attempts creatively to imagine what the play might have looked like. John Fletcher was a generation younger than Shakespeare and succeeded him on his retirement as chief dramatist for the King's Men. His first foray into playwriting was in 1606, when he collaborated with the playwright with whom his name was to be forever connected, Francis Beaumont, on a play titled *The Woman Hater*. A collection of works attributed to Beaumont and Fletcher was published in 1647 – the first dramatic folio after Shakespeare's – although scholars have disagreed about the distribution of their work across these plays. Working up until his death in 1625, Fletcher probably wrote around fifty plays, described by one critic as 'the vast unexplored Amazonian jungle of Jacobean drama'.[54]

Fletcher's first solo play, *The Faithful Shepherdess* (performed, unsuccessfully, in 1607 and published the following year), was important in translating Italian ideas of tragicomedy into the English context, and this had a significant influence on Shakespeare's generic mixing in his later plays such as *The Winter's Tale*. His play *A Woman's Prize, or the Tamer Tam'd* (*c*.1612) takes up the story of Shakespeare's own play *The Taming of the Shrew*. In Fletcher's sequel, Katherine has died and the widowed Petruchio takes a new wife, Maria, who on her wedding night barricades herself in her chamber and taunts her husband:

You have been famous for a woman-tamer,
And bear the feared name of a brave wife-breaker;
A woman now shall take these honours off
And tame you.[55]

This comic riposte to Shakespeare's account of Petruchio and Katherine ends in the reconciliation of the couple: an epilogue for a seventeenth-century revival confirms its ultimate aim 'to teach both sexes due equality / and as they stand bound, to love mutually'.

Fletcher's work was therefore both an influence on and influenced by Shakespeare, and this reciprocity may well have paved the way for their collaborations late in Shakespeare's career. The stylistic differences scholars have found in *Henry VIII* as indicative of shared authorship focus particularly on small, apparently unimportant but revealing words. For instance, it is clear that Shakespeare uses the form 'hath' where Fletcher's preference would be for 'has'. It's interesting, given how we praise Shakespeare's linguistic inventiveness, to note that 'hath' is an old-fashioned or provincial form by this time: you can take the boy out of the country, but you can't take the country out of the boy. Shakespeare speaks the language of his boyhood in this tiny detail, whereas the younger, university-educated Fletcher instinctively adopts the more modern form. Other foci for attribution studies are similarly specific: Shakespeare prefers 'you' and Fletcher 'ye', and Fletcher's contraction ''em' is usually spelled out as 'them' by his older colleague. On this basis, we can suggest that around half of *Henry VIII* is attributable to Fletcher (the same sort of distribution as is conjectured for *The Two Noble Kinsmen*).

One final playwright collaborator whose presence can be traced in the First Folio but who is never acknowledged there is Thomas Middleton (1580–1627). Middleton was a Londoner who attended The Queen's College in Oxford but apparently turned to writing and left without taking a degree. He began writing poetry but soon turned to pamphlets and to drama. Middleton's many plays are characterised by a satirical eye to the nexus of money, sex and self-interest of their contemporary London setting. Although he is usually identified as a strongly Protestant, even Puritan writer, he is far from the modern stereotype of the puritan. *A Chaste Maid in Cheapside* (*c*.1613), for instance, includes a cuckolded man who happily keeps house on the profits of his wife's affair with a nobleman and another hyper-fertile man whose every contact with his wife results in ruinous pregnancy, but who saves their fortunes by fathering a child for a childless couple. It is a distinctly unromantic, but very funny, play world, far from the idealised and largely desexualised comedies set in storybook Italian locations favoured by Shakespeare. Words are promiscuous in Shakespeare's comedies, not people. This distinction between the habitual themes of the two writers may indeed have been what brought them together: Middleton's salty brand of urban satire – so-called city comedy – was highly fashionable, and perhaps Shakespeare, or the King's Men, wanted some of that too.

The play on which Middleton and Shakespeare are generally thought to have collaborated is the satirical tragedy *Timon of Athens*. As discussed in Chapter 1, this previously unprinted play seems to have been a late addition to the collection. It tells the story of a generous philanthrope, Timon, who falls on hard times and finds those who were the recipients of his charity will not return the favour. He retreats, snarling at humanity, into the woods. As in the Fletcher collaboration, Middleton's voice in the play is often marked by its more modern forms, particularly in the use of the now-standard verb form 'I went' rather than, as Shakespeare would prefer, 'I did go'. Others of Shakespeare's plays have been recently identified as bearing the mark of Middleton's input. *Macbeth* is discussed in Chapter 1; the case has also been made for *Measure for Measure* as a Middleton adaptation of an original Shakespeare play, probably to revive it for later performances.

The elusive William Shakespeare

It may seem odd to hold back Shakespeare until the end of this long list of other agents involved in the First Folio. The aim has been to compensate for our general tendency to minimise these other figures and merely to focus on Shakespeare's own creative and individual genius: without the printers, publishers and actors we have already met we would not have Shakespeare's plays. But Shakespeare himself is, of course, the reason they all bothered to labour to bring the First Folio to the bookstalls.

The outline of Shakespeare's life is easy to sketch. He was born in Stratford-upon-Avon in April 1564 (later tradition has given him St George's Day, 23 April, as his birthday, but we cannot be sure of that), the son of a glover who became a prominent local citizen. He almost certainly attended the King's School in Stratford but, like the vast majority of boys of his social status, however clever, did not go on to university. He married Anne Hathaway at the early age of 18 (she, as biographers love to point out, was 26). Their first child, Susanna, was born six months later; twins, Judith and Hamnet, followed in 1585. There are no records of how Shakespeare ended up in London or made his way into the theatrical profession, and these so-called 'lost years' have proved fertile grounds for speculation. Did he travel to Europe? Was he a tutor in a Catholic household? Did he leave Stratford under a cloud for poaching on a local estate? The first reference to him is as an 'upstart crow' and a 'Johannes factotum' (Jack of all trades) in a pamphlet by Robert Greene in 1592, a reference that also parodies *3 Henry VI*, which must have been written by then. Other works of this earliest writing period include *The Two Gentlemen of Verona* and *Titus Andronicus*. In 1594 Shakespeare signed up, with six fellows, as a shareholder in the new Chamberlain's Men playing company. He continued to write comedies and histories based on medieval English subjects during the 1590s, and both he and the company flourished. Shakespeare was an actor as well as a playwright. We can trace his wealth by the purchase of a substantial house in Stratford, New Place, in 1597 (he did not own London property, instead living in a series of lodgings, until buying the gatehouse at Blackfriars in 1613). At the turn of the seventeenth century Shakespeare began to move towards the tragedies that would dominate the next eight years, with *Hamlet*, alongside a couple of more cynical comedies that later critics would call 'problem plays'. After the work on the tragedies, Shakespeare's final plays, which mingle tragedy with romance, comedy and an interest in artifice, show the influence of his sometime collaborator and successor with the King's Men, John Fletcher.

Shakespeare seems to have retired from the theatre around 1613. Some critics believe he was in the process of preparing his plays for publication, perhaps in a kind of rivalry with Ben Jonson, who would publish a volume of his works in 1616. Heminge and Condell may allude to this project when they admit

> It had been a thing, we confess, worthy to have been wished
> that the author himself had lived to set forth and overseen his
> own writings. But since it hath been ordained otherwise, and
> he by death departed from that right, we pray you do not envy
> his friends the office of their care and pain...

The implication is that it is premature death that prevented Shakespeare from fulfilling this task, not the indifference to print that has sometimes been assumed by scholars. That death took place in Stratford in April 1616, three weeks after he had signed his will. Famously, that will seems to marginalise his wife Anne, who is left the 'second-best bed' in a line added to the draft as an afterthought: apologists for their marriage and for Shakespeare as a husband, argue that this would have been the marital bed, steeped in emotional significance, but others read the bequest as a snub.[56]

Shakespeare's traces in the historical record are sparse, like those of most of his contemporaries who were not aristocrats, and, importantly, they reveal little of his inner life. We have no letters or diary by him, nor even any of the explanatory proto-critical material that playwrights were increasingly likely to append to their works in the seventeenth century, outlining their theory of comedy, say, or their sense of their readers. There are no contemporary accounts of his character or personality, and even our abiding visual images of him have been debated as accurate likenesses. Some of the evidence we do have – that he paid for the title of 'gentleman', or that he apparently kept his wife short of money so she needed to borrow from neighbours, or that he supported the plans to enclose formerly common land in Stratford, have been difficult for biographers to square with the wisdom and humanity they read in the plays. One academic, being interviewed about an account of Shakespeare as a hoarder of malt and grain to increase profits, was clear: 'There was another side to Shakespeare besides the brilliant playwright – as a ruthless businessman who did all he could to avoid taxes, maximise profits at others' expense and exploit the vulnerable – while also writing plays about their plight to entertain them.'[57] This is the figure the twentieth-century dramatist Edward Bond wrote about in his harsh dramatic biography *Bingo*. While the description is a harsh one – and perhaps a little too inflected by twenty-first-century ideas and terminology to be entirely accurate – it has its roots in the archival records.

The relative paucity of information, and the apparent discrepancy between the life and the plays, mean that Shakespeare is a difficult author to read biographically. Perhaps this was his intention: he, after all, chose the genre, drama, in which the authorial self is most elusive. Drama has no narrator and no central narrative point of view: it succeeds by making different voices and different perspectives equally convincing and compelling. The biographical

'I' can't easily be found; or, to put it another way, perhaps it is an appropriate genre for someone who is not primarily interested in writing as self-expression. Shakespeare can sometimes seem to be a rather personally evasive figure in his works, and hence the ongoing fascination with, and irresolution of, debates about his own political, religious or sexual orientation. Shakespeare's own experiences do make their way into his plays, but his richest sources were literary ones. Shakespeare got his knowledge (such as it is) of Venice for *The Merchant of Venice*, or Verona for *Romeo and Juliet*, from reading, the same way he had access to ancient Rome or to the way mariners speak to one another in a shipwreck (the opening scene of *The Tempest*) or the spells of witches. Jonson's description of a Shakespeare with 'small Latin and less Greek' in the prefatory poem has sometimes been taken as evidence that Shakespeare was not well educated, but as we find out more about the extent of his reading the opposite seems to have been true.

None of the other descriptions of Shakespeare in the prefatory material to the First Folio suggests direct or personal description of the man, rather than the writing. There is no biographical note, and, as discussed in Chapter 1, no attempt to construct a literary life through the chronology of the plays' composition. Only Ben Jonson's reference to 'Sweet Swan of Avon' locates Shakespeare in his more private capacity, in the provincial town where he bought property to which he returned far from the bustle and fashion of London literary life. The presiding genius of the First Folio is presented only indirectly: Shakespeare is the sum of his writing, not of his biography. And thus it is this first collected edition of his dramatic works that makes him most vitally alive.

FOUR

Printing & Publishing

CHOLAR ROGER STODDARD wrote 'Whatever they may do, authors do not write books.'[1] Stoddard's aim in this apparently paradoxical statement was to draw attention to something often overlooked: the extensive processes and agents involved in producing the book-object. Producing the First Folio was no different. It involved a number of legal, technical and commercial stages, some of them undertaken simultaneously. The project management of this large book must have been demanding: coordinating copy, compositors, suppliers and the messy work of hand-press printing was most likely to have been the day-to-day responsibility of Isaac Jaggard, working on-site at the family's print workshop; perhaps Edward Blount was involved in negotiating rights. Jaggard is associated with this book from the outset: advertised in an English-language list as a local appendix to the Frankfurt Book Fair catalogue, the heading reads: 'Plays, written by M. William Shakespeare, all in one volume, printed by Isaack Jaggard, in fol.' The emphasis on 'one volume' may have been to distinguish it from Thomas Pavier's previous abortive multi-volume edition (see Chapter 2). We will trace the work of Jaggard, Blount and their colleagues as they prepare this book for the marketplace, going behind the scenes at the print shop in London's Barbican, at Stationers' Hall and in the early modern book trade.

The rights to the plays

Half of the plays in the Shakespeare First Folio had been previously printed, and thus the publishers of the collected edition had to acquire the rights from those stationers who had already registered them. There was no early modern copyright, but stationers could pay a small fee and enter details of their title into the Stationers' Register to have their interests protected by the Company. When, for example, Abel Jeffes complained to the court of the stationers that Edward White had published an unauthorised edition of his profitable text, Thomas Kyd's revenge play *The Spanish Tragedy*, in 1592, White was fined and the remaining copies of the offending edition were destroyed. Similarly, work on Ben Jonson's second folio of 1640 was stopped when there was a clash over which stationer owned the rights, exacerbated by the fact that they had not been entered into the Register (entry was not mandatory, but offered additional legal protection in case of dispute). It was in the Stationers' Company's interests – like any professional body – to regulate its own members rather than to submit to further external management.

Isaac Jaggard and Edward Blount paid for a clerk to search back through the Register to see who owned the rights to the plays they wanted to include in the Folio. They needed to negotiate with these fellow stationers over acceptable terms to transfer the rights. Two, John Smithweeke, who owned the rights to *Romeo and Juliet*, *Hamlet*, *Love's Labour's Lost* and *The Taming of the Shrew*, and William Aspley, who owned *2 Henry IV* and *Much Ado About Nothing*, opted for a part-share in the profits of the new edition rather than a fee, and are listed in the colophon at the end of the last page of the Folio. Some publishers may have driven a harder bargain than others: Matthew Law, who owned the rights to the best-selling history plays *Richard II*, *1 Henry IV* and *Richard III*, seems to have been negotiating up to the wire, since there is evidence that work on the Histories section was interrupted for a time and compositors set to work on the Comedies instead. But stationers may have needed persuading to sell their rights both to titles that had proved themselves to be commercially successful – like the reprinted history plays – and to less buoyant books with unsold stock still hanging around their bookstalls.

The acquiring of rights to previously printed plays ran in tandem with negotiations about those that had never before been published. On 8 November 1623, just a few weeks before the First Folio appeared on sale, Jaggard and Blount presented themselves at the headquarters of the publishing industry, Stationers' Hall in Ave Maria Lane, to the west of St Paul's, to pay the fee to enter into the register their rights to the previously unpublished plays. We don't know what arrangement they had come to, presumably through the offices of John Heminge and Henry Condell, with the King's Men over the rights to these manuscripts, nor what they had paid the King's Men for them. The entry lists sixteen plays (PLATE 25), marked as comedies, histories or tragedies and in the order of their publication in the Folio: *The Tempest, The Two Gentleman of Verona, Measure for Measure, The Comedy of Errors, As You Like It, All's Well That Ends Well, Twelfth Night, The Winter's Tale, 3 Henry VI, Henry VIII, Coriolanus, Timon of Athens, Julius Caesar, Macbeth, Antony and Cleopatra* and *Cymbeline.* Presumably during the course of the search for any previous relevant entries, it was discovered that Jaggard already held rights to *As You Like It* and Blount to *Antony and Cleopatra.*

The case of *Troilus and Cressida*

The Catalogue of the plays included in the Folio does not mention *Troilus and Cressida.* Behind this omission is a tussle between stationers over the rights to this play, which we can see recorded in different surviving copies of the First Folio. Getting the rights to previously published plays was clearly an ongoing project even after the printing of the First Folio had begun. Henry Walley had printed a quarto edition of *Troilus and Cressida* in 1609, in two issues. He seems to have been hedging his bets about how best to market this play. One issue carries the title 'The Historie of Troilus and Cressida, as it was lately acted by the Kings Majesty's servants at the Globe', thus marketing the play through its performance associations as was common in quarto publications of the time. By contrast, the other bore no mention of the King's Men, and instead had a preface claiming: 'Eternal reader, you have here a new play, never staled with the stage, never clapper-clawed with the palms of the vulgar, and yet passing full of the palm comical.' This publication stresses the reading qualities of the text, and tries to make a virtue of the fact that it is pristine, unsullied by public performance. Shakespeare's comedies are so 'framed to the life, that they serve for the most common commentaries of all the actions of our lives', and 'all such dull and heavy-witted wordings' then feel 'an edge of wit set upon them'. 'The most displeased with plays, are pleased with his comedies'. 'Amongst all', the publisher assures, 'there is none more witty than this.' It's an interesting sales pitch for a cynical play about an unheroic war and the destruction of a love affair. In any case, both claims in these two 1609 issues can't be true: the play can't both have been performed by the King's Men and never performed at all.

Whatever the publisher was trying to achieve with these marketing devices, the play was not reprinted, and it may have been because he had unsold stock that Walley was so difficult for Blount and Jaggard to deal with. Whatever the reason, at some point negotiations seem to have hit such a stumbling block that plans to include *Troilus* in the Folio were scrapped, and *Timon of Athens* was brought in instead. The substitute play is shorter than

Troilus and thus there is a large 'names of the actors' page to fill up some space caused by the change of plan. The catalogue page was completed with no mention of *Troilus*. A few copies exist with a cancelled sheet following *Romeo and Juliet* printing only the first two pages of *Troilus*, registering this stage of the negotiations; the first copies of the Folio that were sold by London booksellers did not include *Troilus and Cressida*.

For whatever reason, Henry Walley appears to have changed his mind. There is some suggestion in the Stationers' Register that Walley's own rights to the play had not been properly registered – perhaps this came to light when Isaac Jaggard and Edward Blount visited Stationers' Hall to sign up their new plays in early November 1623. This irregularity may have given the Folio publishers some eleventh-hour leverage over Walley. So the play was printed, and squeezed into the volume between the histories and the tragedies. The fact that existing copies of the Folio in bookshops or at Blount's wholesale storage were not bound made it possible for this addition to be interleaved in the existing stack of printed pages for retail. *Troilus and Cressida* has no page numbers after the first couple of pages, and its signatures are not in sequence with the rest of the book. It's an add-in; and at least three extant copies of this book exist without it (there were probably more), registering the experience of the First Folio for its very first buyers in November 1623.

Putting the book together

The Folio is made up of sections of six leaves (or twelve printed pages of text). Where this pattern varies, we get an insight into difficulties or irregularities in the printing process, as around the late inclusion of *Troilus and Cressida*. Some pages are single leaves: for example, the title page is a single leaf, because the process for printing an engraving required different equipment – a rolling press rather than a letterpress. The fact that it is on a single leaf may well have been to simplify the process of contracting this printing job out to another specialist workshop, perhaps even to the engraver Martin Droeshout himself.

Books were not generally printed in order from first page to last, but instead 'by formes'. A forme is a set of pages to be printed on one side of a sheet of paper (two pages, in the case of a folio, which is made from a sheet folded once to create two leaves, each one with a recto (front) and a verso (back)). Distributing the copy into formes enabled different compositors to work simultaneously and also meant that the type from printed pages could be broken up, redistributed and made available for resetting in new pages in an efficient manner. Pioneering detective work on the type in the First Folio enabled Charlton Hinman to highlight some 600 individual pieces of distinctive type that recurred at different points and in different states of damage, and thus prove that it was set by formes (the group of pages set on a single sheet of paper).[2] We also know that printing did not proceed through the book from beginning to end, but that there were numerous interruptions, alterations and asequential passages in the book's preparation.

The copy – whether it was an authorial or theatrical manuscript or an annotated printed play text – was divided up by someone in the printing house responsible for the process known as 'casting off'. This involved estimating how much printed space manuscript or printed copy would require. It was important to judge this accurately because the distribution of copy into pages set the compositors to work on different parts of the book at the same time. Clearly, these separate bits needed to fit together.

Casting off was a job for an experienced press employee, but there were tricks to help adjust where it had been miscalculated. The space around scene divisions or stage directions, for example, could expand or contract if the compositor was worried about the match between copy and page space available. We can see a casting-off problem in the final page of *Much Ado About Nothing* in the Folio (PLATE 26). Here there was too much manuscript to fit comfortably onto the page. All available lines have been used, and there is no spare space at all on this page. We can even see the compositor taking evasive action in the process of typesetting to stop the copy spilling over the end of the page. Gone are the white lines that usually separate off stage directions, halfway down the first column. In the second column the compositor begins to abbreviate to save space, replacing 'and' with '&', and managing to keep Claudio's speech 'I had well hop'd thou wouldst have denied Beatrice' to four lines by abbreviating 'question', 'thou' and 'that' (the expanded version of the y contraction is th). A couple of lines later the entrance of a messenger is sharply condensed, on the same line as Benedick's speech as 'Enter. Mes.' The same happens to 'Dance' and the final 'Finis' at the bottom of the column. The compositor skilfully managed to squeeze too much text into this page layout, compensating for a glitch in the casting-off estimation. He may, also, have made a tactical sacrifice of a single dispensable line. If we compare *Much Ado About Nothing* in its quarto printing of 1600 with the Folio of 1623 at this point, we see that the later text misses out one line 'Here comes the Prince and Claudio', which immediately precedes the stage direction 'Enter Prince and Claudio, with attendants'. One reason for this might be that this explanatory line was unnecessary and therefore was the obvious one to drop to fit the space available. If that is the case, then it suggests a compositor reading his copy with sensitivity and care to try to make an invisible cut.

This may not have always been the case. Charlton Hinman points out a glitch in another crowded page, this time towards the end of *Antony and Cleopatra*. The Folio prints consecutive speeches marked for Proculeius immediately before and after the presumed capture of Cleopatra, for which there is no stage direction. Hinman suggests that it 'seems extremely probable, though it cannot be conclusively proved, that a stage direction calling for the seizure of the Egyptian queen by Caesar's minions has here been lost as a result of inexact casting off'.[3] In that case, the compositor's decision seems less tactful than the case of *Much Ado* outlined above: Cleopatra's arrest is a significant action and probably needed to be reported in the stage direction (PLATE 27).

We can see the opposite problem, when there was not enough copy to fill the page, on other occasions in the Folio. For example, page 157 in *A Midsummer Night's Dream* has a number of additional white lines, especially around the act break, as fillers to pace the text across the printed page. On pages 305–6 in *King Lear*, lines of verse have been broken into half-lines to fill out the available space. In his account of printing, Joseph Moxon described various complicated formulae for casting off, involving arithmetical calculations or even a pair of compasses: these Folio pages show how difficult a job it was to get absolutely right, even for experienced press hands.

Compositorial work

The work of the compositors involved setting individual pieces of type. These 'sorts' were long pieces of lead alloy with a cast reversed-image letter at the tip. Type foundry was a specialised industry, and many sets of type were highly prized elements of a printer's estate, handed on to his heirs. William Jaggard, for instance, had acquired some of his types and ornaments from the printer James Roberts, and the wear and tear visible in the type in the Folio suggests it had been in service for many years. Type letters were cast in different founts – italic, roman and blackletter – and there were different types for Greek, Hebrew and Arabic scripts. A set of roman types probably included a minimum of 130 separate pieces, for letters, punctuation marks, spaces of varying width to fill out the lines, numbers, accents, abbreviations and ligatures (the single piece of type representing tied letters such as *æ*). The First Folio play texts are set in roman type, with italic used for stage directions, for speech prefixes, and for some of the prefatory material, as well as for proper names within the roman text.

Compositors worked in front of a pair of sloping cases divided into compartments. Joseph Moxon describes how the cases needed to be placed 'so as when the compositor is at work the light may come in on his left hand, for else his right hand plying between the window-light and his eye might shadow the letter he would pick up'.⁴ There were ninety-eight boxes in the upper case and fifty-six in the lower (we still use the words for capital letter forms and non-capitals that are derived from this upper/lower case arrangement). The arrangement of the types in the boxes was reflected their frequency of use, 'like the modern QWERTY keyboard', but that layout differed from printing house to printing house, which must have made the readjustments for jobbing compositors moving between casual employment difficult.⁵

Compositors worked from copy pinned in front of them, and thus their job had two distinct parts: the mechanical act of picking out the right type and setting it correctly, but also the interpretative act of reading and understanding their manuscript copy. Difficult handwriting, or a complex or overedited manuscript bristling with interleavings and crossings out, made their task much more difficult. Writing later in the century about the same technological processes (printing did not really change until its mechanisation during the nineteenth century), Moxon described 'bad, heavy, hard work' compared to the 'light, easy work' of setting good copy, lamenting that there was no extra payment for setting illegible scripts 'if a price be already made for a whole book, the good and bad is done at the same price'.[6] Using a slotted wooden composing stick – compositors, but not apprentices, were expected to provide their own – that held a few lines of type, the compositor set each piece of type individually, working in mirror image from left to right, and upside down. The line needed to be justified with blank spaces to the right-hand margin so that the type would not move under printing pressure. He then transferred these lines of type to a wooden paddle called a galley, until the type for the printed page was completed. The type was tied together, and the other pages for the sheet were typeset in the same manner.

The pages of the First Folio all include certain standard elements: a central line dividing the text into two columns, a running header on each page between two lines, and the box lines round the margin. These were not reset for each page, but retained as a kind of skeleton forme. Sometimes this caused problems – there are many instances where the page number in the running header has not been changed from one typeset forme to another, for example. And the last pages of *The Two Gentlemen of Verona* carry the pre-emptive running header of the next play, *The Merry Wives of Windsor*, as a clue to the organisation of the formes across the printing of those two plays.

After printing, the type was broken up – 'distributed'. It had to be cleaned of all traces of ink, dried and returned accurately into the type boxes for efficient reuse. Sometimes compositorial errors might properly be attributed to misdistribution of type. Although the quantity of the different letter types, rather as in the modern board game Scrabble, was probably variable to reflect common usage, it is clear that at some points in the compositorial process, particular frequently used letters became scarce. Play texts are heavy on the upper case italic *E*, for instance, since it is needed for the common words *Exit*, *Exeunt* and *Enter*, and there are examples where Folio pages seem to borrow this letter from other typefaces.

Paper

The leader of the popular rebellion against the king dramatised in *2 Henry VI*, Jack Cade, enunciates his grievances before a nobleman they have captured. Shakespeare presents Cade largely unsympathetically, as a savage and crude demagogue for whom an attack on literacy is a major strand of his radical programme. Cade complains about grammar schools that have 'corrupted the youth of the realm', about the legal system, and, further, that 'thou hast caused printing to be used and, contrary to the King his crown and dignity, thou hast built a paper-mill' (*2 Henry VI*, 4.7.30–35). Cade's complaints are sixteenth- rather than fourteenth-century – no printing press existed in England at the time of the Peasants' Revolt – but even when this play was performed in the 1590s, no paper mill in England produced printing-quality paper. At this point, all high-grade white paper for printing, including that from which the Folio is assembled, was imported from France. The annual level of paper imports in the 1620s has been estimated at around 80,000 reams – a ream was 480 or 500 sheets.[7] Attempts to establish native manufacture for the English book trade during the sixteenth century foundered: one publisher, Richard Tottell (best known now for an important collection of Tudor poems including sonnets by Thomas Wyatt, dubbed *Tottell's Miscellany*, but mainly employed as a law printer) tried and failed, angrily blaming the French for cornering the supply of raw materials (rags) and price-cutting to undermine English rivals.[8]

The poet Thomas Churchyard wrote a commendatory poem on a short-lived paper mill established by German entrepreneur John Spielman, in Dartford in 1588, praising the man and the qualities of his manufacture, and giving a description of the process:

Hammers thump, and make as loud a noise
As fuller doth, that beats his woollen cloth,

In open show, then sundry secret toys
Makes rotten rags, to yield a thickened froth:
When it is stamped, and washed as white as snow,
The skunk on frame, and hanged to dry I trow,
Thus paper straight it is to write upon,
As it were rubbed, and smoothed with slicking stone.
Through many hands, this paper passeth there
Before full form and perfect shape it takes
Yet in short time, this paper ink will bear
Whereon in haste, the workman profit makes.
A wonder sure, to see such rags and shreds
Pass daily through so many hands and heads,
And water too, that paper's enemy is,
Yet paper must take form and shape from this.[9]

This 'wonder sure', the production of high-quality paper, was a specialist craft, in which paper was made one or two sheets at a time. Running water and a supply of rags were the raw material for paper manufacture. Linen rags needed to be sorted and cleaned before fermenting for four or five days, then rinsed and pulverised with wooden tools called stampers to break down the fibres into a pulp. This mixture was formed into sheets on wire moulds and pressed thin between wool blankets called felts: often printed paper in books of this period, including the First Folio, bears the warp and weft imprint of the woven felt fibres. After drying, a gelatine size solution was applied to improve the absorption of printing ink. The paper was stacked to mature. Because it was made of linen, paper was seen as a fabric and handled in large shipments by haberdashers. Crown paper, the type used for printing the Folio, cost about 4*s*–4*s* 6*d* a ream, and was subject to additional taxation on arrival in London (import and purchase taxes rose sharply in the early years of James I's reign). The Folio paper is of medium quality – some copies show damaged corners which may indicate paper weakness, and creases, pleats and other paper-making flaws. On many occasions in the book show-through is visible from the reverse page, especially on title pages and other heavily inked ornamental sections.

Printing

The process of hand-press printing had changed little since Gutenberg and would not change fundamentally for a further two centuries. It involved a number of stages. Two people worked to operate a printing press: one to apply the ink, and the other to place the paper onto the tympan. The lines of set type that made up the forme were locked into a chase to avoid any movement under the pressure of the printing process, and placed horizontally on the bed of the press, and the paper secured on the raised tympan. The type was inked by ink balls – wool-stuffed leather balls on sticks, dipped into ink. Like every part of the process this was a skilled job, since over-inking would result in blots and illegible lettering; under-inking would result in a pale or patchy impression. The tympan was lowered over the forme to form the carriage, which was pushed under the platen. Exerting pressure by pulling the bar forced the platen down onto the tympan, thus pushing the paper into contact with the inked type to make the impression. The bar was released, the carriage returned, the tympan lifted and the inked paper set aside to dry, and the whole process was repeated for the next copy. Describing the speed of this process, Joseph Moxon wrote that, 'If two men work at the press ten quires is an hour; if one man, five quires is an hour': press time was a unit of production, measured in printed pages, rather than a clock unit measured in minutes (PLATE 30).

Work on the Folio was frequently interrupted. Jaggard's role as City Printer and his monopoly on playbill printing both meant that there must have been a constant throughput of small jobs alongside the ongoing project of the Shakespeare volume. In addition, however, we know that a number of other books were being printed concurrently with the Folio, or were completed by suspending work on the Folio. The first sections of the comedies in the Shakespeare book shared the print shop with the third edition of Thomas Wilson's *Christian Dictionary*, a thick quarto volume in double columns that appeared in 1622. Charlton Hinman suggested that after the Wilson book was completed, work proceeded apace on Shakespeare for some months, but that it was again put aside in mid-1622 to complete another commission, a topographical book called *The Description of Leicestershire* by William Burton. A further interruption for Augustine Vincent's book of heraldry, *A Discovery of Errors*, meant that progress continued to be fitful. The pattern of management in Jaggard's printshop during 1622 was that other work was repeatedly prioritised – it's tempting to imagine that the insistently living authors, Burton, Vincent and Wilson, might have been able to keep up the pressure more than the theatre men Heminge and Condell, inexperienced in the world of publishing, negotiating on behalf of a dead playwright.

Other interruptions in the course of printing the history plays apparently attest to difficulties in attaining the copy. The *Henry IV* plays, for instance, were not printed in order, and later there was apparently trouble with the copy for *Henry VIII*. This latter play had not previously been printed, but the prior success of *1 Henry IV* in print may have made its copyholder Matthew Law a difficult man with whom to negotiate. The section of tragedies was the last to be printed: here, the inexpert hand of the new apprentice John Leason (compositor E) is much in evidence. The preliminaries – the dedicatory letters and poems and the catalogue of plays included – were probably printed, as was customary, after the main text (even modern books tend to paginate this material separately). The last of the plays to be printed was *Troilus and Cressida*, probably in October or even November 1623, after lengthy wrangling over the rights.

Corrections

While the press was running off more sheets, an early copy would be given to someone in the printing shop to check for errors. William Jaggard's outfit had recently been slated by one disgruntled author who complained of 'many escapes and mistakings, committed by the Printer whilst my sickness absented me from the press'. The assumption here seems to have been that the author himself would normally be responsible for checking that the compositors had done their job accurately. In the absence of the author in this case, then, it's interesting to look at how far, and by whom, the First Folio has been corrected.

There may well have been points in the publishing process where errors were corrected that have left no trace: a stage of proofreading or of checking before printing began. But our evidence about the practice of correction comes mainly from what are called 'stop-press' corrections: the checking of a sample printed page while the uncorrected pages continue to be printed. A reader in Jaggard's workshop – perhaps Isaac, or perhaps Blount, or perhaps another colleague – read over the pages and marked them up for corrections. By comparing each page of each copy of the Folio, the number of these corrections, or press variants, is clear. Charlton Hinman undertook this painstaking task – he had learned the value of careful scrutiny as a naval cryptanalyst in the Second World War – and found five hundred press variants scattered over a hundred different pages. This seems a relatively low level of correction for a book of over 900 pages, 800,000 words and, most importantly, hundreds of obvious errors. In the fifty or more copies checked by Hinman, 789 of the 939 pages have no press variants, but they do nevertheless have errors of the kind identified earlier that might have been spotted in proofreading – turned letters, missing spaces, and other obvious compositorial mistakes.

Many contemporaneous books have a list of errata, sometimes called slips or faults: in one of his books of the same year, Edward Blount advises readers 'vouchsafe with your pen, the amendment of these few faults, before you begin to read the rest'.[10] There is no such list in the First Folio.

We can see something of how press correction worked because some of the corrected proof sheets have themselves been bound up into copies of the Folio. PLATE 28 shows a page in a copy of the First Folio that once belonged to the actor David Garrick and is now held in the magnificent library dating from the late seventeenth century of The Queen's College, Oxford. It is a page from *King Lear* marked up with print-shop corrections in the margin. It's the moment in the play when Lear, having given up his kingdom to his two older daughters Goneril and Regan, finds them turn against him as he first requests and then pleads for his retinue. The proofreader has picked up a number of small errors we would now call typographical – in that they are mechanical mistakes in setting the type that can be recognised without reference to any manuscript copy. Thus the proofreader notes that 'Nature' needs a stray letter deleted and an inserted 'r'; that there should be a space in 'true need'; that the 'r' in 'Daughters' has slipped or not registered (the term for this unevenly placed type is 'hanging'); that there is a stray comma before 'weep'; and that there is an extra letter at the end of 'mad' that should be deleted. But we can also see at least one error on the page that might have been caught but wasn't – the rogue apostrophe in 'an'ds'.

Plate 29 shows the same page in the Bodleian's copy, where the corrections have been made: we can see the formerly missing letters, but we can also see that correcting the end of the word 'mad' has created an inadvertent 'error'. The compositor has had to insert an extra space to fill out the line, but the edge of the space block was jutting proud and needed to be pushed down to avoid inking. Here

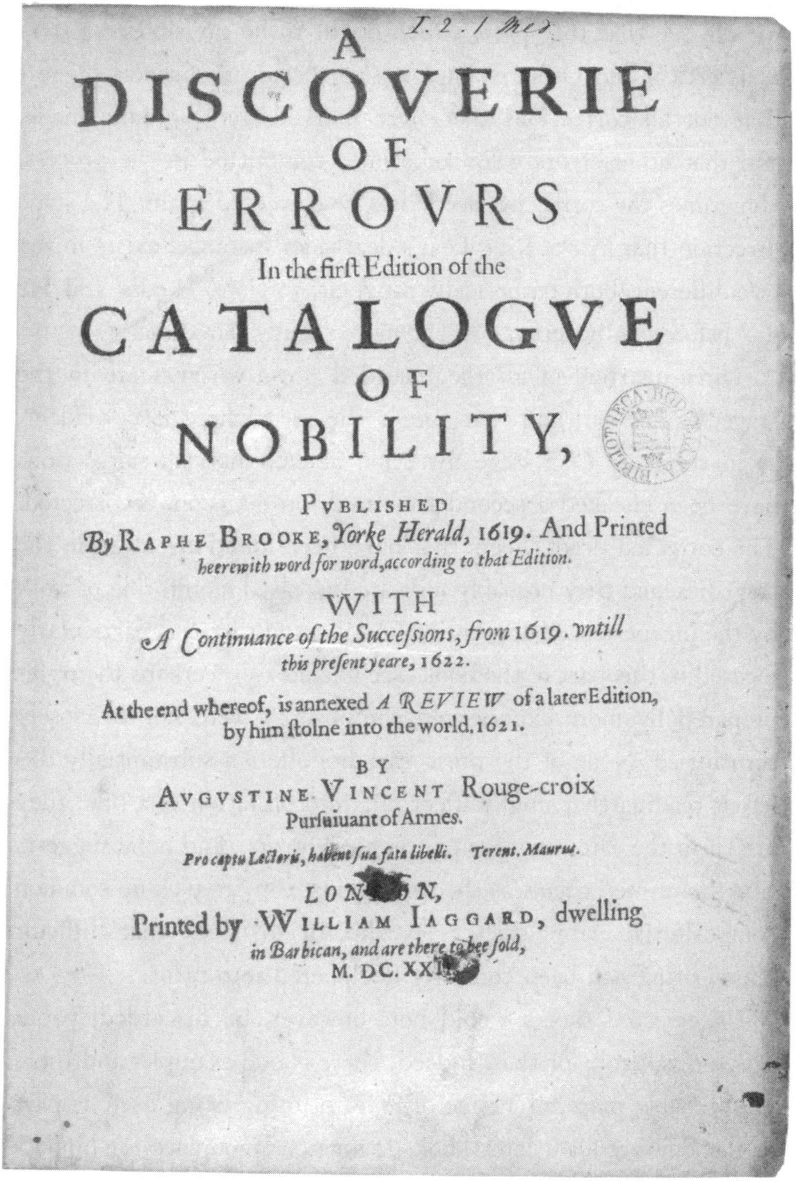

A
DISCOVERIE
OF
ERROVRS

In the firſt Edition of the

CATALOGVE
OF
NOBILITY,

PVBLISHED
By RAPHE BROOKE, *Yorke Herald*, 1619. And Printed
heerewith word for word, according to that Edition.

WITH
A Continuance of the Succeſsions, from 1619. *vntill
this preſent yeare,* 1622.

At the end whereof, is annexed *A REVIEW* of a later Edition,
by him ſtolne into the world, 1621.

BY
AVGVSTINE VINCENT Rouge-croix
Purſuiuant of Armes.

Pro captu Lectoris, habent ſua fata libelli. *Terent. Maurus.*

LONDON,
Printed by WILLIAM IAGGARD, dwelling
in Barbican, and are there to bee ſold,
M. DC. XXII.

FIGURE 8 Vincent's book of heraldry, published by the Folio printer
William Jaggard and used by him to defend himself against shoddy work.
Bodleian Library, I 2.1 *Med.*

we can see that the space, which ought to be invisible, registers as a vertical line. Other examples of corrected proof sheets suggest that not all corrections that were marked were actually made, and that other errors were sometimes committed in the process. Sometimes the correction needed to be corrected again. The stage direction that marks King Lear's death, for instance, exists in the two different, both bathetically misspelt, versions 'H edis' and 'He dis' before finally settling to the more seemly 'He dies'.

Three-quarters of all the recorded press variants are in the tragedies section, and that too is the area where it is evident, as in the *King Lear* stage direction above, that the corrections have been checked a second time and, on occasion, recorrected. The corrected proof sheets that have been found are all from the tragedies, and they probably indicate increased monitoring of work by the inexperienced apprentice John Leason that was particularly focused in this part of the book (see Chapter 3). Perhaps the pages prepared by more experienced compositors were not so closely scrutinised. None of the press variants offers a substantially different reading that might affect our interpretation of a line: they are all in the category of typographical errors. And none suggests that the printed page was checked against copy to pick up common compositorial errors such as eyeslip, or to check that difficult handwriting had been correctly deciphered into print.

Uncorrected sheets would not, however, be discarded: paper was too valuable for that. Indeed, there is one example, and there are probably more, of a page of Folio printing being used as part of the binding for a later book. It was commonplace for binders to buy up printers' waste, and it is assumed that this sheet, a page of *Coriolanus*, came somehow from Jaggard's print shop to be reused in another book.[11] Every copy of the First Folio contains a random distribution of corrected and uncorrected sheets. We tend to think that the printing press creates hundreds of identical printed books, but that is not actually the case in the hand-press period. The singular 'First Folio' used throughout this book is in fact only a hypothetical concept (albeit a useful shorthand): what we have is scores of different texts, different Folios. Each copy is a unique collation. Nor does there seem to have been any attempt to create a perfect copy with all-corrected sheets. The Bodleian used to boast that its First Folio was the prime copy chosen by the publisher as a presentation volume – because it was delivered by the Stationers' Company in early 1624 under the terms of Sir Thomas Bodley's agreement that the library could call a copy of any book printed. This seems like local pride, since there is, unfortunately, no evidence either that this was a general practice or that the Bodleian's copy is any more perfect than any other. The printed book in this period was thus a kind of work in progress, with some sheets at a later stage of development through correction than others.

After printing, the sheets of paper were hung up to dry on wooden racks. This work was probably done by the 'devils' – boys who became black with ink during the course of their work – who were employed in the print shop to fetch and stack paper and run errands. The damp paper must have been very susceptible to marking by inky fingers, and many Folio copies show distinct fingerprints that probably date from this moment in the book's creation (PLATE 15). The dried printed sheets were then gathered together in order according to the signatures. They were bunched into quires and folded in half. The collated sheets were pressed again: left for a day flattened under weights. Two features of the printed page were intended to aid the process of collation. The first, the signature, is a combination of letters and numbers at the foot of the page to organise the page order. The signatures number the quire and then the page, so, for a Folio in sixes like the Shakespeare book, would follow the standard sequence

A, A2, A3, A4, A5, A6, B, B1, B2 and so on. Obviously, those non-standard quires with fewer than six pages would interrupt the sequence. Each of these pages would have a recto side and a verso. Further, each page ended with a word in the bottom right hand margin which anticipated the first word of the next page. The catchword was another feature of the printed book to enable it to be assembled correctly.

Binding

Although books were often sold unbound, we know from something Blount wrote in another volume he published that his bookshop also acted as a bindery, allowing customers to buy a ready-bound First Folio if they did not want the trouble of taking their book elsewhere. Binding was the first act of customisation of the book by its readers – the first way in which they took and began to transform a ready-made object, the printed pages – into a bespoke or personal one. Buyers could thus specify the binding and the decoration that fitted their own library style. Binding came in three basic types, of increasing cost. Vellum (untanned calfskin) or forel (sheepskin or goatskin parchment) could be used in a limp cover, or as covering for boards in hard binding. The other common option, and the most practical one, was dark calf on board. Peter Blayney estimates that standard calf binding would have cost three or four shillings on top of the purchase price of the folio, with the limp vellum at about a shilling, and the vellum or forel boards at two shillings, although he also acknowledges that buyers might well have paid a convenience premium if they got their binding done at Blount's or in another retail bookseller's shop. When the Bodleian Library in Oxford got the copy of the First Folio from which many of the illustrations in this book are taken, they sent it to the local binder William Wildgoose, who returned it in the binding it still has today, complete with printers' waste to stiffen the spine. And while most extant copies of the First Folio have been rebound during the intervening centuries, a handful still register the choices their first buyers made about how to personalise the stack of printed pages, the product of the publishing industry, that they bought in Paul's Churchyard.

CODA

Early Readers

HE LETTER SIGNED by Shakespeare's fellow actors at the head of the Folio addresses 'the great Variety of Readers', and elaborates: 'From the most able to him that can but spell'. It has been a potent myth: the idea that Shakespeare's plays were, from the outset, targeted at a wide demographic, and that their appeal was inclusive. But the economics of the First Folio tell a different story. As discussed in Chapter 2, the Folio was a luxury item only really available to men with a significant disposable income, like the keen shopper Sir Edward Dering, who in December 1623 is its first recorded purchaser. Two other documented early Folio owners were similarly wealthy: Thomas, Lord Arundell and John Egerton, the first Earl of Bridgewater. These are men of similar elite standing to the pair of earls who are the Folio dedicatees, the Herbert brothers: men of means and of education. The Mayor of Hereford, Philip Traherne (uncle to the religious poet Thomas Traherne), must have been an early buyer, since he donated a copy to the library at Hereford Cathedral around 1626. The printer William Jaggard seems to have made a gift of one copy to the herald Augustine Vincent: Vincent, as discussed in Chapter 1, had defended Jaggard's professional honour in a book also printed at his Barbican printshop in 1623, *A Discovery of Errors* (FIGURE 8). Vincent inscribed his copy with the record of the gift.[1]

There's some evidence that Edward Dering was interested in amateur performance. His account book notes a payment of 4s made in 1622 to a Mr Carrington for 'writing out the play of Henry the Fourth', and this document, the 'Dering MS' now in the Folger Shakespeare Library in Washington DC, is a version of both parts together edited down to the length of a single play.[2] Dering may therefore have bought his First Folio with the idea of putting on versions of the plays at his home, Surrenden Manor in Kent.

But most early buyers were probably more focused on reading the text than performing it (it's an awkward volume, after all, to use in practical performance). Humanist theories of reading and of study encouraged reading as an activity undertaken with a pen. To read was simultaneously to mark up, underline, asterisk, or otherwise impose oneself on the printed page: early readers apparently felt none of our reticence about writing in books, even expensive ones. Two early readers in particular have left their marks on copies of the First Folio: William Johnstoone, probably a Scottish reader in the 1620s or 1630s; and a reader associated with the learned social circle centred on Great Tew and the household of Lucius Cary during the 1630s.[3] In describing how their copies suggest their habits of reading, and how the marks in their books indicate what these early readers found valuable or pleasurable about reading the First Folio, the book begins its journey from production into reception.

The Cary copy is now in Glasgow University Library. The only sign of early ownership is an immature-looking signature of 'Lorenzo Cary', the second son of Henry Cary, Lord Falkland, who lived from 1613 to 1641: he may have written on it as a child (many margins in Folio copies seem to have been used for pen practice). Someone, maybe someone else, has clearly marked up this copy with their recollections of seeing plays performed. Perhaps it was Lucius, Lorenzo's older brother (1610–1643), who we know enjoyed both reading and watching drama. One contemporary record has him asking for a manuscript copy of a play, because 'if I valued it so at the single hearing, when mine eyes could not catch half the words what must I do now in the reading when I may pause upon it'.[4] Maybe Lucius paused on the plays of Shakespeare in the First Folio; perhaps this book was part of the literary and intellectual circle he built around himself during the 1630s, when poets, philosophers and theologians met at Great Tew. As one of their number, the lawyer and future historian Edward Hyde, later first Earl of Clarendon, recalled it, theirs was a fellowship 'to study in a purer air, finding all the books they could desire in his library and all the persons together whose company they could wish, and not find in other society'.[5]

Whoever the annotating reader of the Glasgow copy was, he (it probably was he) was unique in tagging the printed book to performance in one very specific way: by marking up 'the names of the principal actors' with apparent reminiscences. Next to the names the reader makes various notes: the word 'know' next to Robert Benfield and Joseph Taylor, 'by report' next to Burbage, 'by eyewitness' at John Lowin, 'hearsay' by William Ostler, and 'so too' by the next names Nathan Field, Nicholas Tooley and William Ecclestone. Next to Shakespeare's name he writes 'least for making' (or, as has been suggested, 'ceased for making'), either reading suggesting that acting was known to be the lesser part of Shakespeare's work for the company (PLATE 31). The comments can help us date the annotations. This is a reader whose playgoing definitely coincided with the long career of Lowin (a King's Men sharer from 1603 to 1642), but appears to have postdated Burbage (who died in 1619). He knows Benfield (a sharer from 1615 to 1642) and Taylor (a sharer from 1619 to 1642, probably as a replacement for Burbage), so it seems that his active theatre attendance was during the 1620s or 1630s. He only knows by hearsay, not direct experience, of Ostler (who died in 1614), Field (who left the company in 1619), Ecclestone (who was playing until 1624) and Tooley (who died in 1623), so that narrows it down to some time after the mid-1620s. It may be relevant to note that the Cary brothers returned from their father's term of office as Lord Deputy of Ireland in 1629, having been there for most of the decade, but we can't identify the annotating reader with any certainty.

The rest of the annotations to the volume are almost all located in the comedies, the plays that come first in the volume. We don't know if this reader enjoyed comedy in particular or was an orderly reader who began at the beginning but was interrupted for some reason. So what did this early reader find in the Folio? First, he was interested, like many contemporaries, in reading as common-placing. Commonplacing was the act of identifying choice phrases or sentiments in the literary work, and marking them, perhaps for copying into a commonplace book. Edward Dering records buying 'two paper books in folio for common-places': blank books awaiting the fruits of his reading. Such books would be organised by thematic heading, such as 'royalty' or 'love'. The point of this anthology of extracts was to have a ready store of good expressions, to reuse or to take as a model in one's own writing. Our reader underlines as commonplaces a large number of speeches and phrases, often adding to these the marginal mark 'ap', short for *approbo*, I approve. The rate of extraction is quite high: a single page of the Folio text gives him an average of eight to ten commonplaces or approved quotations. And he picks a range. On *The Tempest*, for instance, our reader is appreciative of Prospero's lyrical

> These our actors,
> As I foretold you, were all spirits, and
> Are melted into air, into thin air;
> And like the baseless fabric of this vision,
> The cloud-capped towers, the gorgeous palaces,

The solemn temples, the great globe itself,
Yea, all which it inherit, shall dissolve;
And, like this insubstantial pageant faded,
Leave not a rack behind. We are such stuff
As dreams are made on, and our little life
Is rounded with a sleep.   (4.1.148–58)

This is a rightly famous passage that could probably be found in any modern list of Shakespeare quotations. But the reader's tastes extend to the romantic compliments from Ferdinand's suave courtship of Miranda, a young girl who has seen no man except her father and their slave. He also identifies short, expressive insults such as 'thou debauch'd fish' (3.2.26), and the salty sailors' song about Kate 'who loved not the savour of tar nor of pitch, / Yet a tailor might scratch her where'er she did itch' (2.2.51–2), as worthy of notice. This is a reader apparently responsive to a range of linguistic register, enjoying the poetic and rhetorical qualities of Shakespeare's language as well as its comic or bawdy moments: someone, in short, reading Shakespeare for a range of pleasures, some intellectual and others less so. When our reader judges *The Merry Wives of Windsor* as 'very good, light', in one of only a few marginal comments other than 'ap', we get a clear glimpse of his literary tastes. This reader, then, enjoys the specificity of Shakespeare's expression, as well as having a sense of the overall shape and tone of particular plays. For whatever reason, his attention to the text is not sustained beyond the first section of plays, the comedies.

A more thoroughgoing marginal commentary is found in a copy now part of a large collection of folios and other early modern material at Meisei University in Tokyo. This copy also bears a name, 'William Johnstoone'. Although we do not know anything about him, we can deduce from spellings and other linguistic forms that he was probably Scottish, and writing in the late 1620s or 1630.

Johnstoone, if we take him to be the annotating reader, approaches the task of reading the First Folio systematically. Every page of play text is annotated in his neat brown ink in the top margin. His annotations record a combination of plot summary and the extraction and paraphrase of commonplaces. We can recognise, perhaps, the outline of Hamlet's most famous soliloquy, 'To be, or not to be' (3.1.58), in Johnstoone's staccato reworking: 'sting of conscience; question whether we ought to overcome ourselves and our passions by extreme patience or die seeking desperate revenge; miseries and disgraces whereto we are subject; Conscience makes us cowards.' Elsewhere, reading the same play, Johnstoone gives plot summary: 'the Queen, her son Hamlet and Laertes poisoned by the king's treachery'.

Like many – perhaps all – subsequent readers of Shakespeare, Johnstoone tends to read his own preoccupations into the text. He is less concerned about the self-evident strangeness of the double-twins plot in *The Comedy of Errors* than that its Ephesus is a place where 'women [are] unwilling to be controlled', and this theme of transgressive women is prominent throughout his commentary. Whereas our previous reader saw *The Merry Wives of Windsor* as 'light', Johnstoone outlines its central premiss in rather harsh terms: 'hypocritical whore: a wife trusted and left to her own will; bawdry, money makes way everywhere ways to corrupt women' (PLATE 32). The fact that Desdemona is a faithful wife gets much less of his attention in his comments on *Othello* than Iago's scabrous misogyny 'you rise to play and go to bed to work' (2.1.118). In Chapter 1 we saw that the lack of stage directions in the final scene of *The Taming of the Shrew* complicates the interpretation of what actually happens in the theatre during Katherine's long speech of obedience. By contrast, Johnstoone does not find this ending at all difficult, and it's tempting to think he interprets it as he wishes it to be: 'husband commended for making her who when she was a maid and after she was first married was intolerably shrewd and scolding to become loving and obedient; duties of true obedience of a wife to her husband.'

Johnstoone takes Shakespeare's plays seriously, and clearly works on them in a sustained way, annotating every one of the thirty-six in the Folio. His annotations are neatly organised, and fit themselves to the available marginal space on each page. He responds to the plays as plots, by summarising what is happening to whom, sometimes with a particular interpretative logic, but he also responds to the plays as storehouses of quotable poetry and useful philosophy.

These two exemplary readers turn pages that have been imported from France, printed in Jaggard's printshop, and sold in Paul's Churchyard. They understand the plays both as entertainment and as instruction. They identify different passages, exempla and commonplaces because of their own preoccupations and predispositions: they find something relevant to themselves and their concerns in Shakespeare's works. As such, they inaugurate traditions of reading Shakespeare which have persisted through the intervening centuries. Through their marks in the text, they become further participants in a book already bearing the marks of so many other agents: actors, playwrights, poets, compositors, publishers and pressmen. And in doing so they complete the book's journey from production to reception – and start a new one. This book has traced the processes and the individuals behind Shakespeare's First Folio: we are now at the point when a great variety of readers begin their own most creative, idiosyncratic and diverse engagements with this great book.

NOTES

ONE

1. Francis Meres, *Palladis Tamia*, London, 1598, p. 281.
2. *Daily Telegraph*, 21 April 2007.
3. William B. Long, '"Precious Few": English Manuscript Playbooks', in David Scott Kastan, ed., *A Companion to Shakespeare*, Blackwell, Oxford, 1999, p. 414.
4. *The Oxford Authors: Ben Jonson*, ed. Ian Donaldson, Oxford University Press, Oxford, 1985, p. 539.
5. A.W. Pollard, *Shakespeare Folios and Quartos*, Methuen, London, 1909.
6. *Comedies and Tragedies written by Francis Beaumont and John Fletcher*, London, 1647, 'Stationer to the Reader', sig. A4.
7. *Letters of Sir Thomas Bodley to Thomas James*, Clarendon Press, Oxford, 1926, p. 222.
8. Jan Kott, *Shakespeare Our Contemporary*, trans. Boleslaw Taborski, Methuen, London, 1964, p. 9.
9. Fredson Bowers, *Textual and Literary Criticism*, Cambridge University Press, Cambridge, 1966, p. 81.
10. Mary Beth Rose, 'Where Are the Mothers in Shakespeare? Options for Gender Representation in the English Renaissance', *Shakespeare Quarterly* 42 (1991), pp. 291–314.
11. T.H. Howard-Hill, *Ralph Crane and Some Shakespeare First Folio Comedies*, published for the Bibliographical Society of Virginia by the University of Virginia Press, Charlottesville VA, 1972, p. 72.
12. Charlton Hinman, *The Printing and Proof-Reading of the First Folio of Shakespeare*, vol. II, Clarendon Press, Oxford, 1963, p. 347.
13. Jeanne Addison Roberts, 'Ralph Crane and the Text of *The Tempest*', *Shakespeare Studies* 13 (1980), pp. 213–33; p. 214.
14. Diane Purkiss, *The Witch in History: Early Modern and Twentieth Century Representations*, Routledge, London, 1996, p. 199.
15. Gary Taylor and John Lavagnino, *Thomas Middleton: The Complete Works*, Clarendon Press, Oxford, 2007, p. 1165.
16. Jonathan Hope, *The Authorship of Shakespeare's Plays*, Cambridge University Press, Cambridge, 1994, p. 5.

TWO

1. Peter Blayney, 'The Publication of Playbooks', in John D. Cox and David Scott Kastan, eds, *A New History of Early English Drama*, Columbia University Press, New York, 1997, pp. 383–443; Alan B. Farmer and Zachary Lesser, 'The Popularity of Playbooks Revisited', *Shakespeare Quarterly* 56(1) (2005), pp. 1–32; p. 28.

2. Lukas Erne, *Shakespeare and the Book Trade*, Cambridge University Press, Cambridge, 2013, p. 2.

3. Gary Taylor, *Guardian*, 3 May 2004 (www.theguardian.com/stage/2004/may/03/theatre.classics).

4. Gordon McMullan, 'Fletcher, John (1579–1625)', *Oxford Dictionary of National Biography*, Oxford University Press, Oxford, 2004; online edn, October 2006 (www.oxforddnb.com/view/article/9730).

5. Andrew Gurr, *The Shakespeare Company 1594–1642*, Cambridge University Press, Cambridge, 2004, Appendix 4, pp. 281–8.

6. Andrew Gurr, *The Shakespearian Playing Companies*, Clarendon Press, Oxford, 1996, p. 370.

7. John Webster, *The White Devil*, London, 1612, sig. A2v.

8. Francis Meres, *Palladis Tamia*, London, 1598, p. 282.

9. John Dover Wilson, *The Essential Shakespeare: A Biographical Adventure*, Cambridge University Press, Cambridge, 1932, p. 6.

10. William Shakespeare, *Troilus and Cressida*, London, 1609, sig. ¶2v.

11. W.A. Jackson, ed., *Records of the Court of the Stationers' Company 1602–1640*, Bibliographical Society, London, 1957, p. 110.

12. See Sonia Massai, *Shakespeare and the Rise of the Editor*, Cambridge University Press, Cambridge, 2007.

13. William Prynne, *Histrio-Mastix: The players scourge, or, Actors Tragædie* London, 1633, sig. ¶6v.

14. Quoted in James A. Riddell, 'Ben Jonson's Folio of 1616', *The Cambridge Companion to Ben Jonson*, Cambridge University Press, Cambridge, 2000, pp. 152–62; p. 152.

15. Kevin J. Donovan, 'Jonson's Texts in the First Folio', in Jennifer Brady and W.H. Herendeen, eds, *Ben Jonson's 1616 Folio*, University of Delaware Press, Newark, 1991, pp. 23–37; p. 33.

16. Steven K. Galbraith, 'English Literary Folios 1593–1623: Studying Shifts in Format', in John N. King, ed., *Tudor Books and Readers: Materiality and the Construction of Meaning*, Cambridge University Press, Cambridge, 2010, pp. 46–67.

17. Peter W.M. Blayney, *The First Folio of Shakespeare*, Folger Library Publications, Washington DC, 1991, pp. 26–9.

18. Edward Dering's 'Book of Expences', ed. Laetitia Yeandle, www.kentarchaeology.ac/authors/020.pdf.

19. Phoebe Sheavyn, *The Literary Profession in the Elizabethan Age*, Manchester University Press, Manchester, 1909, p. 116.

20. *The Oxford Authors: Ben Jonson*, ed. Ian Donaldson, Oxford University Press, Oxford, 1985, p. 222.

21. Quoted in J. Sears McGee, 'Adams, Thomas (1583–1652)', *Oxford Dictionary of National Biography*, Oxford University Press, Oxford, 2004; online edn, May 2012 (www.oxforddnb.com/view/article/131).

22. Quoted in Mary Morrissey, *Politics and the Paul's Cross Sermons, 1558–1642*, Oxford University Press, Oxford, 2011, pp. 4–5.

23. John Marston, *Antonio's Revenge*, ed. W. Reavley Gair, Manchester University Press, Manchester, 1978, p. 29.

24. Thomas Dekker, *The Gull's Hornbook*, London, 1609, pp. 18–19.

25. Gary Taylor, 'Making Meaning Marketing Shakespeare 1623', in Peter Holland and Stephen Orgel, eds, *From Performance to Print in Shakespeare's England*, Palgrave Macmillan, Basingstoke, 2006, pp. 55–72; p. 56.

26. *The Letters of John Chamberlain*, vol. II, ed. Norman Egbert McLure, American Philosophical Society, Philadelphia PA, 1939, p. 481.

27. Webster, *The White Devil*, sig. A2.

28. Quoted in Laurie Maguire, 'The Craft of Printing', in David Kastan, ed., *A Companion to Shakespeare*, Blackwell, Oxford, 1999, pp. 434–49; p. 434.

29. Samuel Rowlands, *'Tis Merry When Gossips Meet*, London, 1602, sig. A3.

30. Taylor, 'Making Meaning Marketing Shakespeare 1623', pp. 62–3.

31. *The Letters of John Chamberlain*, vol. II, p. 525.

32. See Broadside Ballads Online, http://ballads.bodleian.ox.ac.uk/static/images/sheets/25000/23502.gif.

33. *The Letters of John Chamberlain*, vol. II, pp. 525, 531.

34. Taylor, 'Making Meaning Marketing Shakespeare 1623', p. 68.

35. See Sonia Massai, 'Edward Blount, the Herberts, and the First Folio', in Maria Straznicky, ed., *Shakespeare's Stationers: Studies in Cultural Biography*, University of Pennsylvania Press, Pennsylvania, 2013, pp. 132–46.

36. Peter Blayney, *The Bookshops in Paul's Cross Churchyard*, Occasional Papers of the Bibliographical Society, London, 1990, fig. 2.

37. *The Oxford Authors: Ben Jonson*, p. 386.

38. Anthony J. West, *The Shakespeare First Folio: The History of the Book*, vol. I, Oxford University Press, Oxford, 2001, pp. 5–6.

THREE

1. Jonathan Bate, *The Genius of Shakespeare*, Picador, London, 1987, p. 163.

2. *The Oxford Authors: Ben Jonson*, ed. Ian Donaldson, Oxford University Press, Oxford, 1985, p. 600.

3. Ibid., 'Epistle to My Lady Covell', p. 384; 'My Picture Left in Scotland', p. 324.

4. *The Oxford Authors: Ben Jonson*, p. 601.

5. See Ian Donaldson, 'Jonson, Benjamin (1572–1637)', *Oxford Dictionary of National Biography*, Oxford University Press, Oxford, 2004; online edn, September 2013 (www.oxforddnb.com/view/article/15116).

6. *The Oxford Authors: Ben Jonson*, p. 602.
7. Anne Barton, *Ben Jonson: Dramatist*, Cambridge University Press, Cambridge, 1984, p. 94.
8. *The Oxford Authors: Ben Jonson*, p. 596.
9. Ibid., p. 599.
10. Ibid., p. 604.
11. Ibid., p. 539.
12. Ibid., p. 540.
13. The Oxford edition emends the line back to Jonson's version.
14. Thomas Coryate, *Coryates Crambe*, London, 1611, sig. A2; John Beaumont, *Bosworth Field, with a taste of variety of other poems*, London, 1629, sig. Av; John Selden, *Titles of Honor*, London: 1611, sig. Bv.
15. Thomas Heywood, *The English Traveller*, London, 1633, sig. A3.
16. *Every Man Out of His Humour*, 3.1.
17. See Bart van Es, *Shakespeare and Company*, Oxford University Press, Oxford, 2012.
18. E.A.J. Honigmann and Susan Brock, eds, *Playhouse Wills 1558–1642: An Edition of Wills by Shakespeare and His Contemporaries*, Manchester University Press, Manchester, 1983, p. 165.
19. Andrew Gurr, *The Shakespearian Playing Companies*, Clarendon Press, Oxford, 1996, p. 370.
20. Gabriel Egan, 'John Heminges's Tap-House at the Globe', *Theatre Notebook* 55 (2001), pp. 72–7.
21. Honigmann and Brock, eds, *Playhouse Wills 1558–1642*, p. 167.
22. Van Es, *Shakespeare and Company*, p. 237.
23. *Calendar of State Papers (Domestic) 1598–1601*, p. 578.
24. *The Diary of John Manningham*, quoted in *King Richard III*, ed. Janis Lull, Cambridge University Press, Cambridge, 1999, p. 24.
25. Quoted in van Es, *Shakespeare and Company*, p. 240.
26. Richard Flecknoe, *A Short Discourse of the English Stage*, London, 1664, sig. G7.
27. *The Letters of John Chamberlain*, vol. II, ed. Norman Egbert McLure, American Philosophical Society, Philadelphia PA, 1939, p. 77.
28. Quoted in Michael Brennan, *Literary Patronage in the English Renaissance: The Pembroke Family*, Routledge, London, 1988, p. 140.
29. *The Oxford Authors: Ben Jonson*, p. 260.
30. Brennan, *Literary Patronage in the English Renaissance*, p. 174.
31. David L. Smith, 'Herbert, Philip, first earl of Montgomery and fourth earl of Pembroke (1584–1650)', *Oxford Dictionary of National Biography*; online edn, September 2013 (www.oxforddnb.com/view/article/13042).
32. See Tiffany Stern, '"On each Wall and corner Poast": Playbills, Title-pages, and Advertising in Early Modern London', *English Literary Renaissance* 36 (2006), pp. 57–89.
33. Thomas Heywood, *An Apologie for Actors*, London, 1612, sig. G4v.

34. Ibid.
35. 'The Printer', in Augustine Vincent, *A Discoverie of Errors*, London, 1622, n.pag.
36. Stern, '"On each Wall and corner Poast"', p. 40.
37. Vincent, *A Discoverie of Errors*, n.pag.
38. Peter W.M. Blayney, *The First Folio of Shakespeare*, Folger Library Publications, Washington DC, 1991, p. 8.
39. Gary Taylor, 'Blount, Edward (*bap.* 1562, *d.* in or before 1632)', *Oxford Dictionary of National Biography*; online edn, January 2008 (www.oxforddnb.com/view/article/2686).
40. 'To the Reader', in [Baron Chandos/William Cavendish], *Horae Subsecivae*, London, 1620 sigs A2v–A3v.
41. Christopher Marlowe, *Hero and Leander*, London, 1613, sig. A2.
42. Gary Taylor, 'Making Meaning Marketing Shakespeare 1623', in Peter Holland and Stephen Orgel, eds, *From Performance to Print in Shakespeare's England*, Palgrave Macmillan, Basingstoke, 2006, p. 61.
43. Joseph Moxon, *Mechanick Exercises*, London, 1683–4. Quoted from the edition by Herbert Davis and Harry Carter, *Mechanick Exercises on the Whole Art of Printing*, Oxford University Press, London, 1958, pp. 192–3.
44. This passage is printed on p. 367 of the Oxford Shakespeare: it belongs to 1.3, the scene of Bolingbroke's leave-taking of his father.
45. Richard Sennett, *The Craftsman*, Yale University Press, New Haven CT, 2008, p. 20.
46. Charles Nicholl, *The Lodger: Shakespeare in Silver Street*, Allen Lane, London, 2007, p. 169.
47. Mary Edmond, '"It was for gentle Shakespeare cut"', *Shakespeare Quarterly* 42 (1991), pp. 339–44.
48. Katherine Duncan-Jones, *Times Literary Supplement*, 23 April 2014.
49. Ralph Crane, *The Workes of Mercy, both Corporall and Spiritual*, London, 1621, sig. A6.
50. Modernised from Brian Vickers, ed., *Shakespeare: The Critical Heritage*, vol. I, Routledge & Kegan Paul, London, 1974–81, p. 239.
51. *The Second Part of the Return from Parnassus*, in J.B. Leishman, ed., *The Three Parnassus Plays (1598–1601)*, Ivor Nicholson & Watson, London, 1949, p. 227.
52. J.J.M. Tobin, 'Texture as Well as Structure: More Sources for *The Riverside Shakespeare*', in Thomas Moisan et al., *In The Company of Shakespeare: Essays on English Renaissance Literature in Honor of G. Blakemore Evans*, Fairleigh Dickinson University Press, Madison NJ, 2002, p. 109.
53. Thomas Nashe, *Pierce Penilesse his supplication to the divell*, 1592, sig. F3.
54. Philip Finkelpearl, *Court and Country Politics in the Plays of Beaumont and Fletcher*, Princeton University Press, Princeton NJ, 1990, p. 245.
55. John Fletcher, *The Tamer Tamed* in *Women on the Early Modern Stage*, intr. Emma Smith, Bloomsbury Methuen Drama, London, 2014, p. 138.

56. See Laurie Maguire and Emma Smith, *Thirty Great Myths About Shakespeare*, Wiley–Blackwell, Oxford, 2013.

57. www.telegraph.co.uk/culture/theatre/william-shakespeare/9963602/Shakespeare-was-a-tax-evading-food-hoarder-study-claims.html.

FOUR

1. Roger Stoddard, 'Morphology and the Book from an American Perspective', *Printing History* 9(1) (1987), pp. 2–14; p. 4.

2. Charlton Hinman, *The Printing and Proof-Reading of the First Folio of Shakespeare*, Clarendon Press, Oxford, 1963.

3. *The Norton Facsimile of the Shakespeare First Folio*, intr. Charlton Hinman, 2nd edn, W.W. Norton, New York and London, p. xvii.

4. Joseph Moxon, *Mechanick Exercises*, London, 1683–4. Quoted from the edition by Herbert Davis and Harry Carter, *Mechanick Exercises on the Whole Art of Printing*, Oxford University Press, London, 1958, p. 17.

5. Laurie E. Maguire, 'The Craft of Printing (1600)', in David Scott Kastan, ed., *A Companion to Shakespeare*, Blackwell, Oxford, 1999, pp. 434–49; p. 438.

6. Moxon, *Mechanick Exercises*, in Davis and Carter edition, p. 203.

7. Mark Bland, *A Guide to Early Printed Books and Manuscripts*, Wiley–Blackwell, Oxford, 2010, p. 30.

8. John Bidwell, 'French Paper in English Books', in John Barnard and D.F. Mackenzie, eds, *The Cambridge History of the Book in Britain*, vol. 4, Cambridge University Press, Cambridge, 2002, pp. 583–601; p. 585.

9. Thomas Churchyard, *A Sparke of Frendship and Warme goodwill*, London, 1588, sig. D1v.

10. Edward Blount, 'The Printer to the Curious Reader', in *The Rogue, or the Life of Guzman de Alfarache*, London, 1623, n.pag.

11. William Proctor Williams, 'F1 *Coriolanus* Fragment Found in 17th Century Binding', *Shakespeare Newsletter* 16(2) (1966), p. 12.

CODA

1. Anthony J. West, *The Shakespeare First Folio: The History of the Book*, vol. 1, Oxford University Press, Oxford, 2001, pp. 5–7.

2. Michael Dobson, *Shakespeare and Amateur Performance*, Cambridge University Press, Cambridge, 2011, p. 23.

3. The Johnstoune copy is available online, including a transcription of its annotations by Akihiro Yamada, at shakes-meisei-u-ac-jp.

4. Andrew Gurr, *Playgoing in Shakespeare's London*, Cambridge University Press, Cambridge, 1987, p. 260.

5. Edward Hyde, *The Life of Edward, Earl of Clarendon*, Clarendon Press, Oxford, 1759, p. 22.

FURTHER READING

¶ I have marked two works in each section as a good place to start.

Folio facsimiles

http://firstfolio.bodleian.ox.ac.uk. Bodleian copy, with full facsimile pages and searchable transcriptions.

http://shakes-meisei-u-ac-jp. Heavily annotated in seventeenth-century hand, with a transcription of its annotations by Akihiro Yamada.

The Norton Facsimile of the Shakespeare First Folio, intr. Charlton Hinman, 2nd edn, W.W. Norton, New York and London.

On the First Folio

¶ Peter W.M. Blayney, *The First Folio of Shakespeare*, Folger Library Publications, Washington DC, 1991.

Michael Brennan, *Literary Patronage in the English Renaissance: The Pembroke Family*, Routledge, London, 1988.

Mary Edmond, '"It was for gentle Shakespeare cut"', *Shakespeare Quarterly* 42 (1991), pp. 339–44.

Steven K. Galbraith, 'English Literary Folios 1593–1623: Studying Shifts in Format', in John N. King, ed., *Tudor Books and Readers: Materiality and the Construction of Meaning*, Cambridge University Press, Cambridge, 2010, pp. 46–67.

Charlton Hinman, *The Printing and Proof-Reading of the First Folio of Shakespeare*, Clarendon Press, Oxford, 1963.

T.H. Howard-Hill, *Ralph Crane and Some Shakespeare First Folio Comedies*, published for the Bibliographical Society of Virginia by the University of Virginia Press, Charlottesville VA, 1972.

Sonia Massai, *Shakespeare and the Rise of the Editor*, Cambridge University Press, Cambridge, 2007.

——— 'Edward Blount, the Herberts, and the First Folio', in Maria Straznicky, ed., *Shakespeare's Stationers: Studies in Cultural Biography*, University of Pennsylvania Press, Pennsylvania, 2013, pp. 132–46.

Jeanne Addison Roberts, 'Ralph Crane and the Text of *The Tempest*', *Shakespeare Studies* 13 (1980), pp. 213–33; p. 214.

Gary Taylor, 'Making Meaning Marketing Shakespeare 1623', in Peter Holland and Stephen Orgel, eds, *From Performance to Print in Shakespeare's England*, Palgrave Macmillan, Basingstoke, 2006, pp. 55–72.

¶ Anthony J. West, *The Shakespeare First Folio: The History of the Book*, Oxford University Press, Oxford, 2001.

On early modern printing and textual studies

John Bidwell, 'French Paper in English Books', in John Barnard and D.F. Mackenzie, eds, *The Cambridge History of the Book in Britain*, vol. 4, Cambridge University Press, Cambridge, 2002, pp. 583–601.

Mark Bland, *A Guide to Early Printed Books and Manuscripts*, Wiley–Blackwell, Oxford, 2010, p. 30.

Peter Blayney, 'The Publication of Playbooks', in John D. Cox and David Scott Kastan, eds, *A New History of Early English Drama*, Columbia University Press, New York, 1997, pp. 383–443.

——— *The Bookshops in Paul's Cross Churchyard*, Occasional Papers of the Bibliographical Society, London, 1990.

Fredson Bowers, *Textual and Literary Criticism*, Cambridge University Press, Cambridge, 1966.

Lukas Erne, *Shakespeare and the Book Trade*, Cambridge University Press, Cambridge, 2013.

Alan B. Farmer and Zachary Lesser, 'The Popularity of Playbooks Revisited', *Shakespeare Quarterly* 56(1) (2005), pp. 1–32.

W.A. Jackson, ed., *Records of the Court of the Stationers' Company 1602–1640*, Bibliographical Society, London, 1957.

¶ John Jowett, *Shakespeare and Text*, Oxford University Press, Oxford, 2007.

¶ David Scott Kastan, ed., *A Companion to Shakespeare*, Blackwell, Oxford, 1999.

——— *Shakespeare and the Book*, Cambridge University Press, Cambridge, 2001.

Joseph Moxon, *Mechanick Exercises*, London, 1683–4.

A.W. Pollard, *Shakespeare Folios and Quartos*, Methuen, London, 1909.

Roger Stoddard, 'Morphology and the Book from an American Perspective', *Printing History* 9(1) (1987), pp. 2–14.

William Proctor Williams, 'F1 *Coriolanus* Fragment Found in 17th Century Binding', *Shakespeare Newsletter* 16(2) (1966), p. 12.

On Shakespeare's contemporaries

Philip Finkelpearl, *Court and Country Politics in the Plays of Beaumont and Fletcher*, Princeton University Press, Princeton NJ, 1990.

The Letters of John Chamberlain, ed. Norman Egbert McLure, American Philosophical Society, Philadelphia, 1939.

Edward Dering's 'Book of Expences', ed. Laetitia Yeandle, www.kentarchaeology.ac/authors/020.pdf.

¶ John Fletcher, *The Tamer Tamed* in *Women on the Early Modern Stage*, intr. Emma Smith, Bloomsbury Methuen Drama, London, 2014.

Gordon McMullan, 'Fletcher, John (1579–1625)', *Oxford Dictionary of National Biography*, Oxford University Press, Oxford, 2004; online edn, October 2006 (www.oxforddnb.com/view/article/9730).

Ben Jonson: Dramatist, ed. Anne Barton, Cambridge University Press, Cambridge, 1984.

¶ *The Oxford Authors: Ben Jonson*, ed. Ian Donaldson, Oxford University Press, Oxford, 1985.

Kevin J. Donovan, 'Jonson's Texts in the First Folio', in *Ben Jonson's 1616 Folio*, ed. Jennifer Brady and W.H. Herendeen, University of Delaware Press, Newark, 1991, pp. 23–37.

James A. Riddell, 'Ben Jonson's Folio of 1616', *The Cambridge Companion to Ben Jonson*, Cambridge University Press, Cambridge, 2000, pp. 152–62.

Thomas Middleton: The Complete Works, ed. Gary Taylor and John Lavagnino, Clarendon Press, Oxford, 2007.

J.J.M. Tobin, 'Texture as Well as Structure: More Sources for *The Riverside Shakespeare*', in Thomas Moisan et al., *In the Company of Shakespeare: Essays on English Renaissance Literature in Honor of G. Blakemore Evans*, Fairleigh Dickinson University Press, Madison NJ, 2002, p. 109.

On the early modern theatre

Gabriel Egan, 'John Heminges's Tap-House at the Globe', *Theatre Notebook* 55 (2001), pp. 72–7.

Richard Flecknoe, *A Short Discourse of the English Stage*, London, 1664.

¶ Andrew Gurr, *The Shakespeare Company 1594–1642*, Cambridge University Press, Cambridge, 2004.

Andrew Gurr, *The Shakespearian Playing Companies*, Clarendon Press, Oxford, 1996.

E.A.J. Honigmann and Susan Brock, eds, *Playhouse Wills 1558–1642: An Edition of Wills by Shakespeare and his Contemporaries*, Manchester University Press, Manchester, 1983.

Tiffany Stern, '"On each Wall and corner Poast": Playbills, Title-pages, and Advertising in Early Modern London', *English Literary Renaissance* 36 (2006), pp. 57–89.

¶ Bart van Es, *Shakespeare and Company*, Oxford University Press, Oxford, 2012.

David Wiles, *Shakespeare's Clown: Actor and Text in the Elizabethan Playhouse*, Cambridge University Press, Cambridge, 1987.

On Shakespeare's plays

Jonathan Bate, *The Genius of Shakespeare*, Picador, London, 1987.

Michael Dobson, *Shakespeare and Amateur Performance*, Cambridge University Press, Cambridge, 2011.

Katherine Duncan-Jones, *Shakespeare: Upstart Crow to Sweet Swan*, Arden Shakespeare, London, 2011.

¶ Marjorie Garber, *Shakespeare After All*, Pantheon Books, New York, 2004.

Stephen Greenblatt, *Will in the World: How Shakespeare Became Shakespeare*, Jonathan Cape, London, 2004.

Jonathan Hope, *The Authorship of Shakespeare's Plays*, Cambridge University Press, Cambridge, 1994.

Jan Kott, *Shakespeare Our Contemporary*, Methuen, London, 1964.

Charles Nicholl, *The Lodger: Shakespeare in Silver Street*, Allen Lane, London, 2007.

¶ Laurie Maguire and Emma Smith, *Thirty Great Myths About Shakespeare*, Wiley–Blackwell, Oxford, 2013.

Simon Palfrey, *Doing Shakespeare*, Arden Shakespeare, London, 2011.

Diane Purkiss, *The Witch in History: Early Modern and Twentieth Century Representations*, Routledge, London, 1996.

Mary Beth Rose, 'Where Are the Mothers in Shakespeare? Options for Gender Representation in the English Renaissance', *Shakespeare Quarterly* 42 (1991).

Emma Smith, *The Cambridge Introduction to Shakespeare*, Cambridge University Press, Cambridge, 2007.

Brian Vickers, ed., *Shakespeare: The Critical Heritage*, Routledge & Kegan Paul, London, 1974–78.

John Dover Wilson, *The Essential Shakespeare: A Biographical Adventure*, Cambridge University Press, Cambridge, 1932.

INDEX

Entries in italic type refer to illustrations